THE GARZA WAR IN SOUTH TEXAS

THE GARZA WAR IN SOUTH TEXAS

A Military History, 1890–1893

THOMAS TY SMITH

university of oklahoma press : norman

Library of Congress Cataloging-in-Publication Data

Names: Smith, Thomas T., 1950– author.
Title: The Garza War in South Texas : a military history, 1890–1893/ Thomas Ty Smith.
Description: Norman : University of Oklahoma Press [2023] | Includes bibliographical references and index. | Summary: "Examines three short-lived, but significant, cross-border insurrections between 1890 and 1893 collectively known as the Garza War. These insurrections sought to overthrow the rule of Mexican President Porfirio Díaz. Though the insurrectionists did not pose a martial or material threat to the United States, the U.S. was eventually forced to defend its treaty obligations to the Porfiriato by extinguishing the threat that the Garizstas represented."—Provided by publisher.
Identifiers: LCCN 2023000801 | ISBN 978-0-8061-9288-8 (hardcover)
Subjects: LCSH: Garza, Catarino, 1859–1895. | Ruiz Sandoval, Francisco, active 19th century. | Benavides, Francisco, 1843– | Bourke, John Gregory, 1846–1896. | Shely, Joe, 1853–1910. | Shely, Wash, 1861–1909. | Garza War, 1890–1893. | Insurgency—Texas, South. | United States—Foreign relations—Mexico. | Mexico—Foreign relations—United States. | BISAC: HISTORY / Military / Revolutions & Wars of Independence (see also United States / Revolutionary Period (1775-1800)) | HISTORY / United States / 19th Century
Classification: LCC F391 .S647 2033 | DDC 976.44—dc23/eng/20230420
LC record available at https://lccn.loc.gov/2023000801

The paper in this book meets the guidelines for permanence and durability of the Committee on Production Guidelines for Book Longevity of the Council on Library Resources, Inc. ∞

Copyright © 2023 by the University of Oklahoma Press. Published by the University of Oklahoma Press, Norman, Publishing Division of the University. Manufactured in the U.S.A.

All rights reserved. No part of this publication may be reproduced, stored in a retrieval system, or transmitted, in any form or by any means, electronic, mechanical, photo-copying, recording, or otherwise—except as permitted under Section 107 or 108 of the United States Copyright Act—without the prior written permission of the University of Oklahoma Press. To request permission to reproduce sel ections from this book, write to Permissions, University of Oklahoma Press, 2800 Venture Drive, Norman OK 73069, or email rights.oupress@ou.edu.

▼ ▼ ▼

CONTENTS

introduction ♦ 1

chapter 1
Los Sandovales ♦ 5

chapter 2
Garzistas ♦ 14

chapter 3
The Raid on San Ignacio ♦ 46

chapter 4
Capture and Surrender ♦ 57

Appendix: The Insurrectos, 1890–1893 ♦ 69

Notes ♦ 93

Bibliography ♦ 141

Index ♦ 163

▼ ▼ ▼
INTRODUCTION

My interest in the Garza War began two decades ago when I was researching *The Old Army in Texas*. While looking through the monthly post returns for Fort Ringgold, Texas, I was startled to discover that Captain John Gregory Bourke, Third Cavalry, commanded the post in 1891–92. I had long admired Bourke as one of the beau ideal soldier-scholars of the nineteenth-century US Army. When I was teaching military history at West Point, I had a chance to spend time in the special collections library reading through some of his original diaries of his campaigns in the West as the longtime aide-de-camp to Major General George Crook. Later, looking through his comments in those monthly post returns, I was surprised to see so much activity, cavalry patrols coming and going, the occasional prisoner brought in, and remarks about skirmishes with Mexican revolutionaries. What? This was two decades before the Mexican Revolution of 1910, of which I was very aware, having grown up on the Rio Grande at Del Rio. To find out more I read the annual reports of the commander of the Department of Texas for 1890 through 1893 and discovered a whole guerrilla war I had never heard of, and it was just downriver from my own backyard. I decided that someday I needed to research and write this history.

Finally, the day came when the Garza War could be my next project, and it was March 2020, exactly when archives and libraries all over the country locked their doors against the new pandemic. Fortunately, I had spent years copying the important sections of the nineteenth-century annual reports of the secretary of war and buying microfilm rolls of army post and regimental records from the National Archives. Although I am at heart an old-school pencil-and-yellow-legal-pad guy, just before the year of home quarantine I had managed to overcome my prejudice against digital ones and zeroes and knew how to navigate Ancestry.com and Google Books. Recently a few archives and libraries have begun to open up, while enforcing proper COVID protocols, and as such I owe a debt of gratitude to a number of archivists, librarians, and others. My thanks to Shelby Tisdale and Nik Kendziorski at the Center of Southwest Studies, Fort Lewis College, Durango, Colorado, for access to the microfilm copy of the diaries of Captain John G. Bourke. To Jacqueline B. Davis and Brian P. Howard at the Fort Sam Houston Museum in San Antonio for providing photographs for the book. To Andrew D. Crews and Matt De Waelsche at the Bexar County Central Library in San Antonio for providing email copies of articles from period San Antonio newspapers during the lockdown. To Kathline "Kat" Castiglione at the John Peace Library, University of Texas at San Antonio, for constant aid and patient help while I tried to operate one of the new digital microfilm readers while searching old San Antonio newspapers. And finally, to Professor Robert Wooster, one of America's finest military historians, for his discerning and thoughtful comments on the project, and to Colonel David L. Clark, USA (Ret.), my old friend and trail partner in Texas history, for lending his keen eye for detail and appreciation of the past to the original manuscript.

A word about the Appendix: "The Insurrectos, 1890–1893." In the course of research and writing on the Garza War I began to collect a significant list of 210 names and information on the revolutionaries, most of them Mexican citizens who were exiled to South Texas by choice or by Mexican government threat. I did not want to burden the narrative with a constant barrage of who was arrested, or indicted, or tried, or sentenced, and when. The records of the US Federal Court, Western District, where most of them faced justice, are locked up in the National Archives annex at Fort Worth, which has been closed to visitors since the pandemic began. However, the newspapers of the day, particularly the San Antonio, Brownsville, and Galveston papers, had very detailed information on the names (not always spelled correctly), arrests, trials, sentences, and so on. I thought the information and sources too valuable a historic record to simply stuff in my file cabinet. Many of these revolutionaries had lived in Texas for years, and certainly still have offspring or family ties in Texas. I wanted to provide that list and information, however incomplete or sparse, to history and to those families. These revolutionists of 1890–93 provided the cornerstone ideology, and the historic legacy, for the Mexican Revolution two decades later. For their courage against injustice, they deserve the honor and respect to have their names known.

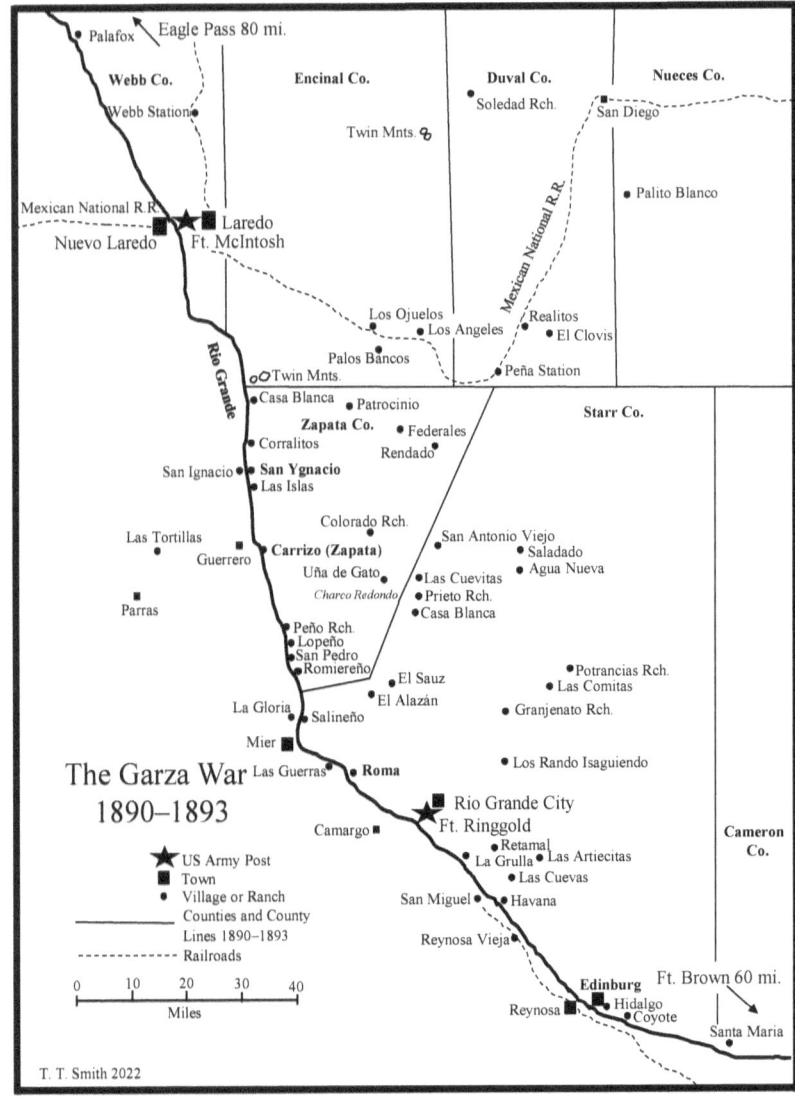

The Garza War, 1890–1893

Map sources: National Archives and Records Administration (NARA) Record Group 393, Records of US Army Continental Commands, 1821–1920, Part 1, Entry 4877, "Letters and Reports Relating to the Garza Revolution," 2 boxes, Box 2, 1893; "Map of the Rio Grande Frontier, Texas, East of Fort McIntosh and South of the Mex. National R.R. Prepared in the Engineer Office, Department of Texas, San Antonio, Texas, February 17, 1893. Official: H. L. Ripley 1st Lieut. 3rd Cavalry, Acting Engineer Officer"; "Map showing the present location of United States and Mexican troops along the lower Rio Grande Frontier, with all available means of communication by rail, water, stage, telegraph (Military and Commercial), and telephone, between all important points. Drawn by 1' Lt. T. W. Griffith, 18' U.S. Inf. under the direction of Col. Anson Mills, 3' U. S. Cavalry. March 8,' 1893"; Entry 4877, Blueprint Maps of Rio Grande Frontier, Department of Texas, 15W2, Map Case 91A, Drawer 4, "Map of the Rio Grande Frontier, Texas, East of Fort McIntosh and South of the Mex. National R.R. Prepared in the Engineer Office, Department of Texas, San Antonio, Texas, December 17, 1892. Official: H. L. Ripley 1st Lieut. 3rd Cavalry, Acting Engineer Officer."

CHAPTER 1

▼ ▼ ▼

LOS SANDOVALES

One of the great ironies of the Garza War in South Texas in the early 1890s was that Porfirio Díaz, president of Mexico, came to power in 1876 by organizing and launching from South Texas his successful revolution against President Lerdo de Tejada with US supporters and funding from American business interests, a clear violation of the neutrality laws of the United States to which Washington turned a blind eye. Three decades later, Díaz railed against that blind eye and bombarded American officials with requests to turn the full power of US judicial, diplomatic, and military force against his opponents in the very same South Texas towns and *rancheros* organizing a revolution against his regime. The Garza War consisted of three significant, but short-lived, cross-border incursions from Texas soil. The first was led by Francisco Ruíz Sandoval in June 1890. In September 1891 Catarino Erasmo Garza, an editor and firebrand, crossed the border with his self-styled Constitutional Army. Finally in December 1892 Garza's second in command, Francisco Benavides, led a brutal attack on the small Mexican garrison across the Rio Grande from San Ygnacio, Texas.

For most of the junior grade US Army officers serving in Texas, the Garza War, in the lower Rio Grande Valley from 1890 to 1893, was their first experience at trying to confront a political insurrection that employed irregular warfare. The army as an institution had not been challenged with a serious political insurrection with international implications in three decades—since 1861 and the Civil War. For senior officers who had served in the Civil War, their experience in that insurrection was largely confined to conventional linear warfare, as irregular guerrilla-style campaigning was a relative rarity. In 1866 and 1870–71, the Irish Fenian Brotherhood, many of whom were Civil War veterans, launched a series of raids from Maine and New York on

Canadian forts and customs posts to try and force the British to withdraw troops from Ireland. However, most of the arrests and weapons confiscations were executed by US law enforcement, the US Army having little role to play in that series of violations of the neutrality law.

Certainly, the army as a corporate body, and many officers both junior and senior, had plenty of experience at irregular warfare in the frontier Indian wars, but the Native Americans were not engaged in a political insurrection—that is, an attempt to overthrow the existing established order and a national government. By and large the objective of Native American raids and larger battles were campaigns of territorial defense or conquest to seize real estate and natural resources from competing tribes, or to defend their own operating area from encroachment of other Indian bands or, even more dangerous, the constantly advancing tribes of the Spanish, Mexicans, or Anglos.

Texas border conflicts, whether caused by Indians, bandits, or revolutionaries, had generated a long history of international tension between Mexico and the United States, particularly when US forces crossed the Rio Grande into Mexico in pursuit of raiders, which the Mexican regimes viewed as an affront to national sovereignty. Staging from US soil in 1850, José María Carbajal, with Anglo, Tejano, and Mexican supporters, attempted to create a separate republic by seizing Camargo, Tamaulipas. Driven back across the border, Carbajal unsuccessfully attacked Mexico again in 1853 but was captured by US troops. In October 1855, James H. Callahan led a force of volunteers across the Rio Grande to attack Lipan Apache who had been raiding Texas. The expedition was intercepted by the Mexican Army and forced to withdraw to Piedras Negras, Coahuila. After setting fire to the town, the Callahan expedition escaped back across the Rio Grande in a retreat covered by US Army troops at Fort Duncan. Raids into Texas by Juan Nepomuceno Cortina, including the capture of Brownsville, set off the 1859–1860 Cortina War, which resulted in a series of cross-border incursions into Mexico by citizen bands and Texas Rangers. Eventually, several pitched battles with Texas Rangers and US Army troops brought an end to Cortina's campaign, which he renewed again during the Civil War. In May 1873, Colonel Ranald S. Mackenzie, with his Fourth Cavalry out of Fort Clark, launched a punitive expedition to attack Kickapoo and Lipan villages near Remolino, Coahuila, sixty miles into Mexico. After destroying the villages and capturing women and children, Mackenzie quickly recrossed the Rio Grande to avoid conflict with the Mexican Army. Lieutenant Colonel William R. Shafter, commanding at Fort Clark, launched a series of incursions into Mexico in 1876 and 1877. In June 1878 Lieutenant Colonel Shafter and Colonel Mackenzie led two columns back to Remolino, where they directly encountered the Mexican Army, but managed to recross the Rio Grande into Texas without bloodshed. This series of invasions incensed the Mexican population and embarrassed the Díaz regime, which began to improve border security against Indian and bandit raids into Texas, improvements that bore fruit in the summer of 1880 when the Mexican and US Armies cooperated against the mutual threat from the Chihenne Apache Victorio, whom the Mexican Army eventually killed.[1]

As a military challenge at the beginning of the last decade of the nineteenth century, the Garza War was unique in several respects. It was a classic case of guerrilla warfare in that the insurgents lived directly among the local population in South Texas, drawing intelligence, as well as political and logistical support, from many sympathetic inhabitants—Tejano, Anglo, and Mexican. It was also distinctive and complex in another respect in that the political and military objective of the insurgents was not intended as a direct martial or material threat to US forces or the US body politic. Their objective was the overthrow of the government of Mexico using neutral ground in Texas as a sanctuary for cross-border incursions with the goal of building a popular revolution. It was that threat to US neutrality laws that brought them into conflict with the US Army and with federal and state law enforcement operating on Texas soil to defend US treaty obligations to the Porfirio Díaz government in Mexico City.

Enforcing the neutrality laws of the United States was complicated for the soldiers on the Rio Grande frontier of Texas. The Posse Comitatus Act of 1878 prevented soldiers from acting as law enforcement and making civilian arrests unless martial law had been declared—it had not and would not be—but if fired upon they had every right to self-defense. They were supposed to aid and protect civil authorities, and on patrol be accompanied by a law officer who was empowered to make arrests. Too many soldiers and too many small patrols meant not enough law officers to accompany the soldiers. Increasingly in the Garza War, both the US Army and law enforcement were forced to discount the restrictions imposed by Posse Comitatus. The federal neutrality law presented its own complexities. A violation of the Neutrality Act was a misdemeanor that could be pursued in federal court by a US district attorney. However, if in the process of catching a revolutionary there was a firefight, which was very often the case, it also became a Texas state or local case for murder, attempted murder, and so on, unless it occurred within federal jurisdiction such as on a local fort. Section 8, Article 1 of the US Constitution gave Congress, not any other persons on US soil or territory, the right to determine or pursue war against another power. The Neutrality Act of 1794 clarified this in detail and remains the basic law of the land. It was modified by the Neutrality Act of 1817, which spelled out the maximum misdemeanor penalties for violation—three years in prison, and up to three thousand dollars in fines. An additional legal complication came with the label that army reports placed on the revolutionaries in South Texas plotting or acting against the Mexican government. If the insurgents, belligerents, rebels, or revolutionaries had legitimate public support and were recognized as such by international consensus, it was possible they could achieve some sort of legal status under international law, but not so if they are merely outlaws or bandits. Army reports initially referred to them as revolutionists, but as time and the Garza War dragged on, those reports increasingly began to call them simply bandits or marauders; interestingly, the reports noted, and rarely denied, the popular support that the revolutionists actually had in South Texas. These were the basic legal aspects for the army being involved in the Garza War of 1890–93.[2]

Five army posts were directly involved in the Garza War to varying degrees. Post at San Antonio was the headquarters of the Department of Texas, commanded by sixty-two-year-old Brigadier General David Sloan Stanley, who had led the department since 1884. Graduating West Point in 1852, Stanley served with the Second Dragoons at Fort Chadbourne in the mid-1850s, so he was very familiar with Texas. Earning a Congressional Medal of Honor at the Battle of Franklin in 1864, he finished the Civil War as a brevet major general and corps commander.[3]

In June 1890 Brigadier General Stanley's 2,298 soldiers in Texas consisted of all twelve troops of the Third Cavalry Regiment; two troops of Fifth Cavalry; the Fifth, Eighteenth, and Twenty-Third Infantry Regiments; and one company of Thirteenth Infantry. This was about 8 percent of a total army of

27,373 with ten cavalry regiments, twenty-five infantry regiments, and five regiments of artillery. The average strength of a twelve-troop cavalry regiment was 706 troopers, while a ten-company infantry regiment averaged 438 riflemen. At Post at San Antonio, founded in 1845 and renamed Fort Sam Houston in September 1890, were thirty-three officers and 607 enlisted men from five troops of the Third Cavalry, six companies of the Twenty-Third Infantry, and a battery of the Third Artillery Regiment.[4]

Of Stanley's total of 2,298 soldiers in Texas, only twenty officers and 426 soldiers were stationed on the portion of the Rio Grande involved at the start of the Garza troubles in June 1890. Camp Eagle Pass, sixty-two acres of leased ground at the site of old Fort Duncan established in 1849, anchored the northern end of the area of operations for the Garza campaign. The post officially closed in August 1883, becoming a sub-post of Fort Clark. The garrison in June 1890 consisted of Captain Charles Morton with one second lieutenant and 55 soldiers of Troop A, Third Cavalry on detached service from Fort Clark. Morton and his troop had been at Eagle Pass several years and were well acquainted with their operating area. In addition to garrison duties, Troop A had detachments conducting routine patrols fifty miles south along the Rio Grande, halfway to Laredo and Fort McIntosh.[5]

One hundred miles downriver at Laredo was the substantial 208-acre post of Fort McIntosh, established in 1849. Colonel Albert G. Brackett, regimental commander of the Third Cavalry, normally commanded the post but had taken leave, so post command fell to Captain Edgar Z. Steever with his Troop G, Third Cavalry. For infantry support he had Companies C and F, Fifth Infantry. Steever had a total of six officers and 95 enlisted men, but in June 1890 the two rifle companies were away in San Antonio conducting annual target practice. Steever and his troopers had spent the past several years at San Antonio, arriving at Fort McIntosh in late May and unfamiliar with the terrain, environment, or the inhabitants.[6]

Down the Rio Grande 103 miles from Laredo, at Rio Grande City, was the 350-acre Fort Ringgold, established as Ringgold Barracks in 1848. Major Edward C. Woodruff had Companies A and B of his own Fifth Infantry, and Troop C, Third Cavalry, a total of seven officers and 123 enlisted men. The Fifth Infantry had several years' service at the post, and also manned a small four-man sub-post at Edinburg, guarding a supply storehouse. Troop C, Third

Cavalry, was unfamiliar with the local geography, having served at Fort Clark before arriving June 22 at Fort Ringgold. Troop C belonged to Captain John G. Bourke, but for many years he had been on detached service, so command of the troop rotated between First Lieutenant Parker W. West and Second Lieutenant George T. Langhorne. Troop C, Bourke, West, Langhorne, and Fort Ringgold would eventually become the very nexus of the Garza War.[7]

At Brownsville, ninety miles below Fort Ringgold, was the Mexican-American War post of Fort Brown, established in March 1846. Commanded by Lieutenant Colonel John J. Upham, Third Cavalry, the 358-acre post was garrisoned by five officers and 153 enlisted men of two troops of the Third Cavalry, and Company D, Fifth Infantry. However, for most of June 1890 Upham had no mounted troops as Troops I and K, Third Cavalry departed June 2 for San Antonio, and their replacements, Troops B and L, Third Cavalry, spent most of the month marching from San Antonio to Forts McIntosh and Ringgold, arriving June 29 at Fort Brown. Major Woodruff also had a small sub-post, Santa Maria, about thirty miles up the Rio Grande, which was manned by a rotating cavalry detachment.[8]

All four posts—Camp at Eagle Pass and Forts McIntosh, Ringgold, and Brown—were commanded by older, seasoned officers, all of whom had served in the Indian campaigns. Three were Civil War veterans—Morton, Woodruff, and Upham—and all but Woodruff had graduated from West Point. However, in June 1890 the cavalry at Forts McIntosh, Ringgold, and Brown were all new to the Rio Grande Valley and generally lacked situational, environmental, and cultural awareness.[9]

Part of that situational awareness was a recognition that among the rural and working classes in the Rio Grande Valley was a general mistrust of governmental authority, as well as resentment toward the US Army. Local elites, Anglo and Tejano, controlled the political, legal, and economic systems with little regard for the voice of the typical *vaquero* or *campesino* who was simply trying to survive in a harsh environment and scratch out a living in a hostile landscape. Law enforcement officers and the US Army were seen as the shields of the system, and of the elites. The lower Rio Grande Valley was also highly populated with Mexican citizens who crossed into Texas to seek economic opportunity, or had fled the increasing repression of the Díaz rule. Díaz had been a general and a hero of the victory over the French, but as president of Mexico he muzzled the press, suppressed opposition, and adopted economic policies that benefited his cronies, the land-owning *hacendados*, and US, British, and German business interests, all to the detriment of the rural poor. The Mexican government privatized the majority of communal lands, selling them off to foreign buyers, dispossessing thousands of poor farmers and dramatically exacerbating Mexico's rural poverty.[10]

Although the political and social resistance to the Porfirian regime had been brewing in the 1880s, the Garza War began on June 24, 1890, not with Catarino Erasmo Garza, but with Francisco Ruíz Sandoval. Sandoval was part of the large Mexican refugee and exile community in the Rio Grande Valley, but was a figure with a murky past, supposedly a onetime Mexican Army officer and Chilean citizen who was deported from Mexico for subversive activities. Living in Laredo, in April and May he organized and armed a band of thirty-five revolutionaries, crossing the Rio Grande on June 24, 1890, intent on capturing Guerrero and Tamaulipas, and expecting the locals to flock to his colors. The manifesto or *proclama* outlining the grievances against the Díaz regime was published in a Laredo paper. Unfortunately for Sandoval, General Bernardo Reyes, the clever but brutal governor of the state of Nuevo León and Díaz's principal counterrevolutionary agent for the South Texas borderlands, had an extensive spy network all through the Rio Grande Valley. Reyes warned Colonel Luis Cerón, in command opposite Laredo, to prepare to meet an invading party. Cerón hardly needed that warning, since mid-June it was common knowledge around Laredo that something revolutionary was afoot. On June 23 Dr. Plutarco Ornelas, the pro-Díaz Mexican consul at San Antonio, sent a letter to Department of Texas commander Brigadier General Stanley warning him that a revolutionary threat to Mexico was brewing at Laredo. On June 24 Deputy US Marshal Eugene Iglesias appealed to department headquarters for help from the army in that he did not have a posse large enough to take on the Sandoval band. At 10:20 p.m. on June 24, the commander of Fort McIntosh received a telegram from department headquarters in San Antonio: "Commanding General directs that you, without delay, send sufficient force to stop the invasion of Mexico. Render all assistance you can to civil authorities."[11]

Sandoval and his party, without firing a single shot, lasted one day on Mexican soil. Pursued by Colonel Cerón's troops, they beat a hasty retreat back to the Rio Grande. Dumping their weapons in the river and swimming nearly naked, they reached the Texas side at sunrise on June 25, going into hiding in the brush at Las Islas, on the Rio Grande thirty-five miles below Fort McIntosh. Just after midnight on June 24, two hours after he received the telegram from headquarters, Captain Edgar Z. Steever with his Troop G, Third Cavalry was in the saddle headed down the Rio Grande from Fort McIntosh. With him were his two troop lieutenants, Francis H. Hardie and Charles A. Hedekin, as well as Deputy US Marshal Eugene Iglesias, and the police chief of Laredo, who claimed to have accurate intelligence on the location of Sandoval. Later evidence emerged that the police chief was moonlighting as part of General Bernardo Reyes's spy ring. Steever and his troops rode all night, reaching the supposed revolutionary rendezvous June 25, just after dawn. Finding nothing, they moved a few miles toward Las Islas. Searching the riverbank, they found Sandoval and ten of his men, helpless, unarmed, in their underwear, preparing to swim back to Mexico. The remainder of the *Sandovales* had already scattered in the brush or had gone back across the Rio Grande. By the end of the day Sandoval and his men were turned over to civil authorities and were in the Laredo jail charged with the federal offense of violating the neutrality laws of the United States.[12]

Hauled to San Antonio, Sandoval and companions were brought before the US circuit court commissioner, who set bond at five thousand dollars. In a matter of a day or two Sandoval's bond, as well as funding for a legal defense, was quickly raised by wealthy and influential businessmen in Laredo, clear evidence of the anti-Díaz sentiment among the Rio Grande Valley's monied elite. Indicted by a grand jury on July 1, Sandoval waited in Laredo for his trial date. Cautious in his movements, he suspected a plot by President Díaz and General Reyes to kidnap him and drag him to Mexico, a scheme that the historical record later proved to be true. The three-day trial for Sandoval and his co-defendants for violating the Neutrality Act occurred in federal court in San Antonio the third week in December 1890. The general public, or at least a number of newspaper editors, assumed it was an open-and-shut case, after all the *pronunciados* were captured red-handed. Sandoval's defense attorney was Bethel Coopwood, one of the Texas super-lawyers of his day. The trial became something of a fiasco as Coopwood, point by point, wrecked the prosecution's evidence in front of a mostly anti-Díaz jury. Two of Sandoval's men who had turned state's evidence during the grand jury suddenly recanted their testimony under Coopwood's questioning. The one remaining state's-evidence witness admitted he was part of the Díaz border spy ring. As to the revolutionary manifesto or proclama issued in Laredo just as Sandoval and friends crossed the border, there was no proof Sandoval wrote it, he did not sign it, and it was probably written by Paulino Martínez, publisher of the Laredo newspaper *El Chinaco* in which it appeared. The prosecutors could not meet the burden of proof required to establish the Sandovales were armed when crossing the border, they fired no weapons, and were unarmed when captured. On December 23, 1890, the jury returned the verdict—not guilty. Sandoval had stated he would return to a quiet life in Laredo, but his actions belayed that claim. In July 1900 the *New York Tribune* reported Sandoval in charge of two steamboats of the Colombian rebel fleet that were captured, and he was jailed in Colombia. His subsequent fate remains an enigma.[13]

The poorly organized, ineptly led Sandoval attempt at producing a revolution did not ring any particular alarm bells at army headquarters, nor with Brigadier General Stanley and his headquarters at San Antonio. In his annual report Secretary of War Redfield Proctor did not mention Mexico or the Texas border, but focused on his policy of concentrating the army in a few large posts and closing as many small posts as possible (sixteen in 1890), which he saw as a "needless extra expense." In his annual report, the commanding general of the army, Major General John M. Schofield, noted that army troops were still required as a deterrent in the West; although Indians were now on reservations, they remained a potential threat as they were "but partially civilized" (written two months before the Sioux troubles and Wounded Knee). Schofield praised the cooperation between the Mexican and US Armies on the lower Rio Grande in halting "lawless incursions," but with prescience noted, "such efficient police work may be required for some years to come." In his report on Texas, Brigadier General Stanley provided a detailed account of the Sandoval incursion and capture, with high praise for Captain Steever and Troop G, Third Cavalry, noting, "The disquiet on the frontier subsided as quietly as it had arisen."[14]

CHAPTER 2

▼ ▼ ▼

GARZISTAS

Department of Texas commander Brigadier General Stanley's quiet frontier lasted through the first half of 1891 as the lower Rio Grande posts resumed routine patrolling for bandits, cattle thieves, and smugglers. Fort McIntosh patrolled upriver halfway to Eagle Pass and downriver to Carrizo (now Zapata), while Fort Ringgold went upriver to Carrizo and downriver to its small detachment at Edinburg. Fort Brown maintained its outpost at Santa Maria and patrolled the lower Rio Grande to its mouth. The first half of 1891 also saw Brigadier General Stanley lose 30 percent of his troop strength, reduced to 1,701 soldiers in Texas. Fort Elliott had closed the previous October and its troops went to the Department of the Missouri. Camp Del Rio and the outpost at Langtry closed in April 1891, and Fort Davis shuttered in July. The headquarters and six companies of the Fifth Infantry were transferred to the Department of the East, and the War Department reduced the strength of every infantry regiment from ten companies to eight, and every cavalry regiment from twelve troops to ten. Brigadier General Stanley was also short of leadership. Of his 153 assigned officers, 87 were present for duty, while 66 (43 percent) were on detached service, leave, or sick leave, or had yet to join their units.[1]

A severe three-year drought in Texas brought crop failures for the farmers and hardship for cavalry mounts in the field with dry waterholes and no grass for grazing. It also brought an unwelcome distraction for Stanley and the staff at the headquarters of the Department of Texas in 1891 in the form of Robert St. George Dyrenforth. Military observers had long held that the tremendous cannonading in big battles often produced rain, although the conviction lacked any proven scientific evidence. Hailing himself as a "concussionist," Dyrenforth convinced someone in Congress to grant the Department of

Agriculture seven thousand dollars to hire him as a special agent to go to Texas and help break the drought gripping much of the state. Somehow the army got stuck with supporting the operation, and the Texas Department adjutant ordered the commander of Fort Bliss to attach Lieutenant Shubiel A. Dyer and a small detachment of the Twenty-Third Infantry to the effort. In August 1891, after shattering the sky near Midland, and then El Paso, with two weeks of explosive balloons, dynamite, a special mortar, and other loud booms it rained two-hundredths of an inch, which Dyrenforth declared a victorious torrent. Then in September and October 1891 the King Ranch sponsored the experiment to continue near Corpus Christi and San Diego, Texas, so Lieutenant Dyer and his detachment were ordered to support the endeavor—"at no expense to the US government." The results were null, and Lieutenant Dyer and his soldiers were ordered back to duty at Fort Bliss at the end of October. The next year, in November 1892, concussionist Dyrenforth tried making rain again, in San Antonio, producing only a rain of glass from shattered windows in Alamo Heights and the Argyle Hotel.[2]

After sending his wife and children to stay with her parents in Omaha, Captain John Gregory Bourke spent a month at Fort McIntosh, arriving at Fort Ringgold on May 15, 1891, taking command of the post and his Troop C, Third Cavalry the next day. A warrior, scholar, ethnographer, anthropologist, scientist, and author, Bourke was one of the most famous officers in the army, made more so by his *On the Border with Crook*, published just as he arrived at post. Born in Philadelphia in 1846, Bourke fought in the Civil War as an enlisted trooper in the Fifteenth Pennsylvania Cavalry, earning a Congressional Medal of Honor at the hard-won Union victory (30 percent casualties) in 1863 at Stone's River, Tennessee. After the war he went to West Point, graduating in 1869 and was commissioned in the Third Cavalry Regiment. Bourke spent most of the next decade and a half as the aide-de-camp to Major General George Crook, with grueling service in a multitude of campaigns against the Apache, Cheyenne, Sioux, and Nez Percé in which he earned several brevet promotions, all of which he declined. He was promoted to captain in June 1882 as the nominal commander of Troop C, Third Cavalry, but spent little time in the position, only from June to September 1885 at Camp Rice, Texas; otherwise he was on detached service for special projects. Prior to being ordered to join his troop he spent five years in Washington, DC, at the direction of the secretary of war, working with the Bureau of Ethnology compiling his voluminous notes for publication. He recorded his first impression of his new command at Fort Ringgold as "the best equipped post of its size I have ever seen in the US Army," but, "Of Rio Grande City, the less said the better." Bourke also recalled, "There was not one single guide or interpreter on the payroll or a map or chart of any portion of that immense district."[3]

Four months later, on September 15, 1891, Catarino Erasmo Garza would change all that, ending the quiet on Brigadier General Stanley's South Texas border frontier. Garza was born on a small farm near Matamoros, Mexico, on November 25, 1859, educated at San Juan College in Matamoros, and briefly served in the Mexican National Guard before moving to Brownsville in 1877 to work in a mercantile. In 1880 he married Carolina Conner, the Irish-Mexican American daughter of the county clerk, and they had two children. As a traveling salesman for the Singer Sewing Machine Company, he lived in multiple towns on both sides of the border, and even briefly in St. Louis, Missouri, before returning to South Texas. He also founded or helped found several Spanish-language border newspapers, including one in Eagle Pass that criticized both the Mexican and US governments, bringing arrest threats from Mexico and an actual US arrest for libel, which cost him a month in the Maverick County jail in 1887.

Fearing extradition, Garza moved farther from the border to Corpus Christi, where he started another newspaper even more critical of the Díaz regime, making personal attacks on General Bernardo Reyes, Díaz's henchman in Nuevo León. Garza also criticized US law enforcement in his newspaper, accusing customs inspector Victor Sebree of murdering in cold blood a prisoner named Abraham Recéndez who had been arrested for robbery. In turn Garza was arrested by Texas Ranger Captain John R. Hughes for libeling Sebree, but was released on bail. Carrying a grudge for Garza's public vilification of him, in September 1888 Sebree shot and badly wounded Garza while he was in a Rio Grande City barbershop, although several versions circulated of exactly how that fight started.

By this time Garza was something of a local political hero among the many anti-Díaz refugees and even Tejano citizens in South Texas who saw him as a champion of Mexican rights. Public reaction to Garza's shooting created a threatening atmosphere that drove Sebree to seek refuge at Fort Ringgold, while the customs inspector at Brownsville, ninety miles away, sent an alarming telegram that an armed mob had taken over Rio Grande City. The Starr County judge informed the Texas governor that a riot was raging and to send Texas Rangers and have the army intervene. A sudden flurry of telegrams from the War Department prompted Brigadier General Stanley to direct the post commander at Fort Ringgold, Lieutenant Colonel David R. Clendenin, to protect Sebree and provide military force in support of law enforcement to end the riot. A large group of Mexicans and Tejanos apparently did go to Fort Ringgold and demand Sebree be turned over to them. Clendenin told them to go away, although newspaper editors hundreds of miles distant manage to turn it into a dramatic confrontation. Garza, the county judge, and Starr County sheriff Warren Washington "Wash" Shely finally calmed down the crowd when the judge promised Sebree would face justice and be brought to trial. Lieutenant Colonel Clendenin reported to Brigadier General Stanley that no property had been destroyed, nor depredations committed: "Condition of affairs not as bad as represented." Sebree was never brought to trial and was transferred to Brownsville as a customs agent, and the great Rio Grande City Riot of 1888, in which there were no recorded injuries, did not merit mention in the monthly post returns of Fort Ringgold, nor in Brigadier General Stanley's annual report.[4]

Divorced in 1889, in May 1890 Catarino Garza married Concepción "Chonita" Gonzáles, daughter of Alejandro Gonzáles, the wealthy owner of the huge Palito Blanco Ranch southeast of San Diego, Texas. Garza was still a Mexican citizen, and among the Mexican refugee population, and even among some Tejano citizens, there was increasing resentment that those of Latino heritage could not find justice in the US legal system. They could not find justice in the Mexican system either, as the Mexican consuls at Laredo, Rio Grande City, Brownsville, and San Antonio seemed only interested in furthering the Díaz regime rather than aiding Mexican citizens in Texas. Essentially, loyalty to either country had so badly eroded to the point where Garza, needing financial and physical support for his growing plans for revolution, found plenty of sympathetic patronage in South Texas from both the monied elite and the simple vaquero. In July 1891 Garza published a scathing personal attack on General Bernardo Reyes, including vulgar comments about

Reyes's mother, remarks that generated a warrant for his arrest for publishing obscene material. When a sheriff went to arrest Garza at Palito Blanco, his father-in-law's ranch, Garza disappeared into the brush, a fugitive.

The fugitive spent the next six weeks organizing and arming his revolution. Principally supplied by his father-in-law, Alejandro Gonzáles, Garza gathered horses, arms, and ammunition from a number of supporting South Texas ranchers and businessmen. The day he picked to start his raid and subsequent revolution had deep cultural and political meaning in Mexico. *Grito de Delores* or *El Grito* celebrated the ringing of church bells in Delores, Mexico, by Father Miguel Hidalgo in 1810 as a call to arms to overthrow Spanish rule, followed by the next day's observance of *Diez y Seis de Septembre*, Mexican independence, gained after an eleven-year struggle. Several hours before sunrise on September 15, 1891, Garza crossed the Rio Grande at La Grulla with about forty men, with another seventy or so crossing at different points, planning to rendezvous in Mexico on the San Juan River, thirty miles above Camargo, Tamaulipas. Riding in the dark a few miles below Camargo, Garza and his band ran into a group of customs guards who immediately opened fire, thinking they were bandits. The Garzistas returned the fire, driving away the custom guards, but Garza lost two horses in the melee. By the end of the day all of the one hundred Garzistas had linked up at the San Juan River and the Garza War became serious, compared to the previous year's inept effort by Francisco Ruíz Sandoval.[5]

At Fort Ringgold that September day were stationed three officers and sixty-two enlisted men of Troop C, Third Cavalry, and Company A, Twenty-Third Infantry. Captain Edward L. Randall commanded Company A, but was in temporary command of the post while Captain John G. Bourke was on leave to see his new baby daughter. On the morning of September 16, Captain Randall telegraphed department headquarters at San Antonio saying he had information that on the previous day one C. E. Garza and fifty armed followers crossed the Rio Grande fourteen miles below post and were attempting a revolution in Mexico. By this time Garza's published revolutionary manifesto or proclama was in the streets of Laredo and Rio Grande City, and was signed C. E. Garza. Department headquarters instructed Captain Randall to send a small detachment to investigate. Randall immediately sent Lieutenant George T. Langhorne and Troop C, Third Cavalry south downriver to gather information. The next day, September 17, Captain Randall telegraphed headquarters that Lieutenant Langhorne learned that a party of sixty armed men, many from Camargo, Mexico, and commanded by C. E. Garza, had crossed in the dark on the fifteenth and they had come from Palito Blanco Ranch in Nueces County, and that Mexican troops in pursuit had an engagement on September 16 at San Miguel, Mexico. Captain Randall quickly received telegraphic instructions that Brigadier General Stanley directed him to go see the US circuit court commissioner and get warrants for Garza and associates, get his command ready to march, and "arrest the revolutionists with or without warrants." No doubt Randall puzzled a bit over the order: the only name he knew for a warrant was Garza, the only cavalry at post had already marched, and even with a warrant, he couldn't legally arrest anyone, martial law had not been declared, and as far as he knew the revolutionaries were still in Mexico.[6]

Nevertheless, Captain Randall followed his orders as best he could. He informed headquarters that he obtained warrants for Garza and four others, although he doesn't explain how he got the names, and on September 18 he sent marching downriver half of his remaining force, a detachment of 10 infantrymen from Company A under Lieutenant Hugh Swain. On September 17, Department of Texas headquarters told Colonel Albert P. Morrow at Fort McIntosh that armed parties had crossed the river into Mexico and he was to scout downriver and find them. Colonel Morrow had eight officers and 172 enlisted men of Troops G, L, and M, Third Cavalry, and Companies C and G, Twenty-Third Infantry. Morrow already had in the field 4 troopers of the Third Cavalry on a routine scout of the river north of the post. After he received his orders, he sent Lieutenant Jesse McI. Carter and 25 men of Troop G, Third Cavalry to scout downriver toward Carrizo. He waited two more days, until September 20, to send Captain Francis H. Hardie and the remainder of Troop G, Third Cavalry south toward Fort Ringgold. Captain John B. Johnson at Fort Brown had himself and the post surgeon as officers, and 57 troopers of Troop B, Third Cavalry. He received orders on September 17, departing post to scout the Rio Grande on September 19, leaving the post surgeon in command of Fort Brown. On September 18, Brigadier General Stanley informed the Mexican consul at San Antonio, Dr. Plutarco Ornelas, that all mounted troops at the three lower Rio Grande posts were in the field searching for any armed bands on the US side. He also informed the adjutant general of the army on the situation as best he knew it. The fact was no one, not even the Mexican Army, knew where Garza and his men were. Over the next several days Stanley received a burst of reports from Mexican and US sources on the location of the Garzistas, none of which proved true. Finally, by the last week in September he began to order troops back to their posts. Captain John G. Bourke had rejoined from leave his Troop C, Third Cavalry and scouted near Carrizo until September 29, returning to Fort Ringgold. Bourke, who was fluent in Spanish and was a master at gaining intelligence, even from an unwilling population—spending years successfully gathering guarded ceremonial and religious anthropological information from the intractable Apache—sent Brigadier General Stanley the first accurate report on Garza's location. Bourke informed him that some of the Garzistas or *Los Catarinos* (their new popular nickname) had broken up into several small groups and had already infiltrated back into Texas.[7]

The Garza raid initially generated a flurry of army orders, but not much combat power. In September the Department of Texas had 1,701 soldiers, of whom 304 (18 percent) were stationed at the three lower Rio Grande posts. Of that 304, 147 (48 percent) were sent to the field after Garza to cover two hundred miles of twisting river border from Fort McIntosh to Fort Brown. The raid also generated a great deal of misinformation in the press. The *Fort Worth Daily Gazette* first reported that the raid was led by Carlos J. Garcia, then Catarino G. Garcia, then Catarino Garsa, an American citizen, and he was accompanied by Francisco Ruíz Sandoval, who was commanding the revolutionary army, and finally, "the whole thing will turn out to be a hoax," and the Mexican secretary of war says, "There is no revolution in Northern Mexico." The *Galveston Daily News* got the name mostly right, Catareo Garza, but observed, "it is believed he will be reinforced by idlers and malcontents on the other side." While Garza's raid was a military failure, in many respects it was a popular publicity victory, particularly in South Texas. Garza's revolutionary goals were ambitious, but not particularly radical, as expressed through his proclama or *manifiesto Plan Revolucionario,* which he did sign. His plans were to depose Díaz and return to the 1857 Constitution; impose one-term limits on politicians; redistribute vacant lands, but not expropriation of *caudillos,* the large land owners; return power to local and state governments; return political freedom, worker protection, free press, and free trade; and curb foreign economic influence.[8]

October and November kept the troops on the lower Rio Grande on constant scouts, checking out reports on Garza's location streaming in from the Mexican Army, local Mexican consuls, and Department of Texas headquarters. Fort Brown maintained a scouting sub-post at Santa Maria, and at Fort McIntosh the bulk of patrols fell to Captain Francis H. Hardie and his Troop G, Third Cavalry. Hardie sent small detachments led by noncommissioned officers north upriver from the post, and personally led scouts south to Carrizo and Roma (257 miles in October), and nearly to Fort Ringgold (644 miles in November). He sent Lieutenant Henry T. Ferguson and a detachment of Company C, Twenty-Third Infantry marching downriver and back, 200 miles. At Fort Ringgold, Company A, Fifth Infantry transferred to Fort Leavenworth, replaced by Captain William B. Wheeler and Company E, Eighteenth Infantry (one officer, thirty-three enlisted men). Based on information from the Mexican consul at Rio Grande City that the insurrectos were at Uña de Gato Ranch, on October 9, 1891, Captain Bourke led a detachment of his Troop C, Third Cavalry forty miles north and carefully inspected the small village of seven families and the area around it, looking for any sign in the brush of fresh camps, campfires, horse manure, or any hint of a group of strange visitors. He found nothing, but he gathered the entire village, wrote down all names and ages, and in Spanish, "I told all these people whom I assembled for the purpose, that I intended to come out and burn their huts to the ground if I learned they were harboring or aiding any of the Mexican revolutionists." Captain Bourke's heavy-handed threat was a clear violation of the civil rights of the villagers, and an example of the army generating hostility from the local population. He no sooner returned to Fort Ringgold than the same Mexican consul came to him again with fresh intelligence: the revolutionaries were now really at Uña de Gato Ranch. By the end of October Bourke came to believe that trying to find these revolutionaries in this wild land among a clearly supportive population was a futile task that wore down men and horses—and the task was better suited to law enforcement, especially US marshals who were intimate with the locals and knew every trail and waterhole. In November Bourke first led a scout to La Grulla, accompanied by a deputy US marshal with the power to arrest. He visited every house in the village and interviewed all eighty-five inhabitants, finding no sign of Garza's band, but suspecting plenty of sympathy for their cause. Bourke then led a scout to Carrizo, while he sent Lieutenant George T. Langhorne and a detachment to Casa Blanca, and Captain Wheeler and a detachment of Company B, Eighteenth Infantry back to Carrizo. At the end of November 1891 Captain Bourke remarked in his monthly post return for Fort Ringgold, "Detachments have been constantly scouting up and down the Rio Grande and to the ranches in this vicinity in pursuit of Mexican Revolutionaries. The information upon which these detachments were sent out proved to be false in every case—Total distance marched about 450 miles!"[9]

The second week in November 1891 the Mexican consul at Rio Grande City, José F. González, asked Captain Bourke to cross the river and go to Guerrero, Tamaulipas, to coordinate his effort against Garza with Colonel Nieves Hernández. Bourke, US Deputy Marshal John Jodon, and a government buckboard driver crossed the Rio Grande on November 10 at Carrizo. Colonel Hernández was not at Guerrero, so they pushed on toward Parras, Nuevo León, twenty-two miles southeast. At Parras they were accosted and arrested by a customs guard whom Bourke described in his diary as "a drunken mescal-soaked ruale" who accused them of being Garzistas. Bourke finally convinced the guard to take them twenty-five miles south to the telegraph station at Cerralvo where they could contact US authorities. Ten miles into that journey the *alcalde* of Agualeguas made them turn over their weapons, which the customs guard had neglected to do. Bourke told them he had all their names and they would be punished for disrespecting US officials. The guard began to apologize as he sobered up, but Bourke would have none of it. Finally reaching Cerralvo, Nuevo León, on November 13, Bourke sent a series of telegrams to US and Mexican consuls; to the Mexican Army headquarters at Monterrey, which immediately ordered his release; and to US consul-general Warner P. Sutton at Nuevo Laredo, who sent a telegram confirming Bourke's identity. Local authorities at Cerralvo tried to make him remain until the next day but Bourke refused, heading for the border in the late afternoon. Reaching the border early the next morning at Mier, Tamaulipas, he was met by General Lorenzo García bearing an official apology. The detention of Captain Bourke and US deputy marshal Jodon created considerable excitement in the press, but Bourke considered the trip worthwhile. Never one to miss an opportunity to gather intelligence, Burke noted seventy-one auxiliary troops guarding Parras, and at Agualeguas were eighty-four cavalry and fifty-six infantry. He formed a low opinion of the Mexican military on this part of the border, but from his quiet conversations with locals he sensed a strong sympathy for Garza and his cause. He was also convinced that Garza himself and some of his men might still be in Mexico.[10]

In November 1891 Brigadier General Stanley became annoyed with not knowing the location or geo-spatial relation of all the local ranch and village names he was reading in the field reports coming in from the Rio Grande, and he suspected his boss, commanding general of the army, Major General John M. Schofield, shared that frustration when Stanley forwarded him the reports. On November 10 Stanley ordered a detailed map survey of the Rio Grande from the Gulf of Mexico to El Paso to be conducted by army officers. Fort Brown would map the southwest corner of Hidalgo County to the Gulf of Mexico; Fort Ringgold to Starr County to Carrizo (Zapata) in Zapata County; Fort McIntosh to Carrizo to the northwest corner of Webb County; Camp at Eagle Pass to Maverick County; Fort Clark to Kinney County through Val Verde County to San Francisco Creek in Pecos County; Camp Peña Colorado to Buchel County to Foley County (both counties absorbed by Brewster County in 1897); the outposts at the villages of Presidio del Norte and Polvo were ordered to map Brewster and Presidio Counties; Fort Hancock to the junction of El Paso, Presidio, and Jeff Davis Counties; and Fort Bliss south to Fort Hancock, "noting all points that may be of interest from a military stand point especially camping grounds and facilities for obtaining fuel and forage . . . points where the river may be fordable and note the most practicable route near or on the river for troops marching from post to post." It took almost a year and a half to complete the mapping.[11]

The scouting routine continued in early December, but the pace suddenly picked up by mid-month. On December 16, 1891, Captain Francis H. Hardie with a detachment of his Troop G, Third Cavalry left Fort McIntosh to scout the brush. The next day near Los Angeles, forty-five miles southeast of the post, they cut a large trail of riders and followed it southwest to a ford of the Rio Grande eight miles above Carrizo. It was apparent that a group of Garzistas had gone back into Mexico. Hardie and his troops followed across the river, spending the day scouting up and down the river on the Mexican side before returning to Texas. Interestingly, the Fort McIntosh monthly post return faithfully reported Hardie's crossing into Mexico, while the Third Cavalry regimental return merely states that Captain Hardie informed the Mexican Army of the Garzistas' incursion. The issue of pursuit and crossing the border was not settled; the older bilateral agreement only agreed to hot pursuit of Indian raiders, and although requested, the United States expressly forbid the Mexican Army from entering South Texas during this period.[12]

Captain Bourke, "with every man that could be gathered together," including the blacksmith, saddler, and nine brand-new recruits, departed Fort Ringgold on December 21, 1891, with twenty-five soldiers from detachments of his Troop G, Third Cavalry, Lieutenant Charles E. Hays and Company E, Eighteenth Infantry, and US Deputy Marshal Manuel Bañados. With the troopers mounted and the infantry in two wagons, the group rode down river toward La Grulla where Bañados, whom Bourke trusted, had learned Garza and some of his band were camped after crossing from Mexico. Near La Grulla, Deputy Bañados arrested and put in irons US Deputy Marshal Tomás Garza, who openly supported the pronunciados. Deputy Garza agreed to lead Bourke to the Garza camp, which was a few miles northeast at Retamal Springs, but warned Bourke that there were one hundred men there, and it was already after sunset. With the infantry mounted, riding behind the cavalrymen, Bourke's group approached the camp in the dark just after midnight. They suddenly came under intense fire from the camp pickets. Returning fire, the troops rushed the camp but the Garzistas scattered into the thick chaparral, and Deputy Tomás Garza managed to escape during the melee. The soldiers captured some equipment, and fortunately had no casualties, but lost a government horse somewhere in the thickets. The next morning, December 22, Bourke sent out two patrols scouting the brush and there were several sharp gunfights, during one of which Lieutenant Hays and Private David Loyd were wounded, and Corporal Charles H. Edstrom, Troop C, Third Cavalry was killed. Corporal Edstrom was apparently thrown or shot from his horse, and then murdered with two shots to his head, fired close enough to leave powder burns on his face, and his ring and his weapons were stolen.[13]

At Fort Ringgold the next day, not having a post chaplain, Captain Bourke presided over Corporal Edstrom's funeral, reading from the Episcopal Book of Common Prayer. It was a very proper military burial with all honors rendered, and widely attended by citizens from Rio Grande City. Born in 1863, Charles H. Edstrom, from Pittsburgh, Pennsylvania, was five-feet-eight inches tall, with blue eyes and brown hair. He listed his occupation as engineer when he originally enlisted for Troop C, Third Cavalry at Cleveland, Ohio, on September 3, 1886. His enlistment was up and he was honorably discharged at Fort Ringgold on September 2, 1891, but two days later he reenlisted, three months before his death at Retamal. Corporal Edstrom served five years with Troop C and was originally buried at Fort Ringgold and later reinterred to the Alexandria National Cemetery at Pineville, Louisiana.[14]

At the strategic level the death of Corporal Edstrom was a footnote, if that. The War Department was still dealing with the fallout of Wounded Knee (thirty-two soldiers killed, forty-nine wounded, over two hundred Sioux killed, including women and children), the violence from the Oklahoma land rush was ongoing, the miners in Idaho were threatening a strike, and there was a continuous range war in Wyoming. At the operational level at Department of Texas headquarters, Corporal Edstrom's death, a state crime, now involved working out cooperative arrangements with state and county law enforcement for warrants, arrests, and local grand juries, in addition to the enduring federal-level enforcement of the neutrality law, as well as constant requests to the War Department for more troops. Brigadier General Stanley did, however, immediately reenforce South Texas with four troops of cavalry, and Texas adjutant general Woodford H. Mabry sent two companies of Texas Rangers under Captains James A. Brooks and James S. McNeel. At the tactical level, the trooper's view from the saddle, the response to the murder of Corporal Edstrom was very simple: the Third Cavalry went to war with the Garzistas.[15]

On Christmas Eve, two days after Corporal Edstrom's burial, Captain Bourke at Fort Ringgold received a telegram from the adjutant general at department headquarters telling him the full force of federal and state judicial systems would prosecute Garza and his band, and he should help gather evidence but, "of course take no unlawful action, but you can assist to the utmost the United States Deputy Marshal." Bourke, who had initially had some sympathy for the anti-Díaz movement now made his commander's intent clear to his troops—shoot on sight any armed insurrectos. Bourke's intent, illegal as it was, was further complicated by the fact that in the brush it was nearly impossible to tell an insurrecto from an innocent rancher or vaquero, nearly all of whom carried firearms. Brigadier General Stanley himself sent a telegram to Bourke, stating his own commander's intent: "We must crush this thing quickly." Stanley immediately ordered four troops of the Third Cavalry from Fort Sam Houston to reinforce the border. The typical duty strength of a Third Cavalry troop was one officer and 39 enlisted men. This 153-trooper reinforcement of the 300 soldiers already at the south Texas Rio Grande posts meant the total force from Fort McIntosh to Fort Brown would be about 450 soldiers. Loading trains at San Antonio on Christmas Eve 1891, Lieutenant William D. Beach's Troop A, Third Cavalry railed to Fort McIntosh and then were to march to join Fort Ringgold. The other three troops were assigned to Fort McIntosh, Troop D, commanded by Captain George F. Chase, would unload and go to the field, and Lieutenant John T. Knight's Troop I would unload and march from Fort McIntosh to Carrizo to establish a patrol base and supply camp. Following a week later, Troop K, commanded by Captain George K. Hunter, railed to Fort McIntosh.[16]

In the last week of December 1891, while the infantry companies at Forts McIntosh and Ringgold guarded Rio Grande fords, the cavalry took to the field. From Fort McIntosh Captain Francis H. Hardie and his Troop G, Third Cavalry scouted southeast toward Los Angeles. In the field Hardie linked up with Texas Ranger Captain James A. Brooks and fifteen rangers of his Company F. From Fort McIntosh Lieutenant William D. Beach and Troop A, Third Cavalry began their march south to Fort Ringgold, but on December 28 Beach intercepted a courier headed for Captain Hardie with a note from Zapata County sheriff Robert A. Haynes saying he had located the Garzista camp and asked Hardie to join him. Beach decided to take his troop and join Hardie as well. Captain Bourke and a detachment of Troop C from Fort Ringgold, with US Deputy Marshal William Van Riper, also joined Hardie on December 29. That evening, nearly in the dark, the entire group attacked the insurrectos at Rendado, about sixty miles southeast of Fort McIntosh. It was a short skirmish, the Garzistas quickly abandoned the camp, scattering for the bush. There were no US casualties, Bourke recovered the government mount that he had lost at Retamal. The group spent two days trying to follow the multitude of tracks in multiple directions and did manage to capture a badly wounded Sixto Longorio, whom Brigadier General Stanley reported was the Garzistas' leader in Bourke's fight at Retamal. Longorio was taken to the guardhouse at Fort Ringgold to be turned over to civil authorities at Brownsville. Bourke interviewed Longorio and was told that Garza himself was at Los Angeles with the men, but left the group when they moved to Rendado as Captain Hardie approached. Longorio told Bourke the Garzistas were losing hope and were despondent with so many soldiers and lawmen now chasing them. He also reported that two of the Garza men were wounded in Bourke's fight at Retamal. Bourke informed Brigadier General Stanley that Longorio's leg had to be amputated because of the wound and he didn't think the man would live long, but in fact Longorio recovered enough to be indicted in February 1893.[17]

At sunrise on December 29 a courier from the field arrived at Fort Ringgold with instructions from Captain Bourke for Lieutenant George T. Langhorne and the remainder of C Troop, Third Cavalry to link up with Captain Francis H. Hardie, and Troop G, Third Cavalry from Fort McIntosh who were somewhere to the north near the Charco Redondo. By the next evening Langhorne and his twenty-nine troopers camped at the Colorado Ranch, about twenty miles southwest of Captain Hardie, who had pushed his command on to Rendado. The next morning at sunrise December 31, Langhorne sent Private Samuel Allen Walker ahead alone with dispatches for Captain Hardie. Fluent in Spanish, the twenty-five-year-old Indiana-born Private Walker was a dependable seven-year veteran of the army. He had been detailed as a quartermaster teamster but asked to join the patrol. Walker rode about six miles northeast to Fandango Creek when he heard voices in the thick chapparal behind him. Hiding in the bush he watched three armed riders approaching, noting white bands on their sombreros, a friend or foe identifier sometimes used by Garzistas. When close he challenged them with his Trapdoor Springfield, firing when they went for their weapons. In the gunfight that followed, Walker shot one from his saddle and killed one of their horses. Very quickly Walker found himself outnumbered and under intense fire as more Garzistas appeared from the brush. Walker beat a hasty retreat but the revolutionaries swarmed after him. For a mile of hard riding he held them off with his accurate pistol fire. Fortunately, Lieutenant Langhorne and his command left camp about a half hour behind Walker and were a few miles away when they heard the firing and came at a gallop, scattering the rebels in every direction. Private Walker led Langhorne back to the scene of his fight and to the dead horse. Walker searched a coat tied to the saddle, finding a trove of documents linked to the Garza organization, documents that would prove valuable to prosecutors in the trials that followed.[18]

Lieutenant Langhorne and his patrol pushed on to Las Cuevitas Ranch, camping for the night. The next morning, New Year's Day 1892, joined by Starr County sheriff Wash Shely, Langhorne rode a few miles toward Prieto Ranch when Sheriff Shely spotted a rider in the brush who immediately tried to dash off, but was soon captured by the group. In Pablo Muñoz's pockets they found his commission as a colonel in Garza's Constitutional Army, and Shely arrested him. Backtracking Muñoz's trail they soon spotted a camp and came under fire. Langhorne dismounted his troops, launching a two-hundred-yard attack through the brush with Private Samuel Allen Walker rushing to the front. The Garzistas scatted into the chaparral, abandoning most of their gear, including some arms and ammunition. Private Walker carefully searched through the equipment, recovering a trove of Garza's commissions and enlistment papers listing a host of names, as well as an order spelling out the organizational structure of the Garza army with names, all priceless evidence in future legal trials. For his single-handed fight with Garza's men on December 31, Private Samuel Allen Walker, Troop C, Third Cavalry was awarded the Congressional Medal of Honor, the only one so earned in the Garza War. Walker went on to serve nearly three decades in the army, becoming a captain leading Philippine Scouts, and after retirement from the army served as a deputy US marshal at Laredo. Lieutenant George Tayloe Langhorne would later become famous in the Big Bend of Texas, first as a major in 1916 while behind the wheel of his Cadillac Touring Car, leading his Eight Cavalry squadron into Mexico and across the Chihuahuan Desert chasing the Glenn Springs raiders, and then in 1917–19 when he was the regimental commander of the Eighth Cavalry who had a dozen fights with Mexican revolutionaries and bandits raiding across the Rio Grande.[19]

At Department of Texas headquarters Brigadier General Stanley had his hands full with the Garza troubles, and also with several of his field commanders. At Fort Sam Houston he had Captain Henry W. Wessells Jr., Troop H, Third Cavalry, placed in arrest for being "insulting, impertinent, insubordinate," to the colonel of the Twenty-Third Infantry. Instead of a court martial he exiled Wessells and his troop to Camp at Eagle Pass with the warning, "If complaint is made of the quarters you will be ordered into tents." More serious trouble occurred with Colonel Albert P. Morrow, the regimental commander of the Third Cavalry and post commander of Fort McIntosh. Morrow was a Civil War volunteer sergeant major who rose to brevet colonel of the Sixth Pennsylvania Cavalry. Commissioned in 1866 as a regular captain of the Seventh Cavalry, in 1883 as a major he had been court-martialed and dismissed for drunkenness on duty, a sentence suspended to half-pay for a year by President Chester A. Arthur. Court-martialed again for drunkenness in 1885, he was held in rank for two years. Morrow became the colonel of the Third Cavalry in February 1891. In December 1891, in the midst of the new Garza troubles, Brigadier General Stanley preferred court-martial charges against Colonel Morrow in that, "from the time this officer took command of the Third Cavalry his official correspondence has been characterized by insolence, impertinence, and insubordination.... He gives us no promise of usefulness here-after and is a dead weight upon the 3rd Regiment of Cavalry." Stanley placed Morrow under house arrest, but two weeks later, in early January 1892, the adjutant general of the army ordered Morrow home to await retirement orders. Brevet Colonel and Major George A. Purington took temporary command of the Third Cavalry.[20]

In January 1892, while Company E, Eighteenth Infantry of Fort Ringgold guarded fords of the Rio Grande, the cavalry was in the saddle. The new post commander, Captain William B. Wheeler, led a scout to Rendado. Lieutenant Charles E. Hays, with a detachment of Third Cavalry, scouted east to Peña Station on the Mexican National Railroad (now Hebbronville, Jim Hogg County). Lieutenant Walter C. Short, attached from the Sixth Cavalry, led a detachment of Troop A, Third Cavalry to Rendado, San Antonio Viejo, and then Colorado Ranch. Captain John G. Bourke, with Lieutenant George T. Langhorne and Troop C, Third Cavalry, went to Havana, then north to Granjenato Ranch where they arrested three suspects. From Fort McIntosh, detachments of Eighteenth Infantry, Company C led by Lieutenant Henry T. Ferguson, and Company G under Lieutenant Stephen O'Conner, guarded fords of the Rio Grande as far south as San Ygnacio. Captain George F. Chase and Lieutenant John W. Heard with Troop D, Third Cavalry set up a scouting camp southeast of San Diego at Palito Blanco, the ranch of Garza's father-in law, Alejandro

Gonzáles. Captain Francis H. Hardie and Lieutenant Jesse McI. Carter with Troop G, Third Cavalry established a camp on the Rio Grande at Salineño, and then moved northeast to a camp near the Mexican National Railroad thirteen miles northwest of Peña Station at Los Angeles (no longer existing; on army maps it was located near present Bruni, Webb County). Lieutenant John T. Knight with Lieutenant Robert C. Williams attached from the First Cavalry, made a camp at Carrizo with Troop I, Third Cavalry. Captain George K. Hunter, and Lieutenant John F. Madden, attached from the Fifth Infantry, with Troop K, Third Cavalry joined the camp at Los Angeles. On the north end of the line Captain Henry W. Wessells Jr. from Camp at Eagle Pass established a patrol base at Indio with detachments of Troop H, Third Cavalry. On the south end of the area of operations at Brownsville, the outpost at Santa Maria was manned by Captain John B. Johnson's Troop B, Third Cavalry. On the surface it seemed like a significant deployment, but the area of operations was huge, about fifteen thousand square miles, and Captain Bourke observed that it was "perfectly clear that the military were confronted with an alien population in full and active sympathy with these marauders, aiding and abetting them in every possible way," and "The military aspects of the Garza business had dwindled down to a pursuit of squads, skulking in the chaparral."[21]

On the afternoon of January 24, 1892, twenty-seven-year-old Richard Harding Davis stepped off the train from Corpus Christi at Peña Station. He was not yet the famous war correspondent of the Boer War or Spanish-American War, but was an ambitious young reporter on a three-month assignment from *Harper's Weekly* to see and report on the American West. It was Davis's first trip to the rapidly vanishing frontier. He came to Peña Station to meet with and do a story on the soldiers engaged in the Garza War. According to Davis, near the station he found Trumpeter Tyler, Third Cavalry (apparently a pseudonym for the only trumpeter at the camp at Los Angeles at the time, Patrick McKrone of Troop K, Third Cavalry). Davis explained he wanted to interview Captain Francis H. Hardie, who had been in the papers as of late.

Hardie's Troop G was camped at Los Angeles, Trumpeter Tyler explained, and he would lead Davis there. Trumpeter Tyler was supposed to meet the train and guide a load of tents and rations, but they didn't arrive, so he was riding back to camp. Trumpeter Tyler explained that Mr. Davis's luggage was too much for a horse. From Davis's trunk he picked out a pair of pants, shirt, and underwear and told him to store the trunk. Davis examined Trumpeter Tyler's horse and gear, carefully recording the soldier had, "a blanket, a overcoat, a carbine, a feed-bag, lariat and iron stake, a canteen, saddle-bags filled with rations on one side and a change of under clothing on the other, a shelter tent done up on a roll, a sword, and a revolver, with rounds of ammunition for it and the carbine worn in a belt around the waist. All this, with the saddle, weighted about eighty pounds."[22]

Trumpeter Tyler led Davis to a store to outfit him for the chaparral with a tin plate, tin cup, iron knife and fork, saddle bags, leather leggings, blanket, and revolver. After a few hours riding west through the brush Davis concluded, "This particular country is the vacant lot of the world." They arrived at Troop G's camp late at night, Trumpeter Tyler sleeping under a wagon, giving Harding his place in a shelter-half with his bunkie. The next morning Davis got an education in soldier field rations. Each soldier had a tin mess kit and a small iron skillet. Daily rations were a hand-sized slab of bacon, coffee, sometimes potatoes or beans, and enough flour to make five or six heavy biscuits the troops called 'dobes after the hard adobe bricks of the border region. Davis learned that the soldiers of Troop G were devoted to their commander, Captain Francis H. Hardie, who was nicknamed "Riding Captain," as he was constantly in the saddle compared to many other officers. Davis had to wait three days to meet Captain Hardie when he came in from a scout. To his credit Davis spent three more days patrolling with the soldiers. Davis's articles for *Harper's Weekly* were illustrated by an up-and-coming artist named Frederic S. Remington who was gaining a reputation for his western scenes and for capturing soldier life. Remington was not with Davis, but was at his home in New Rochelle, New York. The Remington sketches were done from photographs Davis had taken; in fact, the sketch of Captain Hardie has a note at the bottom saying it was done from a bad photograph. Son of Colonel and Civil War Brevet Major General James A. Hardie, Captain Francis H. Hardie was born in California in 1854 and, like his father, went to West Point. However, after attending three years he withdrew and received a direct commission as a second lieutenant in the Third Cavalry in July 1876. Hardie served in the Third, Thirteenth, Fourteenth, and Fifteenth Cavalry Regiments before being medically retired as a lieutenant colonel in

1909. He died in New York City in 1912 and was buried in Arlington National Cemetery.[23]

At Fort Ringgold, Captain John G. Bourke, who had grown weary of chasing the Mexican Army's rumors and poor information, had begun to establish his own intelligence network. He had been lobbying department headquarters to establish an Indian scout company, and wanted to form a battalion of local militia of young Tejanos and Mexicans. In January 1892 headquarters authorized the department quartermaster to begin providing funds to pay for scouts, locals who were familiar with the terrain and population. Hired as scouts for Forts McIntosh and Ringgold were J. C. "Lino" Cuellar, José Maria Santos, Pablo Longorio, Grecencio Benavides, Rufus B. Glover and his brother, and Juan Moreno. The chief scout, Moreno earned seventy-five dollars per month, the others thirty dollars per month. Glover, Cuellar, and Moreno were also deputy US marshals. Bourke never fully trusted some of the scouts, believing they sometimes misdirected a patrol to protect the insurrectos. In fact, Pablo Longorio was later arrested as a Garzista. No doubt working for the army brought the scouts' families and neighbors grief considering the widespread support of Garza's cause. Scouting was also dangerous work now that the conflict had escalated into a shooting war between the Third Cavalry soldiers and the Garzistas. On January 31, 1892, Captain George F. Chase was on patrol with a detachment of Troop D, Third Cavalry out of their camp at Palito Blanco when he sent scouts Glover, Cuellar, and Moreno ahead to Soledad Ranch west of San Diego. Near the ranch the three scouts were ambushed. Glover fell from his horse, shot in the back, Moreno's horse was killed, but he and Cuellar managed to escape. Returning with troops, they found Glover's body behind a pile of rocks surrounded by spent cartridges. Clearly he had put up a fight after being wounded.[24]

In January 1892 the cavalry patrols were operating at a pace and distance that made resupply difficult. To facilitate the logistics burden, Texas department headquarters sent to Fort Ringgold a pack-mule train of a dozen mules under Chief Packer Henry W. Daly. A veteran of the Geronimo Campaign, Daly later became the chief packer of the army from 1903 to 1917. A pack mule carrying 250 pounds could generally keep up with a cavalry patrol in any terrain, whereas the army six-mule wagon had good but limited mobility. A pack train could easily be task-organized to support a three-man patrol with one mule, or a cavalry troop with a half-dozen pack mules.²⁵

Scouting out of his camp at Carrizo in mid-February 1892, Lieutenant John T. Knight with a detachment of Troop I, Third Cavalry, captured Feverion de los Santos, Garza's chief scout and courier. In the dark of night on February 18 Captain Bourke, accompanying Captain Chase and Troop D, Third Cavalry, surrounded Garza's father-in-law's ranch at Palito Blanco, rounding up the inhabitants. Catarino Garza was there but made his escape into the chaparral. Bourke and the soldiers followed Garza's trail the next morning ten miles northwest, where they surprised a camp of Garzistas who scattered into the brush. Among the property Bourke's squad captured was Garza's saddle, overcoat, pistol, papers, and his diary. This was the last verifiable known location of Garza in South Texas, although in May 1893 US district attorney Andrew J. "Jack" Evans received intelligence that Garza was in, or had been in, Key West, Florida, which was true.²⁶

According to Garza's surviving letters, and the testimony of a witness later arrested by Ranger Captain James S. McNeel, Catarino Garza and his brother Encarnación escaped Texas in late February 1892. With the help of two supporters from a ranch near Realitos, the Garza brothers rode to Cuero, and from there Garza went by buggy and his brother by train to Houston, and both by train to New Orleans. Traveling by steamer they went to Key West, where Encarnación remained, while Catarino went to Havana, back to Key West, then to Nassau, then to Costa Rica, where he became a government official in Puerto Limón, often speaking with visiting Americans. In 1894 the United States requested Garza's extradition. Escaping Costa Rica, Garza became involved in the Colombian Revolution and was killed on March 8, 1895, while leading an attack on the jail at Bocos del Toro, Colombia, now Panama. At the cemetery at Palito Blanco Ranch there is no grave for him, but there is a small memorial.²⁷

The absence of Catarino Garza, his escape unknown to the army, did not slow down the Garza War as patrols blanketed the chapparal and the Rio Grande fords as winter set in. By the end of March, with men and horses wearing out, and with no measurable results such as new skirmishes or arrests, Brigadier General Stanley ordered the troops back to their posts. Although the shooting war had paused, the political and judicial war heated up quickly with accusations and counteraccusations. I. H. Broeter, justice of the peace in Nueces County, brought charges against Captain Bourke, his troops, and his scouts for "promiscuous arrests of good citizens without apparent cause," for entering habitations without warrants, and camping troops on private property without permission. Catarino Garza's father-in-law, Alejandro Gonzáles, with his lawyer Robert L. Summerlin, went to see Texas governor James S. Hogg and Texas adjutant general Woodford H. Mabry on February 26 to complain about Captain Bourke, whom Gonzáles claimed slapped him in the face, arrested him without authority, entered his houses at Palito Blanco Ranch without warrants, and generally harassed and mistreated the people of Nueces County. Since he did not control the US Army, Governor Hogg sent him to complain to Brigadier General Stanley. The next day in San Antonio Gonzáles did not have a chance to talk to Stanley because he was promptly arrested for violation of the neutrality laws for providing his son-in-law Garza and his pronunciados with firearms, ammunition, saddles, horses, and money. Gonzáles's attorney Summerlin did meet with Stanley to discuss the peaceful surrender of Catarino Garza. This could have been a ruse to buy time for Garza's escape, or Summerlin did not know Garza had already fled. Stanley told the lawyer it was not an army decision and he would have to negotiate with the US district attorney. The next day Gonzáles went before US Circuit Court commissioner Larkin F. Price, who released him without bail on the promise to show up when called for his later trial. Gonzáles skipped the trial and became himself something of a fugitive.[28]

There was probably an element of truth in Gonzáles's charges given Captain Bourke's change in temperament after the murder of Corporal Edstrom at Retamal, as well as Bourke's failing health from decades in the saddle on hard campaigns with General Crook. However, Brigadier General Stanley informed Governor Hogg that Bourke denied the charges, claiming, "He has never exceeded his lawful authority," and that "county officers elected by revolutionary Mexicans have their own point of view" in that they wanted to be reelected so went with popular support for Garza. Firing a legal volley for the government, E. B. Richardson, U.S. consul at Matamoros, preferred charges for negligence against US Deputy Marshal for the Western District Paul Fricke, claiming Fricke was openly sympathetic to the insurrectos. After Fricke also leveled charges of abuse by the US Army, Stanley fired back too, asking the War Department to request that US attorney general William H. H. Miller remove Fricke from office, saying Fricke has "loafed here in San Antonio instead of going to the border," and was appointed by US Chief Marshal John Jodon, also a Garzista supporter. Bourke accused Fricke of replacing deputies who actually tried to help the Army. Fricke finally left a year later when his term ran out, not renewed by the administration of President Grover Cleveland.[29]

On May 4, 1892, Brigadier General Frank Wheaton assumed command of the Department of Texas upon the retirement of Brigadier General Stanley. From Rhode Island, the fifty-nine-year-old Wheaton was directly commissioned into the First Cavalry in 1855. Although he was the son-in-law of the Confederacy's senior officer, CSA General Samuel Cooper, Wheaton served the Union in nearly all of the Civil War eastern campaigns, initially as colonel of the Second Rhode Island Infantry, but rising to major general of volunteers by the war's end. In 1874 he became the regimental commander of the Second Infantry and spent many years on the Western frontier. Wheaton was something of a stickler and wasted no time proving it. He had his department adjutant general send a note to the commander of Fort Clark, remarking that letters the headquarters received from him are "improperly folded," and that Army Regulation 840 "prescribes letter paper to be folded in three equal folds" and that "the Commanding General directs . . . conform thereto." Shortly afterward, a department circular stated that by command of General Wheaton, "Clerks and messengers at the headquarters will not appear in shirt sleeves during office hours outside of their respective offices."[30]

Just a week after taking command Brigadier General Wheaton was reminded that the Garza War continued in South Texas. On May 11, 1892 a band of Garzistas under Julian Flores, commander of the Libres Fronterizos (Free frontier regiment), crossed the Rio Grande above Mier and ran into Mexican forces at La Mecca. Flores and eight others were killed, including a Black man named Abalado Stringer who went by the alias of Mogro. One Mexican soldier was wounded, and three horses killed. However, things were generally calm in South Texas as the summer wore on. The troops still conducted routine patrols, but with smaller numbers, usually a sergeant and a few troops, while most of the focus at every post was on rifle and pistol target practice with their .45–.70 caliber "Trapdoor" Springfield Model 1888 rifles or Model 1884 "Trapdoor" Carbines, and their .45 caliber Colt or Smith & Wesson pistols. In mid-summer General Wheaton ordered the Detachment of Seminole-Negro Indian Scouts to relocate from the Big Bend to Fort Ringgold. Created by Major Zenas R. Bliss at Fort Duncan in 1870 the Seminole-Negros were originally from Florida and Georgia, and eventually lived in Mexico when Bliss recruited a chief named Siteetastonachy (Snake Warrior), who took the name John Kibbetts, to be the chief scout and his son Bobby to be corporal. The unit settled at Fort Clark with their families and provided many years of dedicated frontier service to the army, with sons, grandsons, uncles, and cousins joining until the scouts were disbanded in 1914. While serving at Fort Ringgold the families remained in their village at the edge of Fort Clark, and the unit sergeant was John (Warrior) Ward, who had earned the Congressional Medal of Honor for saving Lieutenant John L. Bullis in April 1875 during an Indian fight at Eagle Nest Crossing of the Pecos River.[31]

Although Garzista events on the border seemed to settle down in the summer of 1892, Brigadier General Wheaton had other troubles, squabbles, and accusations among his own officers, and most of it revolved around Captain John G. Bourke. Bourke was angry about charges leveled at him by the Starr County court and others. Becoming thoroughly fed up with the legal entanglements of the police action in which he and his troops had been engaged, he informed the new post commander at Fort Ringgold, Captain George A. Drew, that he would not obey any further orders concerning the insurrectos until he had very clear and exact instructions on his duties, a demand that Brigadier General Wheaton ignored. Meanwhile, Captain William B. Wheeler, Eighteenth Infantry, who had temporarily commanded Fort Ringgold from January to April 1892, bypassed the entire War Department chain of command and sent a letter directly to US attorney general William H. H. Miller. The letter delivered charges of arbitrary conduct and illegal acts while pursuing the Garza band against Bourke, and against US district attorney Andrew J. "Jack" Evans. Brigadier General Wheaton demanded that Captain Wheeler produce evidence of his accusations and ordered him to send a written explanation to General of the Army Schofield of why he, Wheeler, had written directly to the attorney general of the United States. Wheaton told Schofield he had investigated and found no merit in Wheeler's charges; that Mrs. Wheeler was a known mischief maker and meddler in official business;

and that Florent B. Jodon, customs collector at Rio Grande City and Garza supporter, had a major hand in this false business. Wheeler claimed he was motivated by the fact that he believed both Bourke and US District Attorney Evans had slandered Mrs. Wheeler. Wheaton let the matter drop.[32]

Captain Bourke, in addition to fending off charges against himself, spent most of the summer testifying as a witness against various Garzistas and supporters at the federal grand jury and trials in San Antonio. He spent so much time in court he eventually rented a house in San Antonio, bringing his wife and children from Omaha to join him. The legal wheels finally started grinding against the insurrectos thanks to Judge Thomas S. Maxey, US federal judge, Western District of Texas, and US district attorney Andrew J. Evans. To this point 130 had been indicted by the federal grand jury and a number already arrested. The trials of insurrectos went on for most of May 1892, all charged in federal district court with violations of the neutrality law. The first couple of Garzistas pled guilty and were given suspended sentences for their relatively minor roles. Then came the most important trial, that of Pablo Muñoz, Garza's second in command during the raid of September 16, 1891. Muñoz was captured New Year's Day by Lieutenant Langhorne's patrol and arrested by Sheriff Shely, who was with the soldiers. The evidence against Muñoz was clear, he was captured with his Constitutional Army commission of colonel signed by Garza in his pocket, and witnesses testified he commanded the regiment named Los Fieles Zaragozans (the faithful of Zaragoza). After a weeklong trial the jury found Muñoz guilty and he was sentenced to eighteen months in prison and a three-thousand-dollar fine. Realizing the guilty verdict meant the government had a strong case and would probably win, most of the remaining defendants in this court session pled guilty, hoping for leniency. One was sentenced to three months' imprisonment, others to five months', three got twelve months', and one was discharged as a case of mistaken identity.[33]

Catarino Erasmo Garza (1859–1895). CN 96.801. https://commons.wikimedia.org/wiki/File:Catarino_Garza_(cropped).jpg. Public domain.

"Garza Revolutionist in the Texas Chaparral," Frederic Remington, *Harper's Weekly*, January 30 1892, 113. The Remington sketches on the Garza War were done from photographs taken by Richard Harding Davis for his articles for *Harper's Weekly*. See https://babel.hathitrust.org/cgi/pt?id=mdp.39015014 1260&view=1up&seq=7&skin =2021. Public domain.

"United States Cavalry Hunting for Garza on the Rio Grande," Frederic Remington, *Harper's Weekly*, March 5, 1892, 220. See https://babel.hathitrust.org/cgi/pt?id=mdp .39015014 1260&view=1up&seq=7&skin=2021. Public domain.

"Third Cavalry Troopers Searching a Suspected Revolutionist," Frederic Remington, *Harper's Weekly*, March 26, 1892, 296. See https://babel.hathitrust.org/cgi/pt?id=mdp.39015014 1260&view=1up&seq=7&skin=2021. Public domain.

"Mexican Guide," Frederic Remington, *Harper's Weekly*, March 26, 1892, 296. See https://babel.hathitrust.org/cgi/pt?id=mdp.39015014 1260&view=1up&seq=7&skin=2021. Public domain.

"Captain Francis H. Hardie, G Troop Third United States Cavalry." Frederic Remington, *Harper's Weekly*, March 26, 1892, 295. See https://babel.hathitrust.org/cgi/pt?id=mdp.39015014 1260&view=1up&seq=7&skin=2021. Public domain.

"Trumpeter Tyler, Third Cavalry." Frederic Remington, *Harper's Weekly*, March 26, 1892, 295. See https://babel.hathitrust.org/cgi/pt?id=mdp.39015014 1260&view=1up&seq=7&skin=2021. Public domain.

The Shely brothers, Company F, Frontier Battalion, 1882: Joe (top row, third from left) and Wash (bottom row, far left). In 1893 Joe was a US deputy marshal, and Wash was the sheriff of Starr County. Raised in South Texas, the biracial, Spanish-speaking brothers were instrumental in running the army's intelligence operation and information campaign to suppress the Garza revolutionaries. Photograph 1409, courtesy the Noah Hamilton Rose Photograph Collection, Western History Collections, University of Oklahoma Libraries.

Captain John Gregory Bourke.
Courtesy Nebraska State
Historical Society Photograph
Collections.

Captain John Gregory Bourke.
Courtesy Nebraska State
Historical Society Photograph
Collections.

Brigadier General David S. Stanley served at Fort Chadbourne in the mid-1850s as a lieutenant in the 2nd Dragoons and commanded the Department of Texas for eight years, 1884–1892. He is shown here at work in his office in the Quadrangle at Fort Sam Houston. Photo courtesy the Fort Sam Houston Museum, San Antonio, Texas.

Brigadier General Frank Wheaton and staff, Fort Sam Houston, 1894. Wheaton (front row, third from left); Wheaton's adjutant Major Arthur MacArthur, father of General Douglas MacArthur (back row, far left); Wheaton's aide-de-Camp Lieutenant George T. Langhorne (back row, sixth from left). Courtesy Fort Sam Houston Museum.

Brigadier General Frank Wheaton, Department of Texas commander, 1892–1895. Courtesy Fort Sam Houston Museum.

CHAPTER 3

▼ ▼ ▼

THE RAID ON SAN IGNACIO

By September 1892 the border was so quiet that Brigadier General Wheaton reported to Secretary of War Stephen B. Elkins and General Commanding the Army John M. Schofield, "The 'Garza' troubles may be considered ended," although there were still the occasional reports of revolutionists, mostly false rumors. This sanguine estimate of the situation evaporated three months later on December 10, 1892. Early that morning about 130 Garzistas divided into three groups and crossed the Rio Grande into Mexico between San Ygnacio and Carrizo. Although accounts differ slightly on the command structure of the Garzistas, on this raid it became evident the leader was a Mexican Army deserter named Francisco Benavides, also known as El Tuerto (One-Eye), who had issued his own revolutionary proclamation the month before. Maximo Martínez apparently commanded one wing of the Garzistas, and also present was Eusebio M. Martínez, known as Mangus de Aqua, whom witnesses identified as the killer of US deputy marshal and scout Rufus Glover back in January 1892. One of the groups ran into a patrol of four Mexican soldiers, killing one while the other three escaped to Guerrero to give warning. Linking up, the large band turned north to attack the small Mexican Army garrison of two officers and forty-one soldiers of Third Squadron, Sixth Cavalry at San Ignacio, Tamaulipas, across the river border from San Ygnacio, Texas. Leaving their horses guarded in the chaparral, the insurrectos advanced dismounted, striking the outpost at noon, the surprise complete. The cavalry troopers were at the stables grooming horses, and in the barracks resting, unprepared for a fight. Captain Rutillio Segura and Lieutenant Manuel Corbarruvias were lunching at the dining table in the captain's quarters, and died in the first volley. The Mexican cavalry troopers fought back for two hours, firing their Remington Model 1871 .50–.70 caliber carbines from the barracks and stables. When they broke open the spare ammunition crates, they discovered the Mexican quartermaster had sent the wrong ammunition. Trooper Francisco Ramírez reported, "We did our duty as soldiers and fought until our ammunition was exhausted." Ramírez was wounded twice, in the left arm and shoulder. The Garzistas set fire to the barracks, forcing the soldiers out and taking them prisoner, along with seven or eight other wounded, marching them to where the horses were held in the chaparral. Francisco Benavides ordered the wounded prisoners to be shot. Private Ramírez and Private Francisco Morales, wounded in the face and hand, both reported that their lives, as well as those of the others wounded with them, were saved by the intercedence of Garza Colonel Rafael Ramírez, a raid leader who lived across the river in San Ygnacio, Texas. Setting fire to the quarters, barracks, stables, and a grocery store, the Garzistas dragged the bodies of the dead captain and lieutenant to one of the burning buildings and tossed them on the fire, doing the same to four wounded soldiers who burned to death. By most accounts it was Benavides who ordered the bodies into the fire. Maximo Martínez had at one time been a servant of Captain Segura; in revenge for mistreatment it was he who supposedly threw the captain's body into the flames. In all, thirteen Mexican cavalrymen were killed and a dozen wounded; two insurrectos were killed, and two wounded. Basillio Martínez, a civilian carpenter, and his son hid in a small jacal house when the firing started. Eventually the insurrectos set fire to the house and he and his son were captured, beaten with rifle butts, and sent to the horses. However, they were soon told they were free to go, which they did. The Garzistas then turned to stealing all they could. Francisco Benavides stole a new sombrero off the head of a Mexican sergeant, Maximo Martínez put a pistol to a woman's breast and robbed her of ten dollars. By 3 p.m. it was over, and twenty-two soldiers and their families had managed to escape across the river to San Ygnacio. The insurrectos gathered all the horses, saddles, arms, ammunition, and equipment they could carry and began to cross the river, taking with them three kidnapped civilians: Pablo Salinas, Refugio Martínez, and Tomás Martínez, a member of the Rurales home guard. Tomás reported that most of the San Ignacio raiders stayed in the brush in Texas for a week near San Ygnacio. He remained with the Garzistas a month before he was freed, but was well treated, and Refugio had escaped after six days.[1]

The raid caused a media sensation and general outrage. Supporters of the Garza movement quickly tried to distance themselves and their cause from the murderous event, even trying to float a disinformation campaign that the attack came from a bunch of angry young Tejano ranchers who were mad at the Mexican soldiers over some incident of honor at a dance at San Ygnacio. One thing is certain: the San Ignacio attack sent shock waves through the War Department, the State Department, Department of Texas headquarters, and the office of the governor of Texas. Army reports and orders generally dropped the term "revolutionist," using the term "bandits." The Zapata County authorities and the local San Ygnacio authorities did not immediately notify the army of the raid, and it took several days for it to hit the papers. Three days after the raid, the head of the Mexican Legation in Washington, DC, Cayetano Romero, sent a letter to Secretary of State John W. Foster officially confirming many of the details of the raid already published in the papers. Dr. Plutarco Ornelas, Mexican consul at San Antonio, wrote to Brigadier General Wheaton claiming the civil authorities at San Ygnacio were holding as prisoners the Mexican soldiers who had escaped the San Ignacio raid. On December 13, Wheaton ordered Captain Francis H. Hardie, temporarily commanding Fort McIntosh, to investigate the charge. Hardie immediately sent Lieutenant Charles A. Hedekin and Troop A, Third Cavalry to San Ygnacio. That same day Major Alexander S. B. Keyes, Third Cavalry, commanding Fort Ringgold, heard about the raid and the prisoner issue from the Mexican consul at Rio Grande City, sending Lieutenant Parker W. West and his Troop I, Third Cavalry who were patrolling near Carrizo to investigate. After interviewing all the officials at San Ygnacio, as well as the Mexican soldiers, West and Hedekin reported that when the survivors of the raid escaped across the river to San Ygnacio they were well treated by the citizens who cared for the wounded, feeding the soldiers and their families, and they were not being held as prisoners. The problem was that the surviving Mexican soldiers did not want to return to Mexico, fearing they would be shot for failing to defend their outpost. After a week or two of negotiations between US border officials and Mexican Army officers over the safe handoff of the Mexican survivors, the soldiers returned to Mexico, except two who were seriously wounded who had been sent to Laredo for medical treatment.[2]

On December 14, 1892, four days after the raid at San Ignacio, Cayetano Romero, the head of the Mexican Legation in Washington, DC, expressing the growing frustrations of the Mexican government over the cross-border raids, wrote to Secretary of State John W. Foster asking the secretary why the troops at Fort McIntosh had not been ordered to the field to chase the bandits. Foster in turn asked the War Department, which was caught flat-footed. Brigadier General Wheaton in Texas had just found out about the event the day before, mainly from the newspapers, as none of the local officials at San Ygnacio or Zapata County had informed the army or state officials, perhaps trying to buy time for the Garzistas to escape. Once he was certain of the facts, Wheaton, on December 17, ordered two troops of Third Cavalry from Fort Sam Houston to Fort McIntosh by rail. Captain George F. Chase and his Troop D, and Captain George K. Hunter and his Troop K, departed San Antonio the next morning. A few days later, on December 21, Wheaton ordered Troop E, Third Cavalry, officered by Captain Oscar Elting and Lieutenant Tyree R. Rivers, to proceed at once by rail from camp at Peña Colorado in the Big Bend to Laredo. Wheaton then ordered Lieutenant Stephen O'Conner and his Company G, Twenty-Third Infantry to rail to Laredo from Fort Sam Houston and take along several ten-man cavalry camp guard detachments from Companies E and F.[3]

On December 17, Wheaton requested an additional cavalry squadron from Major General Schofield commanding the army. Schofield ordered three troops of Seventh Cavalry, five officers and 142 troopers, from Fort Riley, Kansas, to rail to Fort McIntosh. On Christmas Eve 1892 Captain Henry Jackson, commanding the squadron and his own Troop C, loaded the train with his troop, Lieutenant Herbert J. Slocum's Troop D, and Captain Winfield S. Edgerly's Troop G for the thousand-mile trip to Laredo. Jackson and Edgerly were veterans of the December 1890 fight with the Sioux at Wounded Knee, First Sergeant Frederick E. Toy of Troop G wore the Congressional Medal of Honor he earned in the Sioux wars, and since all three of the troops were at Wounded Knee, among them were many veterans of hard campaigning. The soldiers spent Christmas Day on the train, passing through San Antonio, arriving at Fort McIntosh on December 27, marching December 29 for Carrizo. Brigadier General Wheaton sent a clear mission statement to squadron commander Captain Jackson: "The object of your services in the field is to assist as far as possible US Marshals and other officials in making arrests of parties violating, or intending to violate, our neutrality laws. You are directed to capture, or to kill if opposed in capturing, any violators of these laws."[4]

South Texas had suddenly become unusually important to the War Department. Secretary of War Stephen B. Elkins ordered Brigadier General Wheaton to immediately send Captain John G. Bourke to Washington, DC, to brief himself and Major General Schofield on the details of the Garza War. On December 23, Bourke departed San Antonio. Bourke recommended more troops for the Rio Grande Valley, wanted to raise a battalion of young local Tejanos and Mexicans who knew the ground and that such a unit would generate more loyalty to the government, and he wanted more Spanish-speaking government agents such as customs collectors, deputy marshals, and other officers. Bourke also recommended raising a group of Apache scouts as trackers. Most importantly, Bourke recommended pursuing a very aggressive campaign against the Garzistas, to capture or kill until the trouble ended.[5]

As all these troops deployed to the field in South Texas, the army lost a second soldier to the Garza War. On December 23, 1892, near Los Angeles, Private Patrick Lynch of Troop K, Third Cavalry was driving a supply wagon when he accidentally fell off the wagon, the wheels crushing his head. Private Lynch was buried at Fort McIntosh and later reinterred to Fort Sam Houston National Cemetery in 1946. The next day, Christmas Eve, Lieutenant Parker W. West from Fort Ringgold with his Troop I, Third Cavalry, and the Detachment of Seminole-Negro Indian Scouts found a suspicious trail and followed it fifteen miles north of Roma, where it ended at El Alazán and a camp of thirty-five Garzistas. West immediately attacked, killing one insurrecto, wounding and capturing another, along with fourteen horses, saddles, papers, and provisions. The camp scattered, with West following the multitude of trails, but he did not regain contact.[6]

By early January 1893 Brigadier General Wheaton's new operational deployments took shape in a four-line concept of operations—the Rio Grande line, an interior north-south line, several key camps on the east-west Mexican National Railroad, and a southern anchor at the outpost at Santa Maria and

Fort Brown. All of the troops were to act at once upon any information they received, to cooperate when possible, and to thoroughly scout the country, not necessarily confining themselves to special sections.

Brigadier General Wheaton's Four-Line Deployment, January 1893[7]

Rio Grande Line, North to South

Fort McIntosh—Company F, Eighteenth Infantry, First Lieutenant Edward S. Avis, guarding river fords.

San Ygnacio—Troop E, Third Cavalry, Captain Oscar Elting and Lieutenant Tyree R. Rivers.

Carrizo [Zapata]—Troop C, Seventh Cavalry Captain Henry Jackson and Lieutenant Thomas M. Corcoran.

Lopeño—Troop G, Seventh Cavalry, Captain Winfield S. Edgerly and Lieutenant Charles W. Fenton.

Salineño—Troop D, Seventh Cavalry, Lieutenant Herbert J. Slocum.

Fort Ringgold—Troop C, Third Cavalry, Captain John G. Bourke and Lieutenant George T. Langhorne; Troop I, Third Cavalry, Lieutenant Parker W. West; Detachment of Seminole-Negro Indian Scouts, Lieutenant Charles E. Hays; and Company E, Eighteenth Infantry, Captain William B. Wheeler and Lieutenant Everard E. Hatch, guarding river fords.

Interior Line, North to South

Potrancias Ranch—Troop A, Third Cavalry, Captain James O. Mackay and Lieutenant Charles A. Hedekin. Rendado, supply camp—Company G, Twenty-third Infantry, Lieutenant Stephen O'Conner and Lieutenant Hugh Swain. Las Comitas—Troop G, Third Cavalry, Captain Francis H. Hardie and Lieutenant Jesse McI. Carter.

Mexican National Railroad Line, West to East

Los Angeles—Troop K, Third Cavalry, Captain George K. Hunter.

Realitos—Troop D, Third Cavalry, Captain George F. Chase.

Southern End

Santa Maria—Troop B, Third Cavalry, Captain John B. Johnson.

Special Duty

>Telegraph construction, Fort McIntosh to Fort Ringgold, Company B, Eighteenth Infantry from Fort Clark, Captain Charles R. Paul and Lieutenant Thomas W. Griffith.

Brigadier General Wheaton did set some loose boundaries of command responsibilities to avoid duplication of effort. Captain Oscar Elting was to patrol north of his outpost at San Ygnacio and south halfway to Carrizo. Captain Jackson at Carrizo was to patrol north halfway to San Ygnacio and south to Roma, and Fort Ringgold's area of operations was everything south of Roma. To reinforce the difficult logistics of multitudinous patrols in South Texas, Major General Schofield ordered to Texas a large pack train of seventy-five mules and five packers from Fort D. A. Russell, Wyoming, to support Fort McIntosh and Fort Ringgold. These deployments and reinforcements put the numbers of US troops directly in the Garza campaign at twenty-five officers and 691 enlisted men, of which 536 (75 percent) were mounted.[8]

The seriousness of the brutal raid on San Ignacio set off a series of volleys between Secretary of State Foster and Cayetano Romero, the head of the Mexican Legation. Defending his government against earlier criticism from Romero, Foster told Romero the United States had reinforced the border, "at great expense and inconvenience to the Department," adding that the efforts of the United States to stop the raids "seem to receive little cooperation or assistance from the Mexican side of the border. If the same relative force was kept by the Mexican government on their side of the Rio Grande, raids . . . could hardly happen." Romero fired back that Mexico had 2,727 troops on the border compared to, according to the newspapers, the 600 or 800 US troops. Romero provided Foster a very detailed location of Mexican troops sent to him by General Bernardo Reyes, governor of Nuevo León and military commander of the border zone. Reyes's detail of the 2,727 Mexican troops included many that were far north of Nuevo Laredo and had little to do with the Garza War, but there were in fact 2,441 from Laredo south in the actual area of operations, and of those 747 were cavalry. Reyes outlined the following Mexican troop dispositions on or near the Rio Grande in Tamaulipas state:

>Nuevo Laredo—five officers and 99 infantry, Fifth Infantry Squadron; one officer, 318 cavalry, 21 infantry, Thirteenth Regiment.

Guerrero—one officer, 104 cavalry, 10 infantry.

Las Guerras—two officers, 25 cavalry, Fourth Cavalry Regiment; 35 auxiliary infantry.

Mier—three officers, 49 cavalry, Fourth Cavalry Regiment; nine officers, 58 infantry, 64 cavalry, Fifth Auxiliary Battalion; twenty-four officers, 410 infantry, Sixth Infantry Battalion; 49 infantry, 15 auxiliary infantry.

Gloria—16 infantry.

Camargo—three officers, 50 infantry, Sixth Infantry Battalion; two officers, 25 infantry, 25 cavalry, Fourth Cavalry Regiment; one officer, 24 infantry, Tamaulipas Auxiliary.

San Miguel—four officers, 65 infantry, 67 cavalry, Fourth Cavalry Regiment; 10 auxiliary infantry.

Reynosa—ten officers, 65 infantry, 65 cavalry, Fourth Cavalry Regiment; two officers, 25 infantry, Fifth Infantry Squadron.

Matamoros—four officers, 69 infantry, Sixth Infantry Battalion; two officers, 82 infantry, Fifth Infantry Squadron; two officers, 18 infantry, 10 cavalry, Third Auxiliaries; three officers, 19 infantry, 20 cavalry, Fourth Auxiliaries.[9]

Foster wrote back to Romero saying the War Department claimed US troops "in the vicinity of the Rio Grande are about 1,800 men." That number was accurate if "in the vicinity" meant all of Texas, including San Antonio, Fort Clark, Fort Bliss, and Fort Hancock, none of which had much to do with the actual zone of operations in South Texas. The post returns and regimental returns show at this time less than half that number, 716 officers and enlisted men, directly involved in the Garza War. At the War Department Major General Schofield asked Brigadier General Wheaton in Texas his assessment of the Mexican troop numbers. Wheaton wrote back that he had a report from Captain Francis H. Hardie, Third Cavalry, "one of the most intelligent officers in this Department," that between the mouth of the Rio Grande and Nuevo Laredo were 2,000 Mexican soldiers, and that Mexican troops "have moved with commendable promptness and energy."[10]

Brigadier General Wheaton told Major General Schofield and the army chief signal officer, Brigadier General Adolphus W. Greely, the famous Arctic explorer, that he needed a direct telegraph line from Fort McIntosh to Fort Ringgold so that the two posts could quickly communicate and coordinate.

As it was, the Department of Texas headquarters could send a telegram to Fort McIntosh through the railroad system. To telegraph Fort Ringgold it had to send to Brownsville, then Fort Brown, then up to Fort Ringgold via a temporary military telegraph that was installed in 1891 but was down most of the time because the Garzistas cut it, or as the chief signal officer noted, the local cowboys and vaqueros had "a tendency to injure the line by pistol practice on the insulators and lariat practice on the poles," so he needed to put in a duplicate line along the river. On January 8, 1893, the chief signal officer sent one of his flying telegraph trains from Fort Riley, Kansas, to Fort McIntosh. In 1892 Brigadier General Greely developed five of these experimental mobile field telegraph units, each one like a traveling circus complete with wire and wagons, poles and pole wagons, portable telegraph stations, and a signal officer and signal sergeants as operators. The flying telegraph unit could install fifteen miles of line a day and began the line south to Fort Ringgold on January 14, 1893, assisted and escorted by Company B, Eighteenth Infantry from Fort Clark. The demand was so great that Greely soon added his other four telegraph trains, pulled from the rest of the army. In this first successful real time test of the concept, soon several dozen field stations were installed with seventy-four miles of line, while the temporary line to Fort Ringgold advanced.[11]

Recognizing the need for a permanent solution, Congress appropriated seventeen thousand dollars for the construction of the McIntosh-Ringgold Line. In the summer of 1893 the bid went to Sam P. Wreford from Brownsville. In August 1893 the steamship *Bessie* transported the first load of material to Fort Ringgold, and Wreford began building, completing the line by the end of the year, connecting Brownsville, Fort Ringgold, and Fort McIntosh. The line was key to military communication in South Texas and also a benefit to the local citizens as the "only means of immediate communication with the outside world for 200 miles along the Mexican frontier," as the chief signal officer observed. By the end of the decade the military line was annually carrying over seventeen thousand private or business messages.[12]

Having secured his reinforcements and deployed them in a thoughtful mode of operations, and improving his communications through the plan for mobile telegraph units, Brigadier General Wheaton set about building his intelligence organization. He established a special secret fund to pay informants, to offer bribes for information and rewards for capture, and to pay the Shely brothers as scouts to run his spy network. The biracial and fluently bilingual sons of a Kentucky-born Wilson County doctor and a mother born in Mexico, the Shely brothers spent most of their lives on the Rio Grande border. Forty-year-old Josephus "Joe" Shely was a US deputy marshal and former captain of Company F, Texas Rangers in 1882–85. His younger brother, thirty-two-year-old Warren Washington "Wash" Shely, had been a Texas Ranger in his brother's Company F and was elected sheriff of Starr County in 1884, serving for two decades until 1906. As Wheaton explained, "The Mexicans employed as guides proved generally worthless and to be aiding their friends, the bandits, more than the troops." "[U]pon the suggestion of Capt. Chase, whose previous service in the invested region had rendered him familiar with the country, I employed Messrs. Joseph and Washington Shely, . . . both thoroughly acquainted with the country and the people. Through these [two] other men were employed as scouts and were set to work to capture the now scattered violators of our neutrality laws and bring them to justice." Wheaton then had his adjutant communicate his commander's intent to the post commander at Fort Ringgold, saying the Shely brothers were both law enforcement officers and, "are in our service, confidentially employed by General Wheaton's orders to gain information through spies and scouts." The post commander was to keep the information confidential. The Shelys might ask him for assistance or ask to send detachments "away from certain districts" to avoid alarming their go-betweens who were trying to communicate with the bandits, or trying to arrange their capture or surrender. He was to aid the Shelys in any way possible.[13]

The San Ignacio raid of December 10, 1892, was a critical final turning point in the Garza War. The raid put the Mexican and US State Departments publicly at odds over the United States' failure to enforce the neutrality laws, brought the full attention of the US War Department and its resources to South Texas, increased the Justice Department's and federal law enforcement's determination to catch and punish the violators, and—most importantly—the brutality associated with the event began to erode public support in region for the Garza movement. In late December 1892 the Garzistas continued their public relations blunders. On December 23, US deputy marshal Edward F. Hall learned that one of the San Ignacio raiders, Poriciano Palacio, was wounded and was at a ranch near San Ygnacio. Hall went with US deputy marshals Rosendo Guerra and Marcial Benavides and arrested Palacio. Hall returned to San Ygnacio, and Deputies Guerra and Benavides were taking their prisoner to Laredo and camped near Bruni Ranch when they were surprised by a dozen Garzistas who freed Palacio and kidnapped the deputies. The plight of the two Tejano deputies was front-page news and stirred up a hornet's nest of army and law enforcement patrols searching for them. Nearly two weeks later, on January 4, 1893, Lieutenant Charles A. Hedekin with a detachment from Troop A, Third Cavalry found a suspicious trail and followed it until they came upon the group holding the two deputies near San Ygnacio. The Garzistas made a break for the Rio Grande, crossing near Lopeño but soon ran into heavy fire from Mexican soldiers. In the melee Deputies Guerra and Benavides made their escape and were soon helped back to the Texas side by Mexican authorities.[14]

CHAPTER 4

▼ ▼ ▼

CAPTURE AND SURRENDER

US deputy marshal Joe Shely, Sheriff Wash Shely, and Captain George F. Chase, Troop D, Third Cavalry sent out word for a mass conference of Zapata and Starr County ranchers at San Pedro Ranch on the Rio Grande below Carrizo on January 2, 1893. Sheriff Shely told the gathered ranchers that lawlessness must stop, support for the revolutionists was a crime—and for a decade he had risked his life for them, been shot for them, and faithfully protected them from bandits, outlaws, and murderers, but if they continued to support the Garzistas he would resign and leave them to their fate. Further support for the pronunciados, he told them, would only lead to anarchy. Captain Chase said the army was in full cooperation with the law officers and would capture any insurrectos found, and more importantly would capture anyone who supported them, which was a crime. Soldiers were now everywhere, and the army would send even more if needed, which would continue until all the revolutionists and their supporters were found or their activities ceased. It was apparently a very sobering but effective meeting for the locals, and soon the Shely spy network and army patrols began to receive a near overload of tips and information.[1]

Army patrols blanketed South Texas in January 1893, generally keeping the Garzistas in small groups of three to four and constantly moving. Sheriff Shely thought this was counterproductive. He wanted the pace to slow down, giving the revolutionists a chance to assemble so that a large group could be attacked at once. He convinced Brigadier General Wheaton to pull patrols from an area called *federales* in northern Zapata and Starr Counties, and believed his intelligence network would warn when and where the pronunciados would gather if given the opportunity. On January 21, 1893, Lieutenant Joseph T. Dickman of Troop K, Third Cavalry, with Lieutenant

Julius T. Conrad of Troop K, Lieutenant Kirby Walker from Troop D, US deputy marshal Joe Shely, Sheriff Wash Shely, and some state rangers of Company F under Texas Ranger Captain James A. Brooks made a raid on Julian Guerrero's ranch in the *federales* area of northern Starr County, sixty miles north of Rio Grande City. Based on intelligence from Sheriff Shely, there were supposed to be forty bandits there assembled by Francisco Benavides with the intent to attack Camargo, Mexico. Benavides was the leader of the brutal San Ignacio raid of December 10, 1892, and was the most sought after of the Garzistas. The patrol found the camp, and after a sharp fight the insurrectos scattered, but Sergeant Frederick P. Kraup with three men of Troop D saw Benavides and his father-in-law and second-in-command, Prudencio González, in the brush and managed to capture them. Lieutenant Dickman pushed his troops through the chapparal and had another quick fight, wounding and capturing Cecilio Echavarria, a Garza captain and Mexican Army deserter, "who emptied every cartridge in his Winchester before he was captured." Francisco Benavides was taken to Rio Grande City and sent before US Circuit Court commissioner Walter Downs. Benavides refused to talk, making no statement when Downs set bond at two thousand dollars. Unable to meet bond, Benavides remained in jail until his trial. Mexico immediately requested extradition of Benavides and other captured revolutionaries. If done, opined the editor of Brownsville's *Daily Herald,* "there is little doubt that the prisoners will be summarily executed," expressing public opinion and the judgment of most of the legal profession concerning Mexico's due process of Garzistas.[2]

Although actually having reasonable success, there was some frustration among some of the army officers, such as Captain John G. Bourke, thinking that a declaration of martial law might speed the end of the Garza War. Although few spoke publicly, therefore out of school, on what was essentially a political decision by the Harrison and Cleveland administrations, Major Louis T. Morris, Third Cavalry let himself get quoted by the *Daily Herald* on the issue of martial law. The major declared, "Martial law would soon end the Mexican border troubles. Martial law would enable us to make arrests without the slow process of a sheriff's posse, to have prompt and effective trials and punishments before a quickly constituted military tribunal, and to act generally with a vigor that would strike terror into the souls of hostile greasers." On the same page the editor of the *Daily Herald* pushed back against the idea: "Martial law might be a good thing for the bandits, but it would not be welcomed by lawabiding citizens." Martial law enforced by US soldiers was not a distant memory in Texas. Reconstruction had ended less than two decades earlier, which ultimately resulted in the Posse Comitatus Act of 1878, expressly forbidding the US military to act as law enforcement.[3]

Martial law had not been declared, but there was a significant attempt at coordination with Mexican authorities at the highest levels of the US War and State Departments. The Mexican government wanted to coordinate the guarding of all fords on the Rio Grande, to have direct communication between commanders on the ground on each side of the river, and once again raised the issue of the Mexican Army being allow to cross into US territory in hot pursuit of raiders. The secretary of war and Commanding General of the Army Schofield agreed to formal coordination of guarding of fords and agreed that communication across the river by ground commanders was necessary, but refused to support allowing Mexican soldiers to pursue across the Rio Grande. Schofield also pointed out that Mexican and US forces faced different tactical challenges. When in Mexico the raiders were normally in large groups and therefore the Mexican Army had to meet and fight them in large unit formations. When the raiders returned to Texas they usually broke up into small three- or four-man parties. To counter this, US troops had to disperse large units into small patrols to search vast landscapes.[4]

The first two weeks of February 1893 saw a half-dozen captures, arrests, or surrenders of Garzistas as the army and law enforcement tightened its grip on South Texas. In spite of weakening support, the insurrectos continued to use the local legal system to create obstacles for the army. Captain John G. Bourke, with his Troop C, Third Cavalry, and thirteen men of the Detachment of Seminole-Negro Indian Scouts commanded by Lieutenant Percival G. Lowe and US deputy marshal Honsel A. Banda, on February 17, 1893, at the end of a two-week patrol, went to La Grulla on the Rio Grande below Fort Ringgold. Based on intelligence that the ranch was harboring Garzistas, Bourke privately interrogated everyone in the village, taking down all the names, and Deputy Marshal Banda arrested eighteen suspected insurrectos from information and names Bourke had gathered during the interviews. The prisoners were taken to Rio Grande City where US Circuit Court commissioner Walter

Downs held a preliminary hearing and released them. A week later, on February 24, a Starr County grand jury indicted Captain Bourke on charges of false imprisonment and aggravated assault brought by the county district attorney James H. Edwards. The charges claimed that Bourke threatened to shoot La Grulla residents if they didn't name local Garzistas, so the names given and subsequent arrests were made under duress. Supposedly Bourke also hung four residents up by ropes until they talked. On the face of the evidence, the charges against Captain Bourke were probably accurate and demonstrate the local antagonism toward the army. Interestingly, Deputy Marshal Banda—who was with Bourke, was an accomplice, or stood by while Bourke broke the law—was not charged or indicted. Starr County deputy sheriff Pink Barnhill, required to enforce the grand jury indictment, briefly arrested Bourke, but according to Bourke, "upon a trumped up charge . . . for 'false imprisonment' . . . also for assaulting and mistreating them." Barnhill told Bourke to report to his county court trial in March and released him without bond. Upon hearing of the charges, the Brownsville *Daily Herald* opined, "Captain Bourke is regarded . . . as being one of the most fearless and ablest officers in the United States Army. . . . He is a terror to the neutrality law violators. . . . His actions, severe as they may seem, meet with general approval." On March 1, a week after his indictment, Bourke received transfer orders to Chicago to supervise the US Department of State exhibition at the World's Columbian Exposition of 1893. He arrived in Chicago on March 9, just as Starr County district attorney Edwards protested to Governor Hogg, demanding that the governor tell the army to send Bourke back for his trial. The governor ignored the request, as did Brigadier General Wheaton. A week later Bourke received a telegram from Fort Ringgold informing him that Starr County had dropped the charges, provided he never again return to the county.[5]

On February 23 seven Garzistas rode into Captain Henry Jackson's camp at Carrizo and surrendered to him. On that same day, acting on intelligence gained by Sheriff Wash Shely, Lieutenant Percival G. Lowe, Eighteenth Infantry, with two of his Seminole-Negro Indian Scouts and Sheriff Shely, carefully worked their way through the chapparal to a Garzistas camp at dawn, attacking the sleeping revolutionaries. Sheriff Shely pointed his double-barrel shotgun at Eusebio M. Martínez, alias Mangus de Agua, and ordered him to surrender. Martínez raised the Winchester laying beside him and fired at Shely. Shely's buckshot and a bullet fired by a Seminole-Negro scout hit Martínez at the same time. Martínez, a San Ignacio raider and the murderer of US deputy marshal and Army scout Rufus Glover in January 1892, was wearing scout Glover's leggings when he died.[6]

The captures, arrests, and surrenders in March and early April 1893 spelled an end to the Garza movement. Fernandez Salinas, Garza's private secretary, was captured at San Ygnacio on March 8, 1893. On March 22, Maximo Martínez, the most senior Garzista still in the field, surrendered to Captain Jackson at Carrizo. That same day, Seminole-Negro Indian scout John July captured an insurrecto named Juan Manuel Zarrate. Born in Mexico, Corporal John July enlisted in the Seminole-Negro Indian Scouts at age seventeen in 1875, serving twenty-three years until 1898. He died at Fort Ringgold in March 1900. John was one of eight July brothers, cousins, uncles, and offspring who served in the Scouts.[7]

Although the occasional capture or surrender took place through the summer, the principal threat was clearly waning. In mid-April Brigadier General Wheaton began withdrawing troops. Captain James O. Mackay and Lieutenant Charles A. Hedekin, camped at La Retama, were ordered back to Fort McIntosh, arriving April 26. From a field camp at Soladad, Captain Francis H. Hardie with his Troop G, Third Cavalry returned to Fort McIntosh April 27. On April 24 Captain George F. Chase and Lieutenant Kirby Walker with Troop D, Third Cavalry, returned to Fort Sam Houston by rail from Realitos. At Los Angeles Captain George K. Hunter and Lieutenant Julius T. Conrad with Troop K, Third Cavalry railed on April 29 to Fort Sam Houston. Lieutenant Stephen O'Conner and Lieutenant Hugh Swain with Company G, Twenty-Third Infantry abandoned the Rendado supply camp on April 29 and railed back to Fort Sam Houston. Captain Oscar Elting and Lieutenant Frank M. Caldwell with Troop E, Third Cavalry remined in the field at San Ygnacio for two more months until early June, when they joined the Third Cavalry exodus from Texas. At Fort Ringgold Troop C, Third Cavalry temporarily commanded by Lieutenant Joseph T. Dickman of Troop K, and Troop I, temporarily commanded by Lieutenant John W. Heard from Troop D, continued routine short patrols in small detachments until the whole of the Third Cavalry transferred in mid-June to Kansas and the Oklahoma Territory.[8]

Coming from Kansas and the Oklahoma Territory the Fifth Cavalry Regiment replaced the Third Cavalry in June 1893. Colonel James F. Wade and his regimental headquarters departed Fort Reno, Oklahoma Territory, on June 20 and arrived at Fort McIntosh on June 23, railing 648 miles in three days, another demonstration of the revolution in military affairs that railroads caused. In addition to the regimental headquarters, Fort McIntosh also had Captain William P. Hall and Lieutenant Powell Clayton Jr. with fifty-four soldiers of Troop C, Fifth Cavalry, and Captain Early D. Thomas, Lieutenant Joseph E. Cusack and Troop D, Fifth Cavalry with fifty-one troopers. These two troops rotated manning the twenty-man detachment quickly placed at San Ygnacio. To Fort Ringgold went Captain William C. Forbush and Lieutenant Samuel E. Adair with forty-seven soldiers of Troop E, Fifth Cavalry, and Captain Edwin P. Andrus and Lieutenant Solomon P. Vestal and fifty-nine troopers of Troop I, Fifth Cavalry established a detachment outpost at Havana and Hidalgo.[9]

The last to leave the field was the squadron of Seventh Cavalry, which had come from Fort Riley, Kansas, in December 1892. The squadron was to remain in Texas. All three troops broke camp on July 20, 1893, and traveled to their respective stations. Captain Henry Jackson and Lieutenant Thomas M. Corcoran with Troop C, Seventh Cavalry left Carrizo for Fort Hancock on the Rio Grande below El Paso. Lieutenant Herbert J. Slocum and his Troop D, Seventh Cavalry at Salineño were transferred to Fort Sam Houston, and Captain Winfield S. Edgerly and Troop G, Seventh Cavalry, which had been in a field camp at San Pedro, were sent to Fort Clark.[10]

Finally, in December 1893 the secretary of war ordered the discharge of all scouts, guides, and others hired specifically for the Garza War. Brigadier General Wheaton was forced to let go of the Shely brothers—US deputy marshal Joe Shely and Starr County sheriff Wash Shely—and their spy network, of whom Wheaton had told the secretary of war that much of the success was due to the "the intelligent and zealous assistance of . . . Joseph and Washington Shely."[11]

The success, long in coming as it was, was also due to the dedication and discipline of the ordinary soldiers. The discipline and spirit of a military unit can be determined by key indicators like annual desertion rates. In 1893 the average desertion rate for the army that year as a whole was 6.5 percent. For

December 1892 to July 1893, the period of the highest occupation during the Garza War, of the 691 enlisted soldiers in South Texas there were nineteen desertions, or a desertion rate of 2.7 percent, well below the army average. Of the units deployed, the eight troops of Third Cavalry had fourteen desertions and the highest annual desertion rate at 4 percent. The three troops of Seventh Cavalry had three desertions, an annual rate of 2 percent. Company G, Twenty-Third Infantry had one desertion, a rate of 2 percent, and the three companies of Eighteenth Infantry had one desertion, a rate of 0.7 percent. The Detachment of Seminole-Negro Indian Scouts had no desertions. During this last period of the campaign, December 1892 to July 1893, there were seven soldier deaths. Private Patrick Lynch, K Troop, Third Cavalry fell from his wagon and was crushed on December 23, 1892. The exact same thing happened near Laredo on May 16, 1893, when Private Albert Neff, Company, F, Eighteenth Infantry fell from the wagon he was driving. On June 27, 1893, at Fort McIntosh, Private George W. Sample, of the newly arrived Troop G, Fifth Cavalry drowned in the Rio Grande. At Fort Ringgold, Signal Sergeant Benjamin G. Cloud committed suicide on June 28, 1893, and on July 4, 1893, at Carrizo, Private William Pollard of Troop C, Seventh Cavalry committed suicide with his pistol. One private from Troop D, Seventh Cavalry, while on furlough in Chicago, was killed in a railroad accident, and one private from Company B, Eighteenth Infantry died of disease.[12]

In spite of the high degree of discipline, two incidents of soldier mischief on the Rio Grande came to involve the secretary of state, the secretary of war, and the general commanding the army. Cayetano Romero, the head of the Mexican Legation in Washington, DC, complained to the new secretary of state Walter Q. Gresham that, on April 8 and 9, 1893, a Black soldier at Fort Ringgold fired his weapon across the river at the sentry box of the Mexican soldier guarding the customs house opposite the fort. Romero soon complained again to Secretary Gresham that on June 2, 1893, two white soldiers fired on the Mexican sentry box. Secretary Gresham forwarded the complaint to the new secretary of war Daniel S. Lamont, who told General Commanding the Army Schofield to investigate, who told Commander, Department of Texas Brigadier General Wheaton to investigate, who then told Fort Ringgold post commander Major Alexander S. B. Keyes, Third Cavalry to investigate. General Wheaton soon informed the adjutant general of the army that the soldier culprits were young, on their first enlistments, were engaged in a boyish prank, and realized it was a thoughtless act. However, he added, at the general court-martial Seminole-Negro Indian scout Sam Gordon received a ten-dollar-per-month fine for six months. Private John E. Cory and Private Benjamin F. Roberts of Troop C, Third Cavalry received a fine of ten dollars' pay for six months, and six months at hard labor in the Fort Ringgold guardhouse, where they remained when their troop transferred to Fort Riley, Kansas. Both were discharged "without honor" on their release from the guardhouse December 29, 1893.[13]

Secretary of War Lamont summed up the Garza War in his annual report for 1893. "The only active duty the Army has been called upon to perform against armed enemies of good order has been the suppression and punishment of violations of the neutrality laws of this country and Mexico. That duty has been discharged promptly, vigorously, effectively, and to the credit of the troops in the Department of Texas. . . . Of the one hundred and twenty-five bandits engaged in the attack on Mexican troops at San Ygnacio, on the 10th of December, 1892, eighty-six were captured by our troops, and of these, seventy-one were subsequently sentenced by the United States Court. The civil and military authorities of Mexico . . . have expressed their appreciation of the services performed by the United States in suppressing the raids of outlaws that menaced the tranquility of both sides of the border. The general commanding the Department of Texas makes special mention of the officers and men of the Third Cavalry for arduous duty performed in the capture of the offenders." In his annual report on Texas Brigadier General Wheaton noted, "The bandits were kept constantly moving, fleeing from one place of concealment to another in small detachments to better avoid capture, until, their horses being worn out and themselves exhausted by hunger and fatigue, many of them were captured and many others, seeing further escape hopeless, in despair voluntarily surrendered. Of the 132 that have been captured by our troops and scouts 86 have been identified as participants in the San Ygnacio raid." Wheaton added that of the San Ignacio raiders, seventy-one were convicted and sentenced in the May 1893 term of the United States district court.[14]

In summary, the typical sentences handed out to the Garzistas in federal court sessions in late 1892 and early 1893 for violation of the Neutrality

Act were small fines, usually ten dollars, but also either two or three years in federal prison, three years being the maximum allowed under the law. However, the punishments seemed to be lighter in mid-1893, particularly for those who pled guilty. Many of those sentences were suspended, or were limited to a few months in a county jail. On May 17, 1893, Catarino Garza's father-in-law, Alejandro Gonzáles, was arrested at his Palito Blanco ranch for violation of the Neutrality Act and for failure to appear in court. He had forfeited his two-thousand-dollar bond for skipping his earlier trial. He was taken to San Antonio and appeared before Judge Thomas S. Maxey on May 19. Gonzáles pled guilty, and Judge Maxey sentenced him to a sixteen-hundred-dollar fine and one hour in the Bexar County jail. Gonzáles spent his hour in jail and paid his fine in cash. For some it seemed that a federal charge for supporting revolution was a political windfall. Antonio Mateo Bruni, a thirty-seven-year-old Italian immigrant, was a wealthy Laredo businessman and rancher who earned a federal conviction for supporting Garza. Bruni was elected as a Webb County commissioner in 1892 and then held the position of county treasurer until his death in 1931. A Laredo park and elementary school are named for him.[15]

However, some of the insurrectos' cases had long and complicated legal histories that ended up at the US Supreme Court. San Ignacio raiders Juan Duque, Inez Ruiz, and Jesus Guerra served their prison sentences for violation of the neutrality laws but upon release were rearrested by US marshals on an approved request for extradition from Mexico back in July 1893. The three prisoners filed a writ of habeas corpus, and US federal judge Maxey ordered their release, ruling that a violation of US neutrality laws was not an extraditable offense, and that as revolutionists they were essentially political refugees. Representing the government of Mexico in San Antonio was former Texas attorney general James Harvey McCleary. The Díaz regime instructed McLeary to take the cases to the Supreme Court to get a ruling on the status of prisoners and the interpretation of the extradition treaty. On March 16, 1896, the US Supreme Court denied the revolutionaries the status of political refugees, labeling them "banditti" and on April 16 ordered federal officials to turn them over to Mexico for extradition along with a dozen others awaiting the decision. On July 9, 1896, the State Department ordered the surrender to Mexico of Duque and Ruiz.[16]

On September 28, 1897, Starr County sheriff Wash Shely rearrested Jesus Guerra and turned him over to US marshals for extradition. However, the new secretary of state, John Sherman, appointed by President William McKinley, refused to approve the extradition. Sherman had reviewed the file and determined that although Guerra was present at the San Ignacio raid, at his original extradition trial held by US Circuit Court commissioner Larkin F. Price, there were no witnesses who directly accused or proved that Guerra was specifically guilty of murder, kidnapping, or robbery charges in the extradition request, adding that the San Ignacio "expedition" as he called it, was "revolutionary in its origin and purpose ... therefore ... was of a purely political character," thus outside of the scope of the extradition treaty. Cayetano Romero, leading the Mexican Legation in Washington, DC, pushed back, reminding Secretary Sherman that the extradition commissioner and two previous secretaries of state, Gresham and his successor Richard Olney, had approved Guerra's extradition, and that the US Supreme Court had ruled they were bandits and not political actors or refugees. Secretary Sherman refused to approve the transfer, more than likely taking his cue from President McKinley, the Guerra case having more to do with Cuba than Mexico. McKinley was exploring the potential to declare the Cuban revolutionaries as legitimate belligerents, and thus aiding them to rid Cuba, and the Americas, of Spain.[17]

Ironically, the leader of the San Ignacio raid, Francisco Benavides—El Tuerto—also dodged extradition to Mexico, although he did serve three years in a US prison for violation of the Neutrality Act. His original extradition hearing in February 1893 in San Antonio was something of a sensation as the Mexican Army sent witnesses to testify against him, a half-dozen cavalry troopers—in their finest dress uniforms, including large spurs—all veterans of the defense of San Ignacio. Benavides's lawyer, W. E. Cox, argued that Benavides was a US citizen, but the prosecution produced a birth certificate proving he was born in 1843 in Mexico, at Casas Blancas on the Rio Grande. The court found in favor of extradition, but when the request was sent to Washington, Secretary of State Walter Q. Gresham discovered Benavides actually was a US citizen and denied the extradition request. When he was five years old in 1848 Benavides and all the other residents of Casas Blancas, Mexico, suddenly became US citizens because the Treaty of Guadalupe

Hidalgo and the Rio Grande surveys shifted Casas Blancas to the Texas side of the border.[18]

Organizing for revolution on US soil was nothing out of the ordinary for this period. Cuban revolutionists against Spain were using Key West as a base. A rebel vessel from the ongoing Chilean civil war was seized in San Diego, but the rebels outsmarted the US marshal and escaped to sea. Colombia had a series of internal revolts that involved US actors. But clearly the most serious of the violations of the Neutrality Act were in South Texas, where the government spent three years and nearly a quarter million dollars to suppress the activity.

The Garza War became a minor training ground for leader experience and counterinsurgency concepts and tactics that more fully developed a decade later when the army faced a second but much larger political insurgency in the Philippine Insurrection of February 1899–July 1902. All five of the regiments serving in Texas during the Garza War would serve in the Philippine Insurrection, as did many of the officers. For example, Lieutenant George T. Langhorne, who led Troop C, Third Cavalry in the capture of Garza colonel Pablo Muñoz, served as a lieutenant colonel in the Thirty-Ninth US Volunteer Infantry in the Philippine campaign. Lieutenant Joseph T. Dickman, who commanded the Third Cavalry patrol that captured Francisco Benavides, was a lieutenant colonel of the Twenty-Sixth US Volunteer Infantry in the Philippines.[19]

Their Garza War experience, and hard-earned intimate knowledge of the Texas border, served Langhorne and Dickman well later during the Mexican Revolution. Colonel Langhorne commanded the Eighth Cavalry on the Rio Grande, and Major General Dickman commanded the Southern Department, which included all of the Texas border. The US government and the US Army reaction to the Mexican Revolution in 1910 was vastly different from the haphazard approach taken two decades earlier during the Garza War. Most important were troop strength and combat power, which translated into active deterrence directly on the border. Over a dozen regular regiments served on the Rio Grande during this period, and in 1916–17, 110,000 National Guardsmen were sent to the border, with 42,000 in South Texas, and another 18,000 in reserve at San Antonio and Corpus Christi. The neutrality laws were strictly enforced, resulting in very few armed parties organizing in Texas and attacking across the Rio Grande. After US recognition of the presidency of Venustiano Carranza in October 1915, the United States cracked down on border arms smuggling, which had helped fuel the fighting in Mexico. Several US actions also complicated relations with Mexico. In April 1914 US forces seized Veracruz, Mexico, for seven months, and in March 1916 Brigadier General John J. Pershing crossed into Mexico with ten regiments on a what became a one-year campaign to try and capture Francisco "Pancho" Villa, whose forces had raided Columbus, New Mexico. The seizure of Veracruz and the Pershing Expedition generated anger in Mexico but ultimately worked to Venustiano Carranza's advantage. Veracruz helped weaken the regime of President Victoriano Huerta and brought Carranza to presidential power in July 1914, and the Pershing Expedition hastened the decline of Carranza's chief rival, Pancho Villa. The Mexican Revolution had a profound impact on the history of Mexico, and the Garza War of 1890–93 was a smoldering harbinger of a growing anti-Díaz resentment that burst into full flame in 1910.[20]

▼ ▼ ▼

APPENDIX
THE INSURRECTOS, 1890–1893

Aieto, Raiel. Surrendered to US deputy marshal Joe Shely in April 1893. Brought to San Antonio for trial May 4, 1893, by US deputy marshal Joe Shely.[1]

Ajala, Monsicio. Indicted November 13, 1893, by a federal grand jury in San Antonio for violations of the neutrality law.[2]

Alvido, Natiridad. Tried in US federal court in San Antonio May 17, 1892. Pled guilty to violation of US neutrality laws. Sentence suspended by US federal judge Alexander Boarman.[3]

Ansaleo, Motello. Surrendered to US deputy marshal Joe Shely in April 1893 at Carrizo. Brought to San Antonio for trial May 4, 1893, by US deputy marshal Joe Shely.[4]

Arambula, Andres. Surrendered to Captain Henry Jackson, Seventh Cavalry at Carrizo, March 22, 1893. Brought to San Antonio for trial May 4, 1893, by US deputy marshal Joe Shely.[5]

Arsola, Mateo. Captain Henry Jackson, Seventh Cavalry at Carrizo, reported his capture April 12, 1893.[6]

Barrera, Juan. Indicted on November 13, 1893, by a federal grand jury in San Antonio for violations of the neutrality law.[7]

Bazan, Victoriano. In US District Court in San Antonio, May 26, 1892, with US federal judge Alexander Boarman for violation of neutrality laws. Pled guilty and was sentenced to five months in Bexar County jail from time of arrest.[8]

Belmontez, Feleciano. Indicted on November 13, 1893, by a federal grand jury in San Antonio for violations of the neutrality law.[9]

Benavides, Cayetano. In US District Court in San Antonio, May 3, 1893, pled not guilty to violation of the neutrality laws. US federal judge Thomas S. Maxey set trial date for May 4, 1893.[10]

Benavides, Cresencio. Detained in the Fort Ringgold guardhouse as a suspected Garzista, April 3, 1892.[11]

Benavides, Esperidion. In US District Court in San Antonio, May 3, 1893, pled guilty to violation of the neutrality laws. US federal judge Thomas S. Maxey suspended his sentence.[12]

Benavides, Estevan. Garza captain, San Ignacio raider. Captured February 6, 1893, by Lieutenant Parker W. West, Troop I, Third Cavalry from Fort Ringgold and US deputy marshal James Arnold. In US District Court in San Antonio, May 3, 1893, pled guilty to violation of the neutrality laws. US federal judge Thomas S. Maxey suspended his sentence.[13]

Benavides, Francisco. Garza colonel, leader of San Ignacio raid. He had lost an eye so was also known as El Tuerto (One-Eye). He was born in 1843 at Casas Blancas, on the Rio Grande, then part of Mexico. Lived at El Clovis Rancho, northwestern Duval County, Texas. Was Garza's second in command. He led the brutal San Ignacio raid, December 10, 1892. Captured January 21, 1893, by Lieutenant Joseph T. Dickman, Third Cavalry. On January 26, 1893, he appeared before US Circuit Court commissioner Walter Downs at Rio Grande City.

Benavides refused to talk. Downs set his bond at two thousand dollars to appear in district court in San Antonio. Benavides could not make bail and remained in jail. Mexico demanded his extradition for murder. At the extradition hearing in San Antonio in February 1893 his defense attorney, W. E. Cox, that argued he was an American citizen and could not be extradited. The prosecution produced his certificate of birth, signed in Mier, Mexico, three days after his birth. The court found in favor of extradition and forwarded the decision to President Cleveland. On March 22, 1893, Secretary of State Walter Q. Gresham replied back to the court that the request for extradition would be deferred until after the Benavides case went before the Starr County grand jury in May 1893. However, on June 7, 1893, the newspapers reported that the United States denied Mexico's request for extradition of Benavides. Secretary of State Walter Q. Gresham discovered that Benavides actually was a US citizen and denied the extradition request.

When he was five years old Benavides and all the other residents of Casas Blancas, Mexico, suddenly became US citizens in 1848 because the Treaty of Guadalupe Hidalgo and the Rio Grande survey's shifted Casas Blancas to the Texas side of the border. Benavides did serve three years in prison for violations of the Neutrality Act.[14]

Benavides, José María. Arrested by Lieutenant Stephen O'Conner, Company G, Twenty-Third Infantry at San Ygnacio, June 24, 1893.[15]

Bermadez, Leander. Indicted on November 13, 1893, by a federal grand jury in San Antonio for violations of the neutrality law.[16]

Brecina, Jesus. In US District Court in San Antonio, May 3, 1893, case dismissed by US federal judge Thomas S. Maxey.[17]

Briseno, Josne. On trial for violation of US neutrality laws in US District Court in San Antonio, May 8–19, 1893.[18]

Bruni, Antonio Mateo. Born in 1856, Bruni was a wealthy Italian immigrant and businessman in Laredo who was elected Webb County commissioner in 1892, and later county treasurer, a position he held until his death in 1931. He was in US District Court in San Antonio, May 26, 1892, with US federal judge Alexander Boarman for violation of neutrality laws for his support of Garza. The case was delayed until a lawyer could be appointed. Eventually Bruni was convicted of violation of the neutrality laws, a federal conviction that apparently helped his political career. A park and elementary school in Laredo are named for him.[19]

Cadena, Apelinio "Pablo." Son of Santos Cadena. Surrendered February 8, 1893, to Lieutenant Herbert J. Slocum, Troop D, Seventh Cavalry and US deputy marshal O'Donnell.[20]

Cadena, Refugio. Surrendered February 10, 1893, at Peña Ranch to Lieutenant Herbert J. Slocum, Troop D, Seventh Cavalry.[21]

Cadena, Santos. Garza captain. Surrendered February 8, 1893, to Lieutenant Herbert J. Slocum, Troop D, Seventh Cavalry and US deputy marshal O'Donnell. In US District Court in San Antonio, May 3, 1893, pled guilty to violation of the neutrality laws. US federal judge Thomas S. Maxey suspended his sentence.[22]

Cadlor, Guadalupe C. With Francisco Ruíz Sandoval on the Sandoval raid, June 24, 1890. Captured June 25, 1890, at Las Islas by Captain Edgar Z. Steever, Troop G, Third Cavalry and US deputy marshal Eugene Iglesias.

Acquitted for violation of US neutrality laws at trial in San Antonio, December 23, 1890.[23]

Cantu, Lucio. San Ignacio raider. Captured mid-March 1893 by Starr County sheriff Wash Shely and Captain George F. Chase, Third Cavalry. In US District Court in San Antonio, May 3, 1893, pled guilty to violation of the neutrality laws. US federal judge Thomas S. Maxey suspended his sentence.[24]

Cantu, Victor. On trial for violation of US neutrality laws in US District Court in San Antonio, May 8–19, 1893.[25]

Castillo, Molena. Indicted on November 13, 1893, by a federal grand jury in San Antonio for violations of the neutrality law.[26]

Cavazos, Bartolo. Brought to San Antonio May 4, 1893, by US deputy marshal E. F. Hall for trial for violating the Neutrality Act.[27]

Chacon, Jesus. In US District Court in San Antonio, May 3, 1893, pled guilty to violation of the neutrality laws. US federal judge Thomas S. Maxey suspended his sentence.[28]

Cuellar, Tomás. San Ignacio raider, Garza colonel. Born in 1859. Surrendered to Captain Henry Jackson, Seventh Cavalry at Carrizo, March 7, 1893.[29]

Duque, Juan. Garza lieutenant, San Ignacio raider. Captured eight miles from Rio Grande City on March 3, 1893, by Starr County sheriff Wash Shely. After Duque finished his prison sentence for violation of US neutrality laws he was rearrested by US marshals for extradition to Mexico. US federal judge Thomas S. Maxey ordered his release, ruling that a neutrality law violation was not an extraditable offense and the revolutionists were political refugees. The case went to the US Supreme Court, which ruled on March 16, 1896, that they were bandits, not political refugees. On April 16, 1896, the Supreme Court ordered federal authorities to turn Duque and a dozen others over to Mexico for extradition.[30]

Echevarria, Cecilio. San Ignacio raider, captured January 22, 1893, by Lieutenant Joseph T. Dickman, Third Cavalry. Was a captain and deserter from the Mexican Army. On January 25, 1893, when taken before US Circuit Court Commissioner Walter Downs at Rio Grande City, Echevarria admitted to being a revolutionary and to firing at Texas state officers. Downs set his bail at five hundred dollars, which Echevarria paid. Dr. Plutarco

Ornelas, Mexican Consul, San Antonio, Texas. applied to extradite him for crimes in Mexico.[31]

Elizando, Cayetano Garza. Owned a store and ranch at La Grulla. His trial was in US District Court in San Antonio, December 5, 1892. For violations of the Neutrality Act he was sentenced to a ten-dollar fine and two years in prison in Detroit, Michigan, by US federal judge Thomas S. Maxey on December 19, 1892.[32]

Flores, Entiquio. In US District Court in San Antonio, May 26, 1892, with US federal judge Alexander Boarman for violation of neutrality laws. Case delayed until a lawyer could be appointed.[33]

Flores, Galvino. Sandoval raider, June 24, 1890. Captured June 25, 1890, at Las Islas by Captain Edgar Z. Steever, Troop G, Third Cavalry and US deputy marshal Eugene Iglesias. Acquitted at trial in US District Court in San Antonio, December 23, 1890.[34]

Flores, Jesus. Major Alexander S. B. Keyes, Third Cavalry reported his surrender April 17, 1893. In US District Court in San Antonio, May 3, 1893, Flores pled guilty to violation of the neutrality laws. US federal judge Thomas S. Maxey dismissed his case and turned him over to Starr County sheriff Wash Shely for a Starr County murder trial.[35]

Flores, Juan Angel. Indicted on November 13, 1893, by a federal grand jury in San Antonio for violations of the neutrality law.[36]

Flores, Juan Antonio. In San Antonio on December 19, 1892, sentenced by US federal judge Thomas S. Maxey for violations of the Neutrality Act to a ten-dollar fine and three years in prison in Detroit, Michigan.[37]

Flores, Juan Manuel. In US District Court in San Antonio, May 26, 1892, with US federal judge Alexander Boarman for violation of neutrality laws. Case delayed until a lawyer could be appointed.[38]

Flores, Julian. Garza lieutenant. He owned a ranch in Starr County. Flores was commander of the Libres Fronterizos (Free Frontier) regiment. On May 11, 1892, he led a band of several hundred across the Rio Grande above Mier and ran into Mexican forces at La Mecca. Flores and eight others were killed.[39]

Flores, Telesforo. Captain Henry Jackson, Seventh Cavalry at Carrizo, reported his capture April 12, 1893. In US District Court in San Antonio,

May 5, 1893, pled guilty to violation of the neutrality laws. US federal judge Thomas S. Maxey suspended his sentence.[40]

Gaitan, Anastacio. On trial for violation of US neutrality laws in US District Court in San Antonio, May 8–19, 1893.[41]

Galvan, Juaqnio. In US District Court in San Antonio, May 26, 1892, with US federal judge Alexander Boarman for violation of neutrality laws. Pled guilty and was sentenced to five months in Bexar County jail from time of arrest.[42]

Gamez, Pablo. In US District Court in San Antonio, May 3, 1893, pled guilty to violation of the neutrality laws. US federal judge Thomas S. Maxey suspended his sentence. Mexico requested Gamez's extradition.[43]

García, Amador [Amadeo]. With Francisco Ruíz Sandoval on the Sandoval raid, June 24, 1890. Captured June 25, 1890, at Las Islas by Captain Edgar Z. Steever, Troop G, Third Cavalry and US deputy marshal Eugene Iglesias. Acquitted for violation of US neutrality laws at trial in US District Court in San Antonio December 23, 1890.[44]

García, Amando. Surrendered to US deputy marshal Joe Shely in April 1893. In US District Court in San Antonio, May 5, 1893, pled guilty to violation of the neutrality laws. US federal judge Thomas S. Maxey suspended his sentence.[45]

García, Antenacio. Brought to San Antonio May 4, 1893, by US deputy marshal E. F. Hall for trial for violating the Neutrality Act.[46]

García, Antonio. García's extradition trial went before US Circuit Court commissioner Larkin F. Price on November 10, 1893, in San Antonio. Price set bond at two hundred dollars. García could not meet bond and remained in jail.[47]

García, Armando. San Ignacio raider. Surrendered to Captain Henry Jackson, Seventh Cavalry at Carrizo, March 7, 1893.[48]

García, Delfino. Captain George F. Chase, Third Cavalry reported his arrest April 27, 1893.[49]

García, Eusebio. Lieutenant Stephen O'Conner, Twenty-Third Infantry reported his arrest August 1, 1893. Indicted for violation of neutrality laws by federal grand jury in San Antonio, November 13, 1893.[50]

García, Juan. In US District Court in San Antonio, May 26, 1892, with US federal judge Alexander Boarman for violation of neutrality laws. Pled guilty and was sentenced to five months in Bexar County jail from time of arrest.[51]

García, Juan M. P. Surrendered to US deputy marshal Joe Shely in April 1893. Brought to San Antonio for trial May 4, 1893, by US deputy marshal Shely.[52]

García, Julian. Captain Henry Jackson, Seventh Cavalry at Carrizo, reported his capture April 12, 1893.[53]

García, Julio. On trial for violation of US neutrality laws in US District Court in San Antonio, May 8–19, 1893.[54]

García, Louis. Captured at Roma February 8, 1893, by Lieutenant Parker W. West, Troop I, Third Cavalry from Fort Ringgold.[55]

García, Nesario. Captured January 27, 1893, by Starr County sheriff Wash Shely and deputy sheriff Pink Barnhill at Mulas Ranch. He appeared before US Circuit Court Commissioner Walter Downs at Rio Grande City. Downs set his bond to appear in US District Court in San Antonio.[56]

García, Pedro. Wanted for the murder of Corporal Charles H. Edstrom, Troop C, Third Cavalry at Retamal. Captured by Lieutenant Parker W. West, with a detachment of Troop I, Third Cavalry from Fort Ringgold. García was captured thirty-five miles east of post April 19, 1893. Indicted for murder. In US District Court in San Antonio, May 5, 1893, pled guilty to violation of the neutrality laws. US federal judge Thomas S. Maxey suspended his sentence apparently so that his murder trial could proceed.[57]

García, Roman. Surrendered to Captain Henry Jackson, Seventh Cavalry at Carrizo, April 14, 1893. Brought to San Antonio for trial May 4, 1893, by US deputy marshal Joe Shely.[58]

García, Rosillio. In US District Court in San Antonio, May 3, 1893, pled guilty to violation of the neutrality laws. US federal judge Thomas S. Maxey suspended his sentence.[59]

Garza, Bernardo de la. In US District Court in San Antonio, May 27, 1892, for arraignment on charge of violation of the neutrality laws. Trial set for May 31, 1892, by US federal judge Alexander Boarman. Case dismissed by federal district attorney on November 10, 1893, in San Antonio.[60]

Garza, Catarino Erasmo. Born near Matamoros in 1859, Garza became an anti-Díaz firebrand and newspaper editor. Garza led his Constitutional Army from South Texas into Mexico on September 15, 1891. Failing to raise a popular revolution and pursued by US authorities Garza fled Texas in

February 1892. He was killed March 5, 1895, at Boco del Toro, Colombia (now Panama), taking part in the Colombian Revolution.[61]

Garza, Frank. Arrested near San Diego, Texas, January 19, 1892, by Captain George K. Hunter, Troop K, Third Cavalry. Garza admitted he rode with Catarino Garza for a month, but was poorly fed and not paid, so he quit.[62]

Garza, Luis. In US District Court in San Antonio, May 30, 1892, pled guilty to violation of the neutrality laws. Sentenced to two months in jail from time of arrest. Time already served. Discharged by US federal judge Alexander Boarman.[63]

Garza, Rafael. Brought to San Antonio May 4, 1893, by US deputy marshal E. F. Hall for trial for violating the Neutrality Act.[64]

Garza, Rosalio. Captured January 27, 1893, by Starr County sheriff Wash Shely and deputy sheriff Pink Barnhill at Mulas Ranch. He appeared before US Circuit Court commissioner Walter Downs at Rio Grande City. Downs set his bond to appear in US District Court in San Antonio.[65]

Garza, Theodoro. On trial for violation of US neutrality laws in US District Court in San Antonio, May 8–19, 1893.[66]

Garza, Ygnacio. In US District Court in San Antonio, May 27, 1892, for arraignment on charge of violation of the neutrality laws. Trial set for May 31, 1892, by US federal judge Alexander Boarman.[67]

Golindo, Juan M. In US District Court in San Antonio, May 30, 1892, pled guilty to violation of the neutrality laws. Sentenced to eight months in the Starr County jail by US federal judge Alexander Boarman.[68]

González, Alejandro. Catarino E. Garza's father-in-law, owner of Palito Blanco Ranch, and major supporter of the revolutionaries. In US District Court in San Antonio, May 27, 1892, for arraignment on charge of violation of the neutrality laws. Trial set for May 31, 1892, by US federal judge Alexander Boarman. González bonded for two thousand dollars but did not show up for court. González was ordered again to appear in federal court in San Antonio on May 16, 1893, but he sent a note saying he could not come because of family illness. US federal judge Thomas S. Maxey ordered the forfeit of his two-thousand-dollar bond and directed his immediate arrest. On May 17, 1893, González was arrested at his ranch. On May 19, 1893, in San Antonio, he pled guilty to violating US neutrality laws and failure to appear in court. Judge Maxey sentenced him to a sixteen-hundred-dollar fine and an hour in the Bexar County jail. González served his hour and paid the fine in cash.[69]

González, Brunio. Indicted on November 13, 1893, by a federal grand jury in San Antonio for violations of the neutrality law.[70]

González, Concepcíon "Chonita." Daughter of Alejandro González, and Catarino E. Garza's second wife.[71]

González, Francis. In US District Court in San Antonio, May 16, 1892, with US federal judge Thomas S. Maxey for violation of neutrality laws. Arraigned, pled guilty, but sentencing delayed until the court could appoint him a lawyer.[72]

González, Francisco. In US District Court in San Antonio, May 3, 1893, pled guilty to violation of the neutrality laws. US federal judge Thomas S. Maxey suspended his sentence.[73]

González, Manuel. Surrendered to US deputy marshal Joe Shely in April 1893 at Carrizo. Brought to San Antonio for trial May 4, 1893, by Deputy Marshal Shely.[74]

González, Pedro Peña. In US District Court in San Antonio, May 30, 1892, pled guilty to violation of the neutrality laws. Sentenced to eight months in the Starr County jail by US federal judge Alexander Boarman.[75]

González, Prudencio. San Ignacio raider. Born about 1830, lived many years in Aqua Nueva, Texas, had a wife and three daughters, the eldest of whom was married to Francisco Benavides, leader of the San Ignacio raid. Gonzáles was captured with Francisco Benavides January 21, 1893, by Lieutenant Joseph T. Dickman, Third Cavalry. Dr. Plutarco Ornelas, Mexican Consul, San Antonio, Texas, applied to extradite him for arson, robbery, and kidnaping crimes in Mexico. González's extradition trial went before US Circuit Court commissioner Larkin F. Price on April 24, 1893, in San Antonio. Price forwarded a recommendation for extradition to Secretary of State Walter Q. Gresham. In US District Court in San Antonio, May 3, 1893, pled guilty to violation of the neutrality laws. US federal judge Thomas S. Maxey suspended his sentence.[76]

González, Vicente M. Sandoval raider, June 24, 1890. Captured June 25, 1890, at Las Islas by Captain Edgar Z. Steever, Troop G, Third Cavalry and US deputy marshal Eugene Iglesias. Acquitted at trial in US District Court in San Antonio December 23, 1890.[77]

Guebarra, Gregorio. San Ignacio raider. Surrendered to Captain Henry Jackson, Seventh Cavalry at Carrizo, February 23, 1893. Brought to San Antonio for trial May 4, 1893, by US deputy marshal Joe Shely.[78]

Guerra, Antonio. Brought to San Antonio May 4, 1893, by US deputy marshal E. F. Hall for trial for violating the Neutrality Act. Indicted for violation of neutrality laws by federal grand jury in San Antonio, November 13, 1893.[79]

Guerra, Jesus. San Ignacio raider. Guerra was sentenced to prison for violating the Neutrality Act. After he completed his prison term he was rearrested by US marshals for extradition to Mexico. US federal judge Thomas S. Maxey ordered his release, ruling that a neutrality law violation was not an extraditable offense and the revolutionists were political refugees. The case went to the US Supreme Court, which ruled on March 16, 1896, that they were bandits not political refugees. On April 16, 1896, the Supreme Court ordered federal authorities to turn Guerra and a dozen others over to Mexico for extradition. The new secretary of state, John Sherman, appointed by President William McKinley, refused to approve Guerra's extradition. Sherman had reviewed the file and determined that although Guerra was present at the San Ignacio raid, at his original extradition trial held by US Circuit Court commissioner Larkin F. Price, there were no witnesses who directly accused or proved that Guerra was specifically guilty of the murder, kidnapping, or robbery charges in the extradition request, adding that the San Ignacio "expedition," as he called it, was "revolutionary in its origin and purpose . . . therefore . . . was of a purely political character," thus outside of the scope of the extradition treaty. Cayetano Romero, leading the Mexican legation in Washington, DC, pushed back, reminding Secretary Sherman that the extradition commissioner and two previous secretaries of state, Walter Q. Gresham and his successor Richard Olney, had approved Guerra's extradition, and that the US Supreme Court had ruled they were bandits, not political actors or refugees. Secretary Sherman refused to approve the transfer, more than likely taking his cue from President McKinley, the Guerra case having more to do with Cuba than Mexico. McKinley was exploring the potential to declare the Cuban revolutionaries as legitimate belligerents, thus aiding them in ridding Cuba, and the Americas, of Spain.[80]

Guerra, Juan. Surrender reported March 13, 1893, by Captain William B. Wheeler, Eighteenth Infantry. On trial for violation of US neutrality laws in US District Court in San Antonio, May 8–19, 1893.[81]

Guerra, Juan. Surrendered to Lieutenant Parker W. West, Troop I, Third Cavalry and Starr County sheriff Wash Shely about March 4, 1893.[82]

Guerra, Melcher. With Francisco Ruíz Sandoval on the Sandoval raid June 24, 1890. Captured June 25, 1890, at Las Islas by Captain Edgar Z. Steever, Troop G, Third Cavalry and US deputy marshal Eugene Iglesias. Acquitted for violation of US neutrality laws at trial in US District Court in San Antonio December 23, 1890.[83]

Gutiérrez, Amador. Sandoval raider, June 24, 1890. Captured June 25, 1890, at Las Islas by Captain Edgar Z. Steever, Troop G, Third Cavalry and US deputy marshal Eugene Iglesias. Acquitted at trial in US District Court in San Antonio December 23, 1890.[84]

Gutiérrez, Clemente. San Ignacio raider, Garza captain. Born in Guerrero, Mexico, in 1863. Surrendered to Captain Henry Jackson, Seventh Cavalry at Carrizo, February 23, 1893. In US District Court in San Antonio, May 5, 1893, pled guilty to violation of the neutrality laws. US deputy marshal Joe Shely testified that Gutiérrez was instrumental in persuading many of the revolutionists to peacefully surrender. US federal judge Thomas S. Maxey suspended his sentence.[85]

Gutiérrez, Epifano. Indicted on November 13, 1893, by a federal grand jury in San Antonio for violations of the neutrality law.[86]

Gutiérrez, Labrado. Indicted on November 13, 1893, by a federal grand jury in San Antonio for violations of the neutrality law.[87]

Gutiérrez, Liberado. San Ignacio raider, Garza captain. Captured mid-March 1893 by Starr County sheriff Wash Shely and Captain George F. Chase, Third Cavalry. In US District Court in San Antonio, May 3, 1893, pled guilty to violation of the neutrality laws. US federal judge Thomas S. Maxey suspended his sentence.[88]

Gutiérrez, Liberdad. Surrendered to Captain Henry Jackson, Seventh Cavalry at Carrizo, February 23, 1893.[89]

Gutiérrez, Porfirio. Surrendered to Captain Henry Jackson, Seventh Cavalry at Carrizo, March 7, 1893.[90]

Gutiérrez [Gutierras], Procopio. San Ignacio raider, Garza colonel. Born in 1848 in Guerrero, Mexico, and was owner of San Bartola Ranch in Zapata County. Arrested March 8, 1893.[91]

Hernandez, Dario. Arrested February 13, 1893.[92]

Hernandez, David. Captured near Laredo February 16, 1893, by Lieutenant Tyree R. Rivers, Troop E, Third Cavalry.[93]

Hernandez, Nicholas. Charged with violation of US neutrality laws. Case dismissed June 17, 1893 by US district attorney.[94]

Leal, Geraldo. Captured near Laredo February 15, 1893, by Lieutenant Tyree R. Rivers, Troop E, Third Cavalry.[95]

Lemon, Serstones. Major Alexander S. B. Keyes, Third Cavalry, reported his arrest August 2, 1893.[96]

Longorio, Pablo. Former Garzista. Was a guide for Captain George F. Chase, Troop D, Third Cavalry. Was arrested on an old charge of being a horse thief and sentenced to eight years in prison by a Webb County court. The charges and sentence were suspected of being retaliation for helping the army. The Texas governor pardoned Longoria.[97]

Longorio, Sixto. Captured December 29, 1891, at Palito Blanco Ranch by Captain Francis H. Hardie and Troop G, Third Cavalry. Longorio was a prisoner in the guardhouse at Ringgold, then taken to Brownsville and turned over to civil authorities. His wounded leg was amputated and he was not expected to live, but was indicted for violation of the neutrality laws in February 1893. In US District Court in San Antonio, May 16, 1892, with US federal judge Thomas S. Maxey for violation of neutrality laws. Arraigned, pled guilty, but sentencing delayed until the court could appoint him a lawyer.[98]

López, Abelarjo. Sandoval raider, June 24, 1890. Captured June 25, 1890, at Las Islas by Captain Edgar Z. Steever, Troop G, Third Cavalry, and US deputy marshal Eugene Iglesias. Acquitted at trial in US District Court in San Antonio December 23, 1890.[99]

López, Amostacio. Captured mid-March 1893 by Starr County sheriff Wash Shely and Captain George F. Chase, Third Cavalry.[100]

López, Hymio. In US District Court in San Antonio, May 26, 1892, with US federal judge Alexander Boarman for violation of neutrality laws. Case delayed until a lawyer could be appointed.[101]

López, Leonidas. In US District Court in San Antonio, May 26, 1892, with US federal judge Alexander Boarman for violation of neutrality laws. Bond set at one hundred dollars, trial reset for third Monday in November 1892.[102]

López, Manuel. Surrendered to US deputy marshal Joe Shely in April 1893 at Carrizo. Brought to San Antonio for trial May 4, 1893, by Deputy Marshal Shely.[103]

López, Teodoro G. In US District Court in San Antonio, May 5, 1893, pled guilty to violation of the neutrality laws. US federal judge Thomas S. Maxey suspended his sentence.[104]

López, Victoriano. Arrested January 28, 1892, by US deputy marshal Lena Cuellar with Major Louis T. Morris, Third Cavalry. Lopez had a carbine and ammunition of the type carried by Garzistas. Tried in US District Court in San Antonio May 17, 1892. Pled guilty to violation of US neutrality laws. Sentenced by US federal judge Alexander Boarman to twelve months in prison.[105]

Magro, Abeham [Abram]. In US District Court in San Antonio, May 5, 1893, pled guilty to violation of the neutrality laws. US federal judge Thomas S. Maxey suspended his sentence.[106]

Maldonado, Juan. Surrendered to Lieutenant Parker W. West, Troop I, Third Cavalry, and Starr County sheriff Wash Shely about March 4, 1893. On trial for violation of US neutrality laws in US District Court in San Antonio, May 8–19, 1893.[107]

Margo, Estavano. A Black Garzista. Surrendered March 4, 1893, to Starr County sheriff Wash Shely.[108]

Martínez, Ensebio. Arrested June 14, 1893, by US deputy marshal E. F. Hall in Laredo.[109]

Martínez, Eusabio M., alias Mangus de Aqua. San Ignacio raider, killed scout and US deputy marshal Rufus Glover in January 1892. Martínez was killed February 23, 1893, by a Seminole-Negro Indian scout and Starr County sheriff Warren Washington "Wash" Shely on a patrol led by Lieutenant Percival G. Lowe.[110]

Martínez, Felipe. From Laredo, on May 16, 1893, in federal court in San Antonio, he was charged with supplying ammunition to Garza's band.[111]

Martínez, Mateo. Tried in US District Court in San Antonio May 27, 1892. Pled guilty to violation of US neutrality laws. Sentenced by US federal judge Alexander Boarman to three months in the Bexar County jail.[112]

Martínez, Maximo. San Ignacio raider, surrendered to Captain Henry Jackson, Seventh Cavalry, at Carrizo, March 22, 1893. Appeared before US federal judge Thomas S. Maxey on May 30, 1893. Charged with violation of the US neutrality laws. On June 1, 1893, was sentenced to a one-dollar fine and three years in prison in the Anamosa, Iowa, federal penitentiary. Rearrested immediately on an extradition warrant from Mexico for arson, kidnapping, robbery, and murder. Appeared for extradition trial June 5, 1893, before US Circuit Court commissioner Larkin F. Price in San Antonio and pled guilty to all charges. Price forwarded a recommendation for extradition to Secretary of State Walter Q. Gresham. President Cleveland approved the extradition and apparently pardoned Martínez so that he could be turned over to Mexican authorities.[113]

Martivero, Evaristo. Surrendered to Captain Henry Jackson, Seventh Cavalry, at Carrizo, March 22, 1893.[114]

Mendoza, Anastacio. In US District Court in San Antonio, May 3, 1893, pled guilty to violation of the neutrality laws. US federal judge Thomas S. Maxey suspended his sentence.[115]

Mendoza, Francisco L. In US District Court in San Antonio, May 27, 1892, for arraignment on charge of violation of the neutrality laws. Trial set for May 31, 1892, by US federal judge Alexander Boarman.[116]

Mendoza, Pedro. Brought to San Antonio May 4, 1893, by US deputy marshal E. F. Hall for trial for violating the neutrality act.[117]

Meno, Gonzalo. See Sandoval, Marco.

Molina, Jacabo. In US District Court in San Antonio, May 26, 1892, with US federal judge Alexander Boarman for violation of neutrality laws. Pled guilty and was sentenced to five months in Bexar County jail from time of arrest.[118]

Mongao, Innocencio. Charged with violations of the neutrality law, charges dismissed by district attorney in federal court in San Antonio, November 13, 1893.[119]

Montevino, Avisto. Surrendered to US deputy marshal Joe Shely in April 1893 at Carrizo. Brought to San Antonio for trial May 4, 1893, by Deputy Marshal Shely.[120]

Morales, Felipe. Captured mid-March 1893 by Starr County sheriff Wash Shely and Captain George F. Chase, Third Cavalry.[121]

Morales, José María. An ex-priest, was Catarino E. Garza's mentor and teacher in Mexico. Surrendered to Captain Henry Jackson, Seventh Cavalry, at Carrizo, February 23, 1893. In US District Court in San Antonio, May 5, 1893, pled guilty to violation of the neutrality laws. US federal judge Thomas S. Maxey suspended his sentence.[122]

Moreno, Severino. San Ignacio raider. Captured February 6, 1893, by Lieutenant Parker W. West, Troop I, Third Cavalry from Fort Ringgold and US deputy marshal James Arnold. On trial for violation of US neutrality laws in US District Court in San Antonio, May 8–19, 1893.[123]

Moya, Electorio. At US District Court at Brownsville, June 19, 1893, pled guilty to violation of US neutrality laws. Sentenced to one-dollar fine and sixty days in jail by US federal judge Thomas S. Maxey.[124]

Moya, Teodoro. At US District Court at Brownsville, June 19, 1893, pled guilty to violation of US neutrality laws. Sentenced to one-dollar fine and thirty days in jail by US federal judge Thomas S. Maxey.[125]

Muñoz, Pablo. Senior Garza colonel. Born in 1835, came to United States in 1881. Muñoz was captured near Las Cuevitas January 2, 1893, by Lieutenant George T. Langhorne, Third Cavalry. Tried in US federal court in San Antonio May 28, 1892. His defense attorney was Robert L. Summerlin. Muñoz was found guilty of violations of US neutrality laws by an all-Anglo jury. Because of Muñoz's age, US federal judge Alexander Boarman sentenced him to a three-thousand-dollar fine and eighteen months in prison in Detroit, Michigan, half the maximum penalty in prison.[126]

Natividad, Alvado. In US District Court in San Antonio, May 16, 1892, with US federal judge Thomas S. Maxey for violation of neutrality laws. Arraigned, pled guilty, but sentencing delayed until the court could appoint him a lawyer.[127]

Nieto, Rafael. San Ignacio raider. Born in 1853, had a wife and three children. Surrendered in March 1893. In US District Court in San Antonio, May 5, 1893, pled guilty to violation of the neutrality laws. US federal judge Thomas S. Maxey suspended his sentence.[128]

Ortiz, Espiridion. Captured mid-March 1893 by Starr County sheriff Wash Shely and Captain George F. Chase, Third Cavalry. In US District Court in San Antonio, May 5, 1893, pled guilty to violation of the neutrality laws. US federal judge Thomas S. Maxey suspended his sentence.[129]

Palacio, Porician. San Ignacio raider. Wounded in the San Ignacio raid, Palacio was captured December 23, 1892, by US deputy marshal E. F. Hall. While being transported to Laredo by US deputy marshals Rosendo Guerra and Marcial Benavides, the deputies were ambushed by revolutionaries near Bruni Ranch, freeing Palacio and kidnapping the deputies. On January 4, 1893, Lieutenant Charles A. Hedekin with a detachment of Troop A, Third Cavalry attacked the group while they were crossing the Rio Grande into Mexico, and the deputies made their escape in the melee.[130]

Palacios, Antonio. Surrendered to Captain Henry Jackson, Seventh Cavalry, at Carrizo, March 3, 1893.[131]

Palacios, Florencio. Surrendered June 13, 1893, at Laredo to US deputy marshal Eugene Iglesias. Bail was set at two thousand dollars to appear in federal court at San Antonio. On November 10, 1893, pled guilty to violating the neutrality laws, sentenced by US federal judge Thomas S. Maxey to a one-dollar fine and three months in the Webb County jail.[132]

Paz, Ramón. Arrested February 27, 1893. As prisoner at Fort Ringgold, turned over to civil authorities March 5, 1893.[133]

Peña, Juan. In US District Court in San Antonio, May 30, 1892. Charges dismissed by US federal judge Alexander Boarman.[134]

Peña, Navato. Captured in June 1893 in Pecos County by US deputy marshal Joe Shely and Texas Ranger Corporal Kerchner from Captain Frank Jones's Company D.[135]

Peña, Zeon. In US District Court in San Antonio, May 19, 1892, with US federal judge Alexander Boarman for violation of neutrality laws. Indicted and bonded for trial.[136]

Pérez, Juan García. In US District Court in San Antonio, May 30, 1892. Charges dismissed by US federal judge Alexander Boarman.[137]

Pérez, Monico, alias Alezando Perez. Tried in US District Court in San Antonio May 17, 1892. Pled guilty to violation of US neutrality laws. Sentenced by US federal judge Alexander Boarman to twelve months in prison from date of original imprisonment.[138]

Pisusias, Rafael. Indicted on November 13, 1893, by a federal grand jury in San Antonio for violations of the neutrality law.[139]

Poletio, Florentino. One of the party that killed US deputy marshal and scout Rufus Glover, February 2, 1892. [140]

Ponze, Aurelio. On trial for violation of US neutrality laws in US District Court in San Antonio, May 8–19, 1893. [141]

Quellar, Fortunatio. Garza captain, arrested in Laredo February 29, 1892. [142]

Ramírez, Ensenio. Arrested in Laredo in June 1893 by US deputy marshal E. F. Hall. US Circuit Court commissioner S. T. Foster set bail at five hundred dollars. [143]

Ramírez, Eusabio. Indicted on November 13, 1893, by a federal grand jury in San Antonio for violations of the neutrality law. [144]

Ramírez, Francisco. Served in the Libres Fronterizos (Free Frontier) Regiment under Julian Flores. Born in 1849, came to the United States at age thirteen. Tried in US District Court in San Antonio May 27, 1892. Pled guilty to violation of US neutrality laws. Sentenced by US federal judge Alexander Boarman to twelve months in Bexar County jail. [145]

Ramírez, Jesus. Garza captain. Born in Mier, Mexico, in 1861. Captured January 27, 1893, by Starr County sheriff Wash Shely and deputy sheriff Pink Barnhill at Mulas Ranch. He appeared before US Circuit Court commissioner Walter Downs at Rio Grande City. Downs set his bond to appear in US District Court in San Antonio. [146]

Ramírez, Rafael. San Ignacio raider. Born in 1860, lived in San Ygnacio, Texas. Was a Garza colonel, signed most of the Garza officer commissions. Was secretary to Francisco Benavides. Arrested at San Ygnacio March 8, 1893, by Starr County sheriff Wash Shely. Avoided hard-labor prison sentence when Mexican soldiers testified that when Francisco Benavides ordered the wounded prisoners shot, Ramírez interceded and saved their lives. [147]

Ramírez, Secandio (Secundino). Surrendered to Lieutenant Parker W. West, Troop I, Third Cavalry, and Starr County sheriff Wash Shely about March 4, 1893. On trial for violation of US neutrality laws in US District Court in San Antonio, May 8–19, 1893. [148]

Ramírez, Ygnacio. In US District Court in San Antonio, May 19, 1892, for arraignment on a charge of violation of the neutrality laws. Bonded and trial set for May 31, 1892, by US federal judge Alexander Boarman. [149]

Ramón, Severiano M. Captured February 6, 1893, at San Ygnacio by Lieutenant Parker W. West, with a detachment of Troop I, Third Cavalry from Fort Ringgold.[150]

Rangel, Jesus. In US District Court in San Antonio, May 16, 1892, with US federal judge Thomas S. Maxey for violation of neutrality laws. Arraigned, pled guilty, but sentencing delayed until the court could appoint him a lawyer.[151]

Regilado, Juan Sanches. On trial for violation of US neutrality laws in US District Court in San Antonio, May 8–19, 1893.[152]

Rendon, Benito. In US District Court in San Antonio, May 26, 1892, with US federal judge Alexander Boarman for violation of neutrality laws. The district attorney filed *noile prosequi* (prosecutor does not wish to prosecute) in the case.[153]

Reyna, Francisco. Garza captain. In US District Court in San Antonio May 30, 1892, pled guilty to violation of the neutrality laws. Sentenced to eighteen months in prison in Detroit, Michigan, by US federal judge Alexander Boarman.[154]

Rios, Macario. Tried in US federal court in San Antonio May 17, 1892. Case dismissed for mistaken identity.[155]

Rodriguez, Guillermo. At US District Court at Brownsville, June 19, 1893, pled guilty to violation of US neutrality laws. Sentenced to one-dollar fine and sixty days in jail by US federal judge Thomas S, Maxey.[156]

Rodriguez, Mieigio. Indicted November 13, 1893, by a federal grand jury in San Antonio for violations of the neutrality law.[157]

Rodriguez, Moreliano (Molentino). Tried in US District Court in San Antonio May 17, 1892. Pled guilty to violation of US neutrality laws. Sentence suspended by US federal judge Alexander Boarman.[158]

Rodriguez, Narciso. On trial for violation of US neutrality laws in US District Court in San Antonio, May 8–19, 1893.[159]

Rodriguez, Victor. His ranch at Las Mujeras supplied beef to revolutionaries in 1891.[160]

Roman, Eustoigio. In US District Court in San Antonio, May 16, 1892, with US federal judge Thomas S. Maxey for violation of neutrality laws. Arraigned, pled guilty, but sentencing delayed until the court could appoint him a lawyer.[161]

Rosa, Santos. Captured January 27, 1893, by Starr County sheriff Wash Shely and deputy sheriff Pink Barnhill at Mulas Ranch. He appeared before US Circuit Court commissioner Walter Downs at Rio Grande City. Downs set his bond to appear in US District Court in San Antonio. In US District Court in San Antonio, May 3, 1893, pled guilty to violation of the neutrality laws. US federal judge Thomas S. Maxey suspended his sentence.[162]

Ruiz, Inez. Ruiz was sentenced to prison for violating the Neutrality Act. After he completed his prison term he was rearrested by US marshals for extradition to Mexico. US federal judge Thomas S. Maxey ordered his release, ruling that a neutrality law violation was not an extraditable offense and that the revolutionists were political refugees. The case went to the US Supreme Court, which ruled on March 16, 1896, that they were bandits, not political refugees. On April 16, 1896, the Supreme Court ordered federal authorities to turn Ruiz and a dozen others over to Mexico for extradition.[163]

Sais, Cesario. Tried in US District Court in San Antonio May 17, 1892. Pled guilty to violation of US neutrality laws. Sentenced by US federal judge Alexander Boarman to six months in prison from date of original imprisonment.[164]

Sais, Geraldo. On June 1, 1893, in US District Court in San Antonio, sentenced by US federal judge Thomas S. Maxey for violations of the Neutrality Act to eighteen months in the Bexar County jail.[165]

Saiz, Severiano. Captured January 27, 1893, by Starr County sheriff Wash Shely and deputy sheriff Pink Barnhill at Mulas Ranch. He appeared before US Circuit Court commissioner Walter Downs at Rio Grande City. Downs set his bond to appear in US District Court in San Antonio. On trial in US District Court in San Antonio, May 3, 1893, pled guilty to violation of the neutrality laws. US federal judge Thomas S. Maxey deferred his sentence.[166]

Salazar, Devincio. Captured mid-March 1893 by Starr County sheriff Wash Shely and Captain George F. Chase, Third Cavalry.[167]

Salazar, Dioneus (Deonecio, Dionitio). San Ignacio raider, Garza captain. Surrendered to Captain Henry Jackson, Seventh Cavalry, at Carrizo, February 23, 1893. In US District Court in San Antonio, May 5, 1893, pled guilty to violation of the neutrality laws. US federal judge Thomas S. Maxey suspended his sentence.[168]

Salinas, Cecillio. In San Antonio on December 19, 1892, sentenced by US federal judge Thomas S. Maxey for violations of the neutrality act to a ten-dollar fine and three years in prison in Detroit, Michigan.[169]

Salinas, Felipe. On trial for violation of US neutrality laws in US District Court in San Antonio, May 8–19, 1893.[170]

Salinas, Fernandez. Catarino E. Garza's private secretary. Captured at San Ygnacio March 8, 1893, by Starr County sheriff Wash Shely and Captain George F. Chase, Third Cavalry. In US District Court in San Antonio, May 3, 1893, pled guilty to violation of the neutrality laws. US federal judge Thomas S. Maxey suspended his sentence.[171]

Salinas, Luis. On trial for violation of US neutrality laws in US District Court in San Antonio, May 8–19, 1893.[172]

Salinas, Maximo. In US District Court in San Antonio, May 26, 1892, with US federal judge Alexander Boarman for violation of neutrality laws. Pled guilty and was sentenced to five months in Bexar County jail from time of arrest.[173]

Sánchez, Aciano. San Ignacio raider, arrest reported by Fort Ringgold commander, August 5, 1893.[174]

Sánchez, Astano. Indicted on November 13, 1893, by a federal grand jury in San Antonio for violations of the neutrality law.[175]

Sánchez, Juan. In US District Court in San Antonio, May 5, 1893, pled guilty to violation of the neutrality laws. US federal judge Thomas S. Maxey suspended his sentence.[176]

Sánchez, Luis. In US District Court in San Antonio, May 30, 1892. Charges dismissed by US federal judge Alexander Boarman.[177]

Sandoval, Francisco Ruíz. Organized and led first raid June 24, 1890. Captured June 25, 1890, at Las Islas by Captain Edgar Z. Steever, Troop G, Third Cavalry, and US deputy marshal Eugene Iglesias. Acquitted at trial in US District Court in San Antonio, December 23, 1890.[178]

Sandoval, Jesus "Chico." Surrendered to Lieutenant Parker W. West, Troop I, Third Cavalry, and Starr County sheriff Wash Shely about March 4, 1893.[179]

Sandoval, Marco. In the fight at Retamal. Captured while using the alias Gonzalo Meno in June 1893 in Pecos County by US deputy marshal Joe Shely and Texas Ranger Corporal Kerchner from Captain Frank Jones's Company D.[180]

Sandoval, Procopio. Surrendered to Lieutenant Parker W. West, Troop I, Third Cavalry, and Starr County sheriff Wash Shely about March 4, 1893. In US District Court in San Antonio, May 5, 1893, pled guilty to violation of the neutrality laws. US federal judge Thomas S. Maxey sentenced him to five days in jail.[181]

Sandrez, Abren C. Brought to San Antonio May 4, 1893, by US deputy marshal E. F. Hall for trial for violating the Neutrality Act.[182]

Santos, Feverion de los. Supposedly Garza's chief scout and courier. Captured by Lieutenant John T. Knight, Troop I, Third Cavalry, February 18, 1892.[183]

Sarate, Juan Manuel. On trial for violation of US neutrality laws in US District Court in San Antonio, May 8–19, 1893.[184]

Sias, Americano. In US District Court in San Antonio, May 3, 1893, pled guilty to violation of the neutrality laws. US federal judge Thomas S. Maxey suspended his sentence.[185]

Soto, José María. In US District Court in San Antonio, May 3, 1893, pled guilty to violation of the neutrality laws. US federal judge Thomas S. Maxey suspended his sentence.[186]

Soto, Juan Manuel. On trial for violation of US neutrality laws in US District Court in San Antonio, May 8–19, 1893.[187]

Stringer, Abalado. A Black man who supposedly had an alias of Mogro. Was killed by Mexican soldiers on May 11, 1892, at La Mecca, Mexico, during a raid led by Julian Flores.[188]

Trapito, Tebucio, alias Tebucio González. Indicted November 13, 1893, by a federal grand jury in San Antonio for violations of the neutrality law.[189]

Treviño, Amelito. San Ignacio raider. Surrendered in March 1893.[190]

Treviño, Anaclito. Surrendered to Captain Henry Jackson, Seventh Cavalry, at Carrizo, February 23, 1893. In US District Court in San Antonio, May 5, 1893, pled guilty to violation of the neutrality laws. US federal judge Thomas S. Maxey suspended his sentence.[191]

Treviño, Donaciano. In US District Court in San Antonio, May 5, 1893, pled guilty to violation of the neutrality laws. US federal judge Thomas S. Maxey suspended his sentence.[192]

Treviño, Felipe. Garzista, arrest reported by Fort Ringgold commander, August 5, 1893.[193]

Treviño, Juan. Lieutenant Thomas M. Corcoran, Seventh Cavalry, reported his arrest June 23, 1893.[194]

Treviño, Victoriano. Captain Henry Jackson, Seventh Cavalry, at Carrizo, reported his capture April 12, 1893. On trial for violation of US neutrality laws in US District Court in San Antonio, May 8–19, 1893.[195]

Uribe, Santiago. Captain Henry Jackson, Seventh Cavalry, at Carrizo reported his capture April 12, 1893.[196]

Usilio, Santiago. Surrendered to US deputy marshal Joe Shely in April 1893 at Carrizo. Brought to San Antonio for trial May 4, 1893, by Deputy Marshal Shely.[197]

Valdez, Rafael. Captured eight miles from Rio Grande City on March 4, 1893, by Starr County sheriff Wash Shely. In US District Court in San Antonio, May 16, 1893, with US federal judge Thomas S. Maxey for violation of neutrality laws. Arraigned, pled guilty, but sentencing delayed until the court could appoint him a lawyer.[198]

Varrera, Seario. On trial for violation of US neutrality laws in US District Court in San Antonio, May 8–19, 1893.[199]

Vasquez, Feliciano. At US District Court at Brownsville, June 19, 1893, pled guilty to violation of US neutrality laws. Sentenced to one-dollar fine and sixty days in jail by US federal judge Thomas S. Maxey.[200]

Vela, Anicelo. Lieutenant Stephen O'Conner, Twenty-Third Infantry, reported his arrest August 1, 1893.[201]

Vela, Justo. San Ignacio raider, arrest reported by Fort Ringgold commander, August 5, 1893.[202]

Venavidce, Espiridion. On trial for violation of US neutrality laws in US District Court in San Antonio, May 8–19, 1893.[203]

Vidrue, Juan Garza. In US District Court in San Antonio, May 19, 1892, with US federal judge Alexander Boarman for violation of neutrality laws. Released based on mistaken identity.[204]

Ybanes, Blas. Surrendered to Lieutenant Parker W. West, Troop I, Third Cavalry, and Starr County sheriff Wash Shely about March 4, 1893. In US District Court in San Antonio, May 3, 1893, pled guilty to violation of the neutrality laws. US federal judge Thomas S. Maxey suspended his sentence.[206]

Ybanez, Carmen. For violations of the Neutrality Act sentenced to a ten-dollar fine and three years in prison in Detroit, Michigan, by US federal judge Thomas S. Maxey in San Antonio December 19, 1892.[205]

Zapata, Alberto. Indicted November 13, 1893, by a federal grand jury in San Antonio for violations of the neutrality law.[207]

Zapata, Juan Garza. In US District Court in San Antonio, May 26, 1892, with US federal judge Alexander Boarman for violation of neutrality laws. Pled guilty and was sentenced to five months in Bexar County jail from time of arrest.[208]

Zarmosa, Porfirio. In US District Court in San Antonio, May 27, 1892, for arraignment on charge of violation of the neutrality laws. Trial set for May 31, 1892, by US federal judge Alexander Boarman.[209]

Zarrate, Juan Manuel. Captured by Seminole-Negro Indian Scout John July, March 1893.[210]

▼ ▼ ▼
NOTES

Chapter 1

1. Robert Wooster, *The American Military Frontiers: The United States Army in the West, 1783–1900* (Albuquerque: University of New Mexico Press, 2009), 150–51, 214–15; Loyd Uglow, *A Military History of Texas* (Denton: University of North Texas Press, 2022), 203–10, 270–75; Jerry Thompson, ed., *Fifty Miles and a Fight: Major Peter Heintzelman's Journal of Texas & the Cortina War* (Austin: Texas State Historical Association, 1998), 17–33, 131–56; Ernest Wallace, *Ranald S. Mackenzie on the Texas Frontier*, foreword by David J. Murrah (College Station: Texas A&M University Press, 1993), 98–103, 176–80; Paul H. Carlson, *"Pecos Bill": A Military Biography of William R. Shafter* (College Station: Texas A&M University Press, 1989), 100–101, 110–12.
2. Edward K. Kwakwa, *The International Law of Armed Conflict: Personal and Material Fields of Application* (Boston: Kluwer Academic, 1992), 16; Robert E. May, *Manifest Destiny's Underworld: Filibustering in Antebellum America* (Chapel Hill: University of North Carolina Press, 2002), 7; Jules Lobel, "The Rise and Decline of the Neutrality Act: Sovereignty and Congressional War Powers in United States Foreign Policy," *Harvard International Law Journal* 24 (Summer 1983): 1; Theodore B. Olson, "Overview of the Neutrality Act: Memorandum of Opinion for the Attorney General, September 24, 1984," 209–18 at https://www.justice.gov/file/23671; John N. Petrie, *American Neutrality in the 20th Century: The Impossible Dream*, McNair Paper 33 (Washington, DC: National Defense University, Institute for Strategic Studies, January 1953), 25;

John G. Bourke, *Our Neutrality Laws* (Fort Ethan Allen, VT: private printing, 1895), 3.

3. For Stanley's biography see Francis B. Heitman, *Historical Register and Dictionary of the United States Army,* 2 vols. (Washington, DC: Government Printing Office, 1903), 1:915; West Point Alumni Foundation, *The Register of Graduates and Former Cadets of the United States Military Academy 1802–1970,* Cullum Memorial Edition (West Point, NY: West Point Alumni Foundation, 1970), 245; Ezra J. Warner, *Generals in Blue: Lives of the Union Commanders* (Baton Rouge: Louisiana State University Press, 1964), 470–71; Thomas W. Cutrer, "David Sloan Stanley," in *The New Handbook of Texas,* ed. Ron Tyler, Douglas E. Barnett, Roy R. Barkley, Penelope C. Anderson, and Mark F. Odintz, 6 vols. (Austin: Texas State Historical Association, 1996), 4:57–58. For a broader look at Stanley, see D. S. Stanley, *Personal Memoirs of Major General D. S. Stanley, U.S.A.* (Cambridge, MA: Harvard University Press, 1917), and Samuel W. Fordyce IV, ed., *An American General: The Memoirs of David Sloan Stanley* (Santa Barbara, CA: Narrative Press, 2003).

4. "Report of the Major-General Commanding the Army, October 23, 1890," in "Report of the Secretary of War, 1890," House Exec. Docs., no. 1, vol. 2, pt. 2, 51st Cong., 2nd sess., serial 2831, 58, 79; National Archives and Records Administration (NARA), Records of the United States Army Adjutant General's Office, 1780–1917, Record Group 94, Returns from United States Military Posts 1800–1916, NARA Microfilm No. M617, roll 1085, Post Returns San Antonio, Texas, January 1883–August 1890, and roll 1079, Post Returns Fort Sam Houston, Texas, September 1890–December 1900; Thomas T. Smith, *The Old Army in Texas: A Research Guide to the U.S. Army in Nineteenth-Century Texas,* 2nd ed. (Austin: Texas State Historical Association, 2020), 94–95, 144–45.

5. NARA Microfilm No. M617, roll 215, Post Returns Fort Clark, Texas, January 1882–December 1892; National Archives and Records Administration, Records of the United States Army Adjutant General's Office, 1780–1917, Record Group 391, Records of the United States Regular Army Mobile Units, 1821–1942, Returns from Regular Army Cavalry Regiments, 1833–1916, NARA Microfilm No. 744, roll 32, Regimental Returns, Third Cavalry, 1885–1893; "Report of the Quartermaster-General, October 9,

1890," in "Report of the Secretary of War, 1890," House Exec. Docs., no. 1, vol. 2, pt. 2, 51st Cong., 2nd sess., serial 2831, 846; Smith, *The Old Army in Texas,* 66.

6. NARA Microfilm No. M617, roll 683, Post Returns, Fort McIntosh, Texas, January 1881–December 1891, and roll 684, Post Returns, Fort McIntosh, Texas, January 1892–December 1902; Regimental Returns, Third Cavalry, May 1890; "Report of the Quartermaster-General, October 9, 1890," 849; Smith, *The Old Army in Texas,* 79–80.

7. NARA Microfilm No. M617, roll 1022, Post Returns Fort Ringgold, Texas, January 1885–December 1894; "Report of the Quartermaster-General, October 9, 1890," 850; Smith, *The Old Army in Texas,* 91–92.

8. NARA Microfilm No. M617, roll 153, Post Returns, Fort Brown, Texas, January 1887–December 1902; "Report of the Quartermaster-General, October 9, 1890," 844; Smith, *The Old Army in Texas,* 55–56.

9. On the background of the officers see Heitman, *Historical Register and Dictionary of the United States Army,* 1:730, 920, 978, 1057.

10. Arnoldo De León, *They Called Them Greasers: Anglo Attitudes toward Mexicans in Texas, 1821–1900* (Austin: University of Texas Press, 1983), 60–61, 93–94, 97; James N. Leiker, *Racial Borders: Black Soldiers along the Rio Grande* (College Station: Texas A&M University Press, 2002), 121–122.

11. Elliott Young, *Catarino Garza's Revolution on the Texas-Mexico Border* (Durham: Duke University Press, 2004), 59, 78–80; "Report of Brigadier General Stanley, September 12, 1890," in "Report of the Secretary of War, 1890," House Exec. Docs., no. 1, vol. 2, pt. 2, 51st Cong., 2nd sess., serial 2831, 184–85; "Brigadier General David S. Stanley, Commander, Department of Texas, to Dr. P. Ornelas, Consul of Republic of Mexico, San Antonio, Texas, June 25, 1890," and "Lieutenant David J. Rumbough, aide-de-camp, Commanding General, Department of Texas, to Commanding Officer, Fort McIntosh, Telegram, 10:20 PM, June 24, 1890," (quote), National Archives and Records Administration (NARA), Records of the United States Army Adjutant General's Office, 1780–1917, Record Group 393, Records of US Army Continental Commands, 1821–1920, NARA Microfilm No. M1114, Letters Sent by Headquarters, Department of Texas, 1870–1894 and 1897–1898, Roll 9, vol. 29, January 2,

1890-December 31, 1891; "Revolution in Mexico," *Galveston Daily News* June 24, 1890, 6. For the text of the proclamation or *proclama*, see "The Day In Courts," *San Antonio Express News*, December 20, 1890, 3.
12. "Report of Brigadier General Stanley, September 12, 1890," 184–85; Post Returns, Fort McIntosh, June 1890; Regimental Returns, Third Cavalry, June 1890; "Arrest Expected for Violation of the United States Neutrality Law," *Fort Worth Daily Gazette*, June 25, 1890, 2; "Nipped in the Bud," *Fort Worth Daily Gazette*, June 26, 1890, 2.
13. Young, *Catarino Garza's Revolution on the Texas-Mexico Border*, 80–85; "The Temples of Law," *San Antonio Express News*, December 19, 1890, 6; "The Day In Courts," *San Antonio Express News*, December 20, 1890, 3; "Jury Still Out," *San Antonio Express News*, December 22, 1890, 3; "The Mills of Justice," *San Antonio Express News*, December 23, 1890, 3; "Sandoval's Case," *Fort Worth Gazette*, December 20, 1890, 2; "Sandoval's Case," *Fort Worth Daily Gazette*, December 22, 1890, 1; "The Trial of Mexican Revolutionist," *Galveston Daily News*, June 27, 1890, 2; "General Sandoval Acquitted," *Galveston Daily News*, December 23, 1890, 1; Margery H. Krieger, "Bethel Coopwood (1827–1907)," in Tyler et al., eds., *The New Handbook of Texas*, 2:316; "The News This Morning," *New York Tribune*, July 18, 1900, 8.
14. "Report of the Secretary of War, November 15, 1890," House Exec. Docs., no. 1, vol. 2, pt. 2, 51st Cong., 2nd sess., serial 2831, 15–16 (first quote); "Report of the Major-General Commanding the Army, October 23, 1890," 44 (second quote), 46 (third and fourth quotes); "Report of Brigadier General Stanley, September 12, 1890," 185 (fifth quote).

Chapter 2

1. "Report of Brig. Gen. Stanley, September 9, 1891," in "Report of the Secretary of War, 1891," House Exec. Docs., no. 1, vol. 1, 52nd Cong., 1st sess., serial 2921, 156, 159; Post Returns, Fort McIntosh, Texas, January–September 1891; Post Returns, Fort Ringgold, Texas, January–September 1891; Post Returns, Fort Brown, Texas, January–September 1891, Regimental Returns, Third Cavalry, January–September 1891; Smith, *The Old Army in Texas*, 67, 97, 149–150.

2. Dyrenforth's final report was presented to the US Senate in March 1892 in which he concluded there were not enough experiments conducted to produce sufficient data to reach a definite conclusion on the effectiveness of concussionism. "Rain Experiments," *Fort Worth Daily Gazette*, March 3, 1892, 3; S. C. Gwynne, "Rain of Error," *Texas Monthly*, August 2003, 39–46 (first quote); "Lieutenant Colonel James P. Martin, Assistant Adjutant General (AAG), Department of Texas, to Commanding Officer, Fort Bliss, Texas, September 21, 1891," (second quote); and "Lieutenant Colonel James P. Martin, Assistant Adjutant General (AAG), Department of Texas, to Lt. S. A. Dyer, US Army at Corpus Christi, Texas, September 26, 1891," "Lieutenant Colonel James P. Martin, Assistant Adjutant General (AAG), Department of Texas, to Lt. S. A. Dyer, US Army at San Diego, Texas, October 20, 1891," Letters Sent by Headquarters, Department of Texas, Roll 9, vol. 29; Donald R. Haragan, "Weather Modification," in Tyler et al., eds., *The New Handbook of Texas*, 6:859–60; "The Rain Maker's Record," *El Paso International Daily Times*, September 16, 1891, 4; "Rain Makers," *Fort Worth Daily Gazette*, September 19, 1891, 1.

3. Post Returns, Fort Ringgold, May 1891, Regimental Returns, Third Cavalry, June 1882, June–September 1885; Joseph C. Porter, *Paper Medicine Man: John Gregory Bourke and His American* West (Norman: University of Oklahoma Press, 1986), 282–83; Joseph C. Porter, "John Gregory Bourke, (1846–1896)," in Tyler et al., eds., *The New Handbook of Texas*, 1:662; Joseph C. Porter, "John G. Bourke," in Paul Andrew Hutton, *Soldiers West: Biographies from the Military Frontier* (Lincoln: University of Nebraska Press, 1989), 137–57; F. W. Hodge, "John Gregory Bourke," *American Anthropologist* 9 (July 1896): 245–48; Heitman, *Historical Register and Dictionary of the United States Army*, 1:232; "John Gregory Bourke Diary," Roll 8, vol. 102, 41–108, 109, May 14, 1891 (first quote), 111 (second quote), Microfilm Collection 1, entry 032, Center of Southwest Studies, Fort Lewis College, Durango, Colorado; Bourke, *Our Neutrality Laws*, 6–7 (third quote).

4. Young, *Catarino Garza's Revolution on the Texas-Mexico Border*, 16, 31, 39, 43, 52, 66–69; Gilbert M. Cuthbertson, "Catarino E. Garza and the Garza War," *Texana* 12 (1974): 335–47; Gilbert M. Cuthbertson, "Catarino

Erasmo Garza (1859–1895)," in Tyler et al., eds., *The New Handbook of Texas*, 3:106–7; Alicia A. Garza, "Rio Grande City Riot of 1888," in Tyler et al., eds., *The New Handbook of Texas*, 5:585; De León, *They Called Them Greasers*, 60–61, 93–94, 101; "Lieutenant O. M. Smith, Assistant Adjutant General (AAG), Department of Texas, to Commanding Officer Fort Ringgold, September 25, 1888, telegram," and "Brigadier David S. Stanley to Adjutant General's Office, Division of the Missouri, September 27, 1888, telegram," (quote), Letters Sent by Headquarters, Department of Texas, Roll 9, vol. 27.

5. Young, *Catarino Garza's Revolution on the Texas-Mexico Border*, 52–54, 73–77, 98–103; Cuthbertson, "Catarino E. Garza and the Garza War," 338–40; Joe R. Baulch, "Garza War," in Tyler et al., eds., *The New Handbook of Texas*, 3:113; Jerry Thompson, *A Wild and Vivid Land: An Illustrated History of the South Texas Border* (Austin: Texas State Historical Association, 1997), 131–33; J. M. Hunter, "The Garza Revolution in 1890," *Frontier Times* 19 (January 1942): 135–36; "Campaign of the Border," *Daily Express* (San Antonio), May 21, 1893, 9.

6. Post Returns, Fort Ringgold, September 1891; Regimental Returns, Third Cavalry, September 1891; Daniel Lewis, *A Guide to the Microfilm Edition of the Garza Revolution, 1891–1893: Records of the U.S. Army Continental Commands, Department of Texas* (Bethesda, MD: UPA Collection, LexisNexis, Reed Elsevier, 2009), 1, 2, at https://media2.proquest.com/documents/103936.pdf; "Lieutenant Colonel James P. Martin, Assistant Adjutant General (AAG), Department of Texas, to Commanding Officer, Fort Ringgold, Texas, September 16, 1891, telegram," and "Lieutenant Colonel James P. Martin, Assistant Adjutant General (AAG), Department of Texas, to Commanding Officer, Fort Ringgold, Texas, September 17, 1891, telegram," (quote), Letters Sent by Headquarters, Department of Texas, Roll 9, vol. 29.

7. Post Returns, Fort Ringgold, Texas, September 1891; Post Returns, Fort McIntosh, Texas, September 1891; Post Returns, Fort Brown, Texas, September 1891; Regimental Returns, Third Cavalry, September 1891; Lewis, *A Guide to the Microfilm Edition of the Garza Revolution*, 2; "Lieutenant Colonel James P. Martin, Assistant Adjutant General (AAG), Department of Texas, to Commanding Officer, Fort McIntosh,

Texas, September 17, 1891, telegram"; "Lieutenant Colonel James P. Martin, Assistant Adjutant General (AAG), Department of Texas, to Commanding Officer, Fort Brown, Texas, September 17, 1891, telegram"; "Brigadier General David S. Stanley, Commander, Department of Texas to Dr. Plutarco Ornelas, Mexican Consul, San Antonio, Texas, September 18, 1891"; "Brigadier General David S. Stanley, Commander, Department of Texas, to Adjutant General's Office, Washington, D.C., September 18, 1891"; "Lieutenant Colonel James P. Martin, Assistant Adjutant General (AAG), Department of Texas, to Capt. Johnson, 3rd Cav. in field near Santa Maria, September 23, 1891"; "Lieutenant Colonel James P. Martin, Assistant Adjutant General (AAG), Department of Texas, to Commanding Officer Fort McIntosh, October 2, 1891," Letters Sent by Headquarters, Department of Texas, Roll 9, vol. 29; Porter, *Paper Medicine Man*, 283.

8. Post Returns, Fort Ringgold, Texas, September 1891; Post Returns, Fort McIntosh, Texas, September 1891; Post Returns, Fort Brown, Texas, September 1891; Regimental Returns, Third Cavalry, September 1891; "Dangerous," *Fort Worth Daily Gazette*, September 17, 1891, 7; "Another Account," *Fort Worth Daily Gazette*, September 17, 1891, 7; "Only a Namesake," *Fort Worth Daily Gazette*, September 18, 1891, 1; "A Plan of Revolution," *Fort Worth Daily Gazette*, September 18, 1891, 1; "The Garza Affair," *Fort Worth Gazette*, September 19, 1891, 1 (first quote); "No Revolution," *Fort Worth Daily Gazette*, September 23, 1891, 1 (second quote); "Invading Mexico," *Galveston Daily News*, September 17, 1891, 1 (third quote); Young, *Catarino Garza's Revolution on the Texas-Mexico Border*, 3–5, 113–16.

9. Post Returns, Fort Ringgold, Texas, October–November 1891 (second quote); Post Returns, Fort McIntosh, Texas, October–November 1891; Post Returns, Fort Brown, Texas, October–November 1891; Regimental Returns, Third Cavalry, October–November 1891; "Lieutenant Colonel James P. Martin, Assistant Adjutant General (AAG), Department of Texas, to Commanding Officer, Fort Ringgold, Texas, November 2, 1891," Letters Sent by Headquarters, Department of Texas, Roll 9, vol. 29; "John Gregory Bourke Diary," Roll 8, vol. 106, 78–88, 81, October 9, 1891 (first quote); Porter, *Paper Medicine Man*, 284–86; Lewis, *A Guide to the Microfilm Edition of the Garza Revolution*, 3–4.

10. "John Gregory Bourke Diary," Roll 8, vol. 106, 149–92, 165, November 11, 1891 (quote); Porter, *Paper Medicine Man*, 286; Young, *Catarino Garza's Revolution on the Texas-Mexico Border*, 108–11; Lewis, *A Guide to the Microfilm Edition of the Garza Revolution*, 4; "Suspicious Mexican," *Fort Worth Daily Gazette*, November 15, 1891, 8; "Held as Suspects," *Fort Worth Daily Gazette*, November 16, 1891, 7.

11. "Lieutenant Colonel James P. Martin, Assistant Adjutant General (AAG), Department of Texas, to Post Commanders, November 10, 1891" (quote), Letters Sent by Headquarters, Department of Texas, Roll 9, vol. 29; "Report of Brig. Gen. Wheaton, August 18, 1893," in "Report of the Secretary of War, November 27, 1893," House Exec. Docs., no. 1, vol. 2, pt. 2, 53rd Cong., 2nd sess., serial 3198, 140–45; "Lieutenant Colonel James P. Martin, Assistant Adjutant General (AAG), Department of Texas, to Adjutant General, Washington, D.C., August 22, 1893," Letters Sent, Department of Texas, Roll 10, vol. 31, January 2–December 31, 1893. The maps are the basis for the map accompanying this article and those of South Texas can be found at National Archives and Records Administration (NARA) Record Group 393, Records of United States Army Continental Commands, 1821–1920, Part 1, Entry 4877, "Letters and Reports Relating to the Garza Revolution," 2 boxes, Box 2, 1893, and are titled "Map of the Rio Grande Frontier, Texas, East of Fort McIntosh and South of the Mex. National R.R. Prepared in the Engineer Office, Department of Texas, San Antonio, Texas, February 17, 1893. Official: H. L. Ripley 1st Lieut. 3rd Cavalry, Acting Engineer Officer," and "Map showing the present location of United States and Mexican troops along the lower Rio Grande Frontier, with all available means of communication by rail, water, stage, telegraph (Military and Commercial), and telephone, between all important points. Drawn by 1' Lt. T. W. Griffith, 18' U.S. Inf. under the direction of Col. Anson Mills, 3' US Cavalry. March 8,' 1893." Copies of the two maps above plus a December 17, 1892, Ripley Map are also found in National Archives and Records Administration (NARA) Record Group 393, Records of United States Army Continental Commands, 1821–1920, RG393-I, E 4877, Blueprint Maps of Rio Grande Frontier, Department of Texas, 15W2, Map Case 91A, Drawer 4, "Map of the Rio Grande Frontier, Texas, East of Fort McIntosh and South of the Mex. National R.R. Prepared in the Engineer Office,

Department of Texas, San Antonio, Texas, December 17, 1892. Official: H. L. Ripley 1st Lieut. 3rd Cavalry, Acting Engineer Officer."

12. Post Returns, Fort McIntosh, Texas, December 1891; Regimental Returns, Third Cavalry, December 1891.

13. "Brigadier General David S. Stanley, Commander, Department of Texas, to Adjutant General's Office, Washington, D.C., December 23, 1891," Letters Sent by Headquarters, Department of Texas, Roll 9, vol. 29; "Report of Brig. Gen. Wheaton, September 13, 1892," in "Report of the Secretary of War, 1892," House Exec. Docs., no. 1, vol. 1, pt. 2, 52nd Cong., 2nd sess., serial 3077, 133–35; Post Returns, Fort Ringgold, Texas, December 1891; Post Returns, Fort McIntosh, Texas, December 1891; Regimental Returns, Third Cavalry, December 1891; "John Gregory Bourke Diary," Roll 8, vol. 107, 136–45, 136, November 22, 1891 (quote); Lewis, *A Guide to the Microfilm Edition of the Garza Revolution*, 5; Porter, *Paper Medicine Man*, 286–88; "A Skirmish with Garza," *Galveston Daily News*, December 23, 1891, 1.

14. Records of the Adjutant General's Office, 1780–1917, National Archives Record Group 94, NARA Microfilm M233, "Register of Enlistments, 1798–1914," volume 1885–90 A–K, roll 44, 7, and volume 1891–92 A–Z, roll 46, 172, Ancestry.com; Office of the Quartermaster General, 1774–1985, National Archives Record Group 92, "U.S. Burial Registers, Military Posts and National Cemeteries, 1862–1960," "Record Book of Fort Ringgold, Texas Cemetery," and "Record Book of National Cemetery at Alexandria, Louisiana," 118, Ancestry.com; "John Gregory Bourke Diary," Roll 8, vol. 107, 145, December 23, 1891; "Corporal Edstrom's Funeral," *Galveston Daily News* January 2, 1892, 2; "Corporal Edstrom's Funeral," *Daily Express* (San Antonio), January 1, 1892, 2.

15. "Report of Major-General Commanding the Army, September 24, 1891," in "Report of the Secretary of War, 1891," House Exec. Docs., no. 1, vol. 1, 52nd Cong., 1st sess., serial 2921, 55–56; "Report of Major-General Commanding the Army, September 30, 1892," in "Report of the Secretary of War, 1892," House Exec. Docs., no. 1, vol. 2, pt. 2, 52nd Cong., 2nd sess., serial 3077, 45, 46; "Report of Brig. Gen. Stanley, September 9, 1891," in "Report of the Secretary of War, 1891," House Exec. Docs., no. 1, vol. 1, 52nd Cong., 1st sess., serial 2921, 156–57, 159; Porter, *Paper Medicine*

Man, 287; "The Chase for Garza," *Daily Express* (San Antonio) 28 (no. 1), January 1, 1893, 1.

16. "Report of Brig. Gen. Wheaton, September 13, 1892," 134; "Brigadier General David S. Stanley, Commander, Department of Texas, to Commanding Officer, Fort Ringgold, Texas, December 23, 1891, telegram"; "Lieutenant Colonel James P. Martin, Assistant Adjutant General (AAG), Department of Texas, to Commanding Officer, Fort Ringgold, Texas, December 24, 1891, telegram" (first quote); "Brigadier General David S. Stanley, Commander, Department of Texas, to Commanding Officer, Fort Ringgold, Texas, December 26, 1891, telegram" (second quote), Letters Sent by Headquarters, Department of Texas, Roll 9, vol. 29; Post Returns, Fort Ringgold, Texas, December 1891; Post Returns, Fort McIntosh, Texas, December 1891; Regimental Returns, Third Cavalry, December 1891; Porter, *Paper Medicine Man*, 287.

17. "Report of Brig. Gen. Wheaton, September 13, 1892," 134–35; "Brigadier General David S. Stanley, Commander, Department of Texas, to Major General Schofield, Washington, D.C., January 1, 1892"; "Brigadier General David S. Stanley, Commander, Department of Texas, to Major General Schofield, Washington, D.C., January 5, 1892"; "Brigadier General David S. Stanley, Commander, Department of Texas, to Major General Schofield, Washington, D.C., January 9, 1892," Letters Sent by Headquarters, Department of Texas, Roll 10, vol. 30; Post Returns, Fort Ringgold, Texas, December 1891; Post Returns, Fort McIntosh, Texas, December 1891; Regimental Returns, Third Cavalry, December 1891; Bourke, *Our Neutrality Laws*, 19–20; Porter, *Paper Medicine Man*, 287; Lewis, *A Guide to the Microfilm Edition of the Garza Revolution*, 5; "Fight with Garza's Men," *Galveston Daily News*, January 2, 1891, 2; Paul N. Spellman, *Captain J. A. Brooks, Texas Ranger* (Denton: University of North Texas Press, 2007), 72–75.

18. "Brigadier General David S. Stanley, Commander, Department of Texas, to Major General Schofield, Washington, D.C., January 1, 1892"; "Brigadier General David S. Stanley, Commander, Department of Texas, to Major General Schofield, Washington, D.C., January 3, 1892," Letters Sent by Headquarters, Department of Texas, Roll 10, vol. 30; Post Returns, Fort Ringgold, Texas, December 1891, January 1892; Regimental Returns,

Third Cavalry, December 1891, January 1892; Bourke, *Our Neutrality Laws*, 19; Lewis, *A Guide to the Microfilm Edition of the Garza Revolution*, 6; Charles M. Neal Jr., *Valor across the Lone Star: The Congressional Medal of Honor in Frontier Texas*, foreword by Jerry Thompson, (Austin: Texas State Historical Association, 2002), 239–52, 324–25.

19. "Brigadier General David S. Stanley, Commander, Department of Texas, to Major General Schofield, Washington, D.C., January 3, 1892," Letters Sent by Headquarters, Department of Texas, Roll 10, vol. 30; Neal Jr., *Valor across the Lone Star*, 250–51, 324–25; Lewis, *A Guide to the Microfilm Edition of the Garza Revolution*, 6. From Patriot, Indiana, Samuel Allen Walker served twenty-seven years in the army. As a sergeant in 1901 he was commissioned as a first lieutenant in the Philippine Scouts, where he served until the scouts disbanded in 1911. Reverting from captain to his enlisted rank of sergeant major, Walker retired in 1911 and moved to Laredo, Texas, where he became a deputy US marshal and then US marshal for the Southern District until 1924. Walker died September 10, 1954, and is buried in the Catholic cemetery in Laredo. Neal, *Valor across the Lone Star*, 324–25. From Kentucky, twenty-four-year-old Lieutenant George Tayloe Langhorne graduated from West Point in 1889. He was a military attaché in Brussels, served in the Cuba and Puerto Rico military occupation, in 1904–6 was with Captain John J. Pershing's Moro Expedition during the Philippine Insurrection. He was the aide-de-camp for General Leonard Wood for five years, and was then in Berlin as a military attaché. As an Eighth Cavalry squadron commander and then regimental commander, he spent another half-decade on the Texas border before returning to the Philippines in 1923. Colonel Langhorne retired in 1931 and died January 25, 1962 in Chicago. Thomas T. Smith, *The Old Army in the Big Bend of Texas, 1911–1921: The Last Cavalry Frontier* (Austin: Texas State Historical Association, 2018), 35–36, 53.

20. "Brigadier General David S. Stanley, Commander, Department of Texas, to Adjutant General's Office, Washington, D.C., telegram, January 27, 1891" (first quote); "Second Lieutenant Daniel B. Devore, aide-de-camp, Commanding General, Department of Texas, to Captain Henry W. Wessells Jr., Fort Sam Houston, Texas, September 9, 1891" (second quote); "Brigadier General David S. Stanley, Commander, Department of

Texas, to Adjutant General's Office, Washington, D.C., December 23, 1891" (third quote); and "Lieutenant Colonel James P. Martin, Assistant Adjutant General (AAG), Department of Texas, to Colonel Morrow, Fort McIntosh, Texas, December 23, 1891"; "Brigadier General David S. Stanley, Commander, Department of Texas, to Adjutant General's Office, Washington, D.C., January 21, 1892," Letters Sent by Headquarters, Department of Texas, Roll 9, vol. 29, and Roll 10, vol. 30; Adjutant General's Office, *General Court-Martial Orders, Adjutant General's Office, 1883* (Washington, DC: Government Printing Office, 1884), General Court-Martial Orders No. 53, November 15, 1883; Adjutant General's Office, *General Court-Martial Orders, Adjutant General's Office, 1885* (Washington, DC: Government Printing Office, 1886), General Court-Martial Orders No. 20, February 24, 1885; Heitman, *Historical Register and Dictionary of the United States Army,* 1:729.

21. "Brigadier General David S. Stanley, Commander, Department of Texas, to Major General Schofield, Washington, D.C., January 9, 1892," Letters Sent by Headquarters, Department of Texas, Roll 10, vol. 30; Post Returns, Fort Ringgold, Texas, January 1892; Post Returns, Fort McIntosh, Texas, January 1892; Regimental Returns, Third Cavalry, January 1892; Bourke, *Our Neutrality Laws,* 18 (first quote), 20 (second quote).

22. Regimental Returns, Third Cavalry, December 1891, January–February 1892; Jno. Gilmer Speed, "The Hunt for Garza," *Harper's Weekly,* January 30, 1892, 103, 113; Richard Harding Davis, "West from a Car Window: Part I, From San Antonio to Corpus Christi," *Harper's Weekly,* March 5, 1892, 220–22; Richard Harding Davis, "West from a Car Window: Part II, "Our Troops on the Border," *Harper's Weekly,* March 26, 1892, 294 (quote), 295, from https://babel.hathitrust.org/cgi/pt?id=mdp.39015014260&view=1up&seq=7&skin=2021.

23. Davis, "West from a Car Window: Part II, Our Troops on the Border," 295 (quotes); Peggy and Harold Samuels, *Frederic Remington: A Biography* (Garden City, NY: Doubleday & Company, 1982), 164. On Hardie, see Adjutant General's Office, *Official Army Register for 1911* (Washington, DC: War Department Document No. 383, Adjutant General's Office, December 1, 1910), 416; Heitman, *Historical Register and Dictionary of the United States Army,* 1:499–500; West Point Alumni Foundation, *The*

Register of Graduates and Former Cadets of the United States Military Academy, 1802–1970, 273; Warner, *Generals in Blue,* 204–5; "Find a Grave," Ancestry.com.

24. "Lieutenant Colonel James P. Martin, Assistant Adjutant General (AAG), Department of Texas, to Chief Quartermaster, Department of Texas, February 26, 1892"; and "Brigadier General David S. Stanley, Commander, Department of Texas, to Major General Schofield, Washington, D.C., February 2, 1892," Letters Sent by Headquarters, Department of Texas, Roll 10, vol. 30; Post Returns, Fort Ringgold, Texas, February 1892; Post Returns, Fort McIntosh, Texas, February 1892; Regimental Returns, Third Cavalry, February 1892; Porter, *Paper Medicine Man,* 289; Lewis, *A Guide to the Microfilm Edition of the Garza Revolution,* 9; "Garza's Men Growing Bolder; They Shot and Killed a Scout from Ambush," *New York Times,* February 3, 1892, 1. The US Marshals Service has a webpage honoring US deputy marshal Rufus B. Glover at https://www.odmp.org/officer/19659-deputy-us-marshal-rufus-b-glover.

25. Post Returns, Fort Ringgold, Texas, January 1892; Emmett M. Essen, *Shavetails & Bell Sharps: The History of the U.S. Army Mule* (Lincoln: University of Nebraska Press, 1997), 7, 106–7.

26. "Brigadier General David S. Stanley, Commander, Department of Texas, to His Excellency Governor J. S. Hogg, Austin, Texas, February 25, 1892," Letters Sent by Headquarters, Department of Texas, Roll 10, vol. 30; Post Returns, Fort Ringgold, Texas, February 1892; Post Returns, Fort McIntosh, Texas, February 1892; Regimental Returns, Third Cavalry, February 1892; "John Gregory Bourke Diary," Roll 8, vol. 108, 33–34, November 18, 1892; Porter, *Paper Medicine Man,* 289; Lewis, *A Guide to the Microfilm Edition of the Garza Revolution,* 9, 10; "Garza at Key West," *Daily Express* (San Antonio), May 18, 1892, 5.

27. Young, *Catarino Garza's Revolution on the Texas-Mexico Border,* 268–84, 295–96, 303–4; Cuthbertson, "Catarino Erasmo Garza (1859–1895)," 3:106–7; Thompson, *A Wild and Vivid Land,* 131; "Garza Is in Luck," *Daily Express* (San Antonio), December 17, 1893, 6.

28. "Report of Brig. Gen. Wheaton, September 13, 1892," 133–35; Post Returns, Fort Ringgold, Texas, February–March 1892; Post Returns, Fort McIntosh, Texas, February–March 1892; Regimental Returns, Third Cavalry,

February–March 1892; Secretary of the Interior, *Official Register of the United States, Containing a List of Officers and Employés in the Civil, Military, and Naval Service on the First of July, 1891*, 2 vols. (Washington, DC: Government Printing Office, 1892), 1:981; "Worse, More of It," *Fort Worth Daily Gazette*, March 3, 1892, 3 (quote); "Talk it Over," *Fort Worth Daily Gazette*, March 1, 1892, 8.

29. "Brigadier General David S. Stanley, Commander, Department of Texas, to His Excellency Governor J. S. Hogg, Austin, Texas, March 1, 1892" (quote); "Brigadier General David S. Stanley, Commander, Department of Texas, to Major General Schofield, Washington, D.C., February 2, 1892" (second quote), Letters Sent by Headquarters, Department of Texas, Roll 10, vol. 30; "The Fricke Case," *Fort Worth Daily Gazette*, March 4, 1892, 4; "No Successor Appointed," *Brownsville Herald*, 1893, 3; "News by Wire," *Brownsville Herald*, April 16, 1893, 2; Porter, *Paper Medicine Man*, 288–89.

30. "Lieutenant Colonel James P. Martin, Assistant Adjutant General (AAG), Department of Texas, to Commanding Officer, Fort Clark, Texas, May 3, 1892" (first, second, third quotes); "Department of Texas Circular, August 5, 1893" (fourth quote), Letters Sent by Headquarters, Department of Texas, Roll 10, vol. 30; Warner, *Generals in Blue*, 553–54; Heitman, *Historical Register and Dictionary of the United States Army*, 1:1022.

31. "Lieutenant Colonel James P. Martin, Assistant Adjutant General (AAG), Department of Texas, to Lieut. P. G. Lowe, 18th Infantry, Commander, Seminole-Negro Indian Scouts, Camp at Polvo, Texas, July 20, 1892," Letters Sent by Headquarters, Department of Texas, Roll 10, vol. 30; Post Returns, Fort Ringgold, Texas, July–September 1892; Post Returns, Fort McIntosh, Texas, July–September 1892; Regimental Returns, Third Cavalry, July–September 1892; "Made a Bad Break, Garza Revolutionist Try to Cross the River," *Galveston Daily News*, May 13, 1892, 1; Thomas T. Smith, Jerry D. Thompson, Robert Wooster, and Ben E. Pingenot, eds., *The Reminiscences of Major General Zenas R. Bliss, 1854–1876* (Austin: Texas State Historical Association, 2007), 429–31; Don A. Swanson, *Seminole, Lipan, Cherokee, Creek, Indian Scouts Enlistment Records, Fort Clark* (Bronte, TX: Ames-American Printing Co., n.d.), 46; "Garzaites Trial," *Daily Express* (San Antonio), May 20, 1892, 3.

32. "Report of Brig. Gen. Wheaton, September 13, 1892," 133; "Lieutenant Colonel James P. Martin, Assistant Adjutant General (AAG), Department of Texas, to Commanding Officer, Fort Ringgold, July 20, 1892"; "Lieutenant Colonel James P. Martin, Assistant Adjutant General (AAG), Department of Texas, to Captain William B. Wheeler, 18th Infantry, Fort Ringgold, Texas, September 22, 1892"; "Lieutenant Colonel James P. Martin, Assistant Adjutant General (AAG), Department of Texas, to Captain William B. Wheeler, 18th Infantry, Fort Ringgold, Texas, November 10, 1892"; "Lieutenant Colonel James P. Martin, Assistant Adjutant General (AAG), Department of Texas, to Captain William B. Wheeler, 18th Infantry, Fort Ringgold, Texas, December 7, 1892"; "Brigadier General Frank Wheaton, Commander, Department of Texas, to Adjutant General's Office, Washington, D.C., December 5, 1892," Letters Sent by Headquarters, Department of Texas, Roll 10, vol. 30; Porter, *Paper Medicine Man*, 288–90.

33. Porter, *Paper Medicine Man*, 290. Judge Maxey, born in Mississippi, served in the Confederate Army, earned his law degree from the University of Virginia, was in the Mississippi state legislature before moving to Texas in 1871, and was a federal judge from 1888 to 1916. Walter Prescott Webb, "Thomas Sheldon Maxey (1846–1921)," in Tyler et al., eds., *The New Handbook of Texas*, 4:581; Andrew J. Evans was born in South Carolina, moved to Texas in 1857, and served in the Texas legislature. He was a Unionist in the Civil War, and was a postwar state senator. Appointed as a district attorney by President Grant in 1872, Evans served the post for several decades. Jennifer Eckel, "Andrew Jackson Evans (1832–1897)," in Tyler et al., eds., *The New Handbook of Texas*, https://www.tshaonline.org/handbook/entries/evans-andrew-jackson. On the trials see Young, *Catarino Garza's Revolution on the Texas-Mexico Border*, 177–78; "Garzaites Trial," *Daily Express* (San Antonio), May 20, 1892, 3; "Trial of Munoz," *Daily Express* (San Antonio), May 21, 1892, 6; "Rest Their Case," *Daily Express* (San Antonio), May 24, 1892, 6; "Ended the Trial," *Daily Express* (San Antonio), May 25, 1892, 6; "Munoz Convicted," *Daily Express* (San Antonio), May 26, 1892, 6; "Garza Revolutionaries," *Daily Express* (San Antonio), May 27, 1892, 5; "From the Border," *Daily Express* (San Antonio), May 28, 1892, 6; "Revolutionist in Court," *Daily Express* (San

Antonio), May 31, 1892, 6; "Garza Revolutionist," *Galveston Daily News*, May 17, 1892, 7; "Trying a Garzaite," *Galveston Daily News*, May 20, 1892, 4; "Trial of Garza's Lieutenant," *Galveston Daily News*, May 25, 1892, 4; "The First in Sixty Years," *Galveston Daily News*, May 26, 1892, 3; "The Garza Cases," *Galveston Daily News*, May 27, 1892, 3; "Pablo Munoz Sentenced," *Galveston Daily News*, May 28, 1892, 5.

Chapter 3

1. "Report of Brig. Gen. Wheaton, September 13, 1892," 133 (quote); "Report of Brig. Gen. Wheaton, August 18, 1893," 140–45; "Brigadier General Frank Wheaton, Commander, Department of Texas, to Adjutant General's Office, Washington, D.C., December 17, 1892," Letters Sent by Headquarters, Department of Texas, Roll 10, vol. 30; Post Returns, Fort Ringgold, Texas, December 1892; Post Returns, Fort McIntosh, Texas, December 1892; Regimental Returns, Third Cavalry, December 1892; Lewis, *A Guide to the Microfilm Edition of the Garza Revolution,* 12–13; Young, *Catarino Garza's Revolution on the Texas-Mexico Border,* 126–29; "Freebooters," *Fort Worth Daily Gazette*, December 13, 1892, 1; "Bandits Battle," *Fort Worth Daily Gazette*, December 14, 1892, 1; "He Was a Traitor," *Fort Worth Daily Gazette*, December 15, 1892, 1; "The Men Roasters," *Fort Worth Daily Gazette,* December 17, 1892, 1; "Story of Two Captives," *Daily Express* (San Antonio), February 11, 1893, 3; "Battle of San Ygnacio," *Daily Express* (San Antonio), February 12, 1893, 6; "Story of the Fight," *Daily Express* (San Antonio), February 14, 1893, 6; "Testimony of a Soldier," *Daily Express* (San Antonio), February 15, 1893, 6 (quote); "Skirmish at San Ygnacio," *Daily Express* (San Antonio), February 16, 1893, 8; James B. Hughes Jr., *Mexican Military Arms: The Cartridge Period, 1866–1967* (Houston: Deep River Armory, 1968), 4–5, 8–10.
2. "Señor Cayetano Romero, Mexican Legation of Mexico, Washington, D.C., to Mr. Foster, Department of State, Washington, D.C., December 13, 1892," US Department of State, *Papers Relating to the Foreign Relations of the United States, with the Annual Message of the President, Transmitted to Congress December 3, 1893* (Washington, DC: Government Printing

Office, 1894), 424–25; "Report of Brig. Gen. Wheaton, August 18, 1893," 140–45; "Brigadier General Frank Wheaton, Commander, Department of Texas, to Adjutant General's Office, Washington, D.C., December 17, 1892"; "Assistant Adjutant General (AAG), Department of Texas, to Commanding Officer, Fort McIntosh, Texas, December 19, 1892"; "Brigadier General Frank Wheaton, Commander, Department of Texas, to Dr. Plutarco Ornelas, Mexican Consul, San Antonio, Texas, December 24, 1891," Letters Sent by Headquarters, Department of Texas, Roll 10, vol. 30; Post Returns, Fort Ringgold, Texas, December 1892; Post Returns, Fort McIntosh, Texas, December 1892; Regimental Returns, Third Cavalry, December 1892; "Bandits Battle," *Fort Worth Daily Gazette*, December 14, 1892, 1; "Lonely Woman," *Fort Worth Daily Gazette*, December 16, 1892, 1; "The Cause of the Trouble," *Fort Worth Daily Gazette*, December 16, 1892, 1; "No Truth in It," *Fort Worth Daily Gazette*, December 21, 1892, 1; "Where Are They," *Fort Worth Daily Gazette*, December 24, 1892, 1.
3. "Señor Cayetano Romero, Mexican Legation of Mexico, Washington, D.C., to Mr. Foster, Department of State, Washington, D.C., December 14, 1892," US Department of State, *Papers Relating to the Foreign Relations of the United States . . . 1893*, 424–25; "Report of Brig. Gen. Wheaton, August 18, 1893," 140–141; "Assistant Adjutant General (AAG), Department of Texas, to Captain George F. Chase, Third Cavalry, Fort Sam Houston, Texas, December 17, 1892," Letters Sent by Headquarters, Department of Texas, Roll 10, vol. 30; Post Returns, Fort Ringgold, Texas, December 1892; Post Returns, Fort McIntosh, Texas, December 1892; Regimental Returns, Third Cavalry, December 1892; National Archives and Records Administration (NARA), Records of the United States Army Adjutant General's Office, 1780–1917, Record Group 94, Returns from Regular Army Infantry Regiments June 1821–December 1916, Microfilm No. M665, roll 239, Twenty-Third Infantry Regiment, January 1891–December 1897, Regimental Returns, Twenty-Third Infantry, December 1892.
4. "Report of Brig. Gen. Wheaton, August 18, 1893," 141; "Assistant Adjutant General (AAG), Department of Texas, to Commanding Officer, Fort McIntosh, Texas, December 27, 1892"; "Assistant Adjutant General (AAG), Department of Texas, to Captain Henry Jackson, Seventh

Cavalry, December 28, 1892" (quote), Letters Sent by Headquarters, Department of Texas, Roll 10, vol. 30; National Archives and Records Administration, Records of the United States Army Adjutant General's Office, 1780–1917, Record Group 391, Records of the United States Regular Army Mobile Units, 1821–1942, Returns from Regular Army Cavalry Regiments, 1833–1916, NARA Microfilm No. 744, roll 74, Seventh Cavalry, 1889–1896, Regimental Returns, Seventh Cavalry, December 1892.

5. "Brigadier General Frank Wheaton, Commander, Department of Texas, to Major General Schofield, Washington, D.C., December 23, 1892," Letters Sent by Headquarters, Department of Texas, Roll 10, vol. 30; Porter, *Paper Medicine Man,* 289; "Capt. J. G. Bourke," *Fort Worth Daily Gazette,* December 29, 1892, 1.

6. "Report of Brig. Gen. Wheaton, August 18, 1893," 142; Post Returns, Fort Ringgold, Texas, December 1892; Post Returns, Fort McIntosh, Texas, December 1892; Regimental Returns, Third Cavalry, December 1892; Office of the Quartermaster General, "US National Cemetery Interment Control Forms," and "US Military Burial Registers, 1768–1921, Record Book of Interments in the Post Cemetery, Fort McIntosh, Texas," Ancestry.com ; "A Soldier Died," *Fort Worth Daily Gazette,* December 24, 1892, 1; "The Border War," *Fort Worth Daily Gazette,* December 27, 1892, 1.

7. "Report of Brig. Gen. Wheaton, August 18, 1893, 142"; Post Returns, Fort Ringgold, Texas, January 1893; Post Returns, Fort McIntosh, Texas, January 1893; Post Returns, Fort Brown, January 1893; Regimental Returns, Third Cavalry, January 1893; Regimental Returns, Seventh Cavalry, January 1893; National Archives and Records Administration (NARA), Records of the United States Army Adjutant General's Office, 1780–1917, Record Group 94, Returns from Regular Army Infantry Regiments June 1821–December 1916, Microfilm No. M665, Roll 196, Eighteenth Infantry Regiment, January 1890–December 1897, Regimental Returns, Eighteenth Infantry, January 1893.

8. "Lieutenant Colonel James P. Martin, Assistant Adjutant General (AAG), Department of Texas, to Captain Oscar Elting, Troop E, Third Cavalry, San Ignacio, Texas, December 28, 1892"; "Lieutenant Colonel James P. Martin, Assistant Adjutant General (AAG), Department of Texas, to Captain Oscar Elting, Troop E, Third Cavalry, San Ignacio,

Texas, December 30, 1892"; "Lieutenant Colonel James P. Martin, Assistant Adjutant General (AAG), Department of Texas, to Commanding Officer, Fort McIntosh, Texas, December 23, 1892"; "Lieutenant Colonel James P. Martin, Assistant Adjutant General (AAG), Department of Texas, to Commanding Officer, Fort Ringgold, Texas, May 6, 1893," Letters Sent by Headquarters, Department of Texas, Roll 10, vol. 30, and Roll 10, vol. 31; Post Returns, Fort Ringgold, Texas, January 1893; Post Returns, Fort McIntosh, Texas, January 1893; Post Returns, Fort Brown, January 1893; Regimental Returns, Third Cavalry, January 1893; Regimental Returns, Seventh Cavalry, January 1893; Regimental Returns, Eighteenth Infantry, January 1893; Regimental Returns, Twenty-Third Infantry, January 1893.

9. "John W. Foster, Headquarters, Department of State, Washington, D.C., to Señor Cayetano Romero, Mexican Legation of Mexico, Washington, D.C., December 27, 1892"; "Señor Cayetano Romero, Mexican Legation of Mexico, Washington, D.C., to Mr. Foster, Department of State, Washington, D.C., January 1, 1893," US Department of State, *Papers Relating to the Foreign Relations of the United States . . . 1893*, 430 (quotes), 434, 435, 437.

10. "John W. Foster, Headquarters, Department of State, Washington, D.C., to Señor Cayetano Romero, Mexican Legation of Mexico, Washington, D.C., January 4, 1893," US Department of State, *Papers Relating to the Foreign Relations of the United States . . . 1893*, 435 (first quote); "Brigadier General Frank Wheaton, Commander, Department of Texas, to Major General Schofield, Washington, D.C., December 23, 1892" (second, third quotes), Letters Sent by Headquarters, Department of Texas, Roll 10, vol. 30.

11. "Brigadier General Frank Wheaton, Commander, Department of Texas, to Adjutant General's Office, Washington, D.C., December 30, 1892"; "Brigadier General Frank Wheaton, Commander, Department of Texas, to Chief Signal Officer, Washington, D.C., December 31, 1892," Letters Sent by Headquarters, Department of Texas, Roll 10, vol. 30; "Report of the Chief Signal Officer, October 10, 1892," in "Report of the Secretary of War, 1892," House Exec. Docs., no. 1, vol. 1, pt. 2, 52nd Cong., 2nd sess., serial 3077, 594–95; "Report of the Chief Signal Officer, October 9, 1893,"

in "Report of the Secretary of War, November 27, 1893," House Exec. Docs., no. 1, vol. 2, pt. 2, 53rd Cong., 2nd sess., serial 3198, 645–47; "Report of the Chief Signal Officer, October 1, 1894," in "Report of the Secretary of War, November 26, 1894," House Exec. Docs., no. 1, vol. 4, pt. 2, 53rd Cong., 3rd sess., serial 3295, 484 (quote); Thomas T. Smith, *The U.S. Army and the Texas Frontier Economy, 1845–1900* (College Station: Texas A&M University Press, 1999), 169–70; "The Military Telegraph Line," *Daily Herald* (Brownsville), January 16, 1893, 3; "Commenced Construction," *Daily Herald* (Brownsville), January 24, 1893, 3.

12. "Report of the Chief Signal Officer, 1894," 483–84, 502; "Report of the Chief Signal Officer, October 1, 1895," in "Report of the Secretary of War, November 26, 1895," House Exec. Docs., no. 2, vol. 3, 54th Cong., 1st sess., serial 3370, 574–75; "Report of the Chief Signal Officer, 30 September 1896," in "Report of the Secretary of War, November 24, 1896," House Exec. Docs., no. 2, vol. 2, 54th Cong., 2nd sess., serial 3478, 596 (quote); "Report of the Chief Signal Officer, October 5, 1900," in Report of the Secretary of War, November 30, 1900," House Exec. Docs., no. 2, vol. 2, 56th Cong., 2nd sess., serial 4071, 1006; Smith, *The U.S. Army and the Texas Frontier Economy, 1845–1900*, 170; "Military Items," *Daily Herald* (Brownsville), May 8, 1893, 3; "Material for Construction," *Daily Herald* (Brownsville), August 16, 1893, 3.

13. "Report of Brig. Gen. Wheaton, August 18, 1893," 142 (first quote); "Lieutenant Colonel James P. Martin, Assistant Adjutant General (AAG), Department of Texas, to Major Alexander S. B. Keyes, Third Cavalry, Fort Ringgold, Texas, February 20, 1893" (second and third quotes), Letters Sent by Headquarters, Department of Texas, Roll 10, vol. 31. The son of Kentucky-born physician William Washington Shely, and mother, Mary, born in Mexico, Josephus "Joe" Shely was born in Indianola 1853, was married to Mary Hunter Shely, and died in San Antonio May 20, 1910, and was buried in Cuero, Texas. Joe's younger brother Warren Washington "Wash" Shely was born in 1861 and was married to Lucinda, whose father was born in Germany and mother was born in Mexico. "Wash" Shely died March 19, 1909, in Rio Grande City and is buried there in the Downtown Historic Cemetery. On the Shely brothers, see US Bureau of the Census, Ninth Census of the United States, 1870, NARA

Microfilm Publication M593, roll 1609, Wilson County, Texas, Precinct 4; US Bureau of the Census, Tenth Census of the United States, 1880, NARA Microfilm Publication T9, roll 1332, Webb County, Texas, Precinct 3, Enumeration District 145; Twelfth Census of the United States, 1900, NARA Microfilm Publication T623, Starr County, Texas, Justice Precinct 01, Enumeration District 074; "Bexar County, Texas Probate Records, 1837–1913," in "Texas, US Wills and Probate Records, 1833–1974," Ancestry.com; "Report of Brig. Gen. Wheaton, August 18, 1893," 142; "Warren Washington 'Wash' Shely" at https://www.ancestry.com/mediaui/tree/40645530/person/28070962537/media/; Christina Stopka, Texas Ranger Research Center, comp., "Partial List of Texas Ranger Company and Unit Commanders," 37, at https://www.texasranger.org/wp-content/uploads/2019/10/HISTORY_RangerCommanders2019.pdf; Evan Anders, "Manuel Guerra (1856–1915)," in Tyler et al., eds., *The New Handbook of Texas*, 3:369; "The Right Man in the Right Place," *Daily Herald* (Brownsville), May 17, 1893, 3; Chuck Parsons, *Texas Ranger Lee Hall: From the Red River to the Rio Grande* (Denton: University of North Texas Press, 2020), 156; Young, *Catarino Garza's Revolution of the Texas-Mexico Border*, 104, 173; Sammy Tise, *Texas County Sheriffs* (Hallettsville, TX: Tise Genealogical Research, 1989), 473; "Campaign of the Border," *Daily Express* (San Antonio), May 21, 1893, 9.

14. Lewis, *A Guide to the Microfilm Edition of the Garza Revolution*, 9; "Found at Last," *Fort Worth Daily Gazette*, December 25, 1892, 2; "Escaped from the Bandits," *Daily Herald* (Brownsville), January 16, 1893, 2.

Chapter 4

1. Lewis, *A Guide to the Microfilm Edition of the Garza Revolution*, 20; "Campaign of the Border," *Daily Express* (San Antonio), May 21, 1893, 9.
2. "Brigadier General Frank Wheaton, Commander, Department of Texas, to Adjutant General's Office, Washington, D.C., January 23, 1893" (first quote); "Brigadier General Frank Wheaton, Commander, Department of Texas, to Adjutant General's Office, Washington, D.C., January 25, 1893," Letters Sent by Headquarters, Department of Texas, Roll 10, vol.

31; Lewis, *A Guide to the Microfilm Edition of the Garza Revolution*, 16–17; "A Big Capture," *Daily Herald* (Brownsville), January 23, 1893, 3; "Another Capture," *Daily Herald* (Brownsville), January 27, 1893, 3; "Mexico," *Daily Herald* (Brownsville), January 30, 1893, 2 (second quote).

3. "A Suggestion by Major Morris," *Daily Herald* (Brownsville), February 9, 1893, 2 (quotes).
4. "Señor Alberto Leal, Consulate of Mexico, Rio Grande City, Texas to Señor Mariscal, December 16, 1892"; "John W. Foster, Headquarters, Department of State, Washington, D.C., to Señor Cayetano Romero, Mexican Legation of Mexico, Washington, D.C., January 19, 1893"; "Secretary of War S. B. Elkins to Secretary of State John W. Foster, January 19, 1893"; "General Schofield to Secretary of War S. B. Elkins, January 17, 1893"; "General Schofield to Mr. Lamont, February 20, 1893," US Department of State, *Papers Relating to the Foreign Relations of the United States . . . 1893*, 438, 439–40, 446–47; "Lieutenant Colonel James P. Martin, Assistant Adjutant General (AAG), Department of Texas, to Commanding Officer, Fort McIntosh, Fort Ringgold, Camps at Carrizo, San Ygnacio, February 2, 1893," Letters Sent by Headquarters, Department of Texas, Roll 10, vol. 31.
5. After the Chicago exposition, Captain John G. Bourke rejoined his Troop C, Third Cavalry at Fort Riley, Kansas, where he wrote *Our Neutrality Laws* about his experiences in South Texas. Bourke and the troop transferred to Fort Ethan Allen, Vermont, in 1894 where Bourke finished his critical essay on South Texas, "The American Congo," published in *Scribner's Magazine*. After a lingering illness he died on June 8, 1896. One of the great soldier-scholars of the nineteenth century was buried without fanfare in Arlington National Cemetery at age forty-nine. "Brigadier General Frank Wheaton, Commander, Department of Texas, to Adjutant General's Office, Washington, D.C., February 18, 1893," Letters Sent by Headquarters, Department of Texas, Roll 10, vol. 31; Post Returns, Fort Ringgold, Texas, February 1893; Regimental Returns, Third Cavalry, February 1893; "John Gregory Bourke Diary," Roll 9, vol. 111, 35, February 24, 1893 (first quote); Lewis, *A Guide to the Microfilm Edition of the Garza Revolution*, 17, 19; Porter, *Paper Medicine Man*, 290–91; De León, *They Called Them Greasers*, 101; "Another Capture," *Daily Herald*

(Brownsville), February 6, 1893, 2; "More Garza News," *Daily Herald* (Brownsville), February 8, 1893, 3; "Capt. Bourke Accused of Working the Third Degree," *Daily Herald* (Brownsville), March 3, 1893, 1 (second quote); "Rio Grande City Notes," *Daily Herald* (Brownsville), March 6, 1893, 3; "Capt. Bourke Arrives," *Daily Herald* (Brownsville), March 9, 1893, 1; "Starr County Attorney Protests to the Governor," *Daily Herald* (Brownsville), March 10, 1893, 2.

6. "Report of Brig. Gen. Wheaton, August 18, 1893," 143; "Brigadier General Frank Wheaton, Commander, to Adjutant General's Office, Washington, D.C., February 24, 1893," Letters Sent by Headquarters, Department of Texas, Roll 10, vol. 31; Post Returns, Fort Ringgold, Texas, February 1893; Lewis, *A Guide to the Microfilm Edition of the Garza Revolution*, 19; "Campaign of the Border," *Daily Express* (San Antonio), May 21, 1893, 9; "The Dead Bandit," *Daily Herald* (Brownsville), February 25, 1893, 3; US Marshals Service, page for US deputy marshal Rufus B. Glover, at https://www.odmp.org/officer/19659-deputy-us-marshal-rufus-b-glover.

7. "Brigadier General Frank Wheaton, Commander, Department of Texas, to Adjutant General's Office, Washington, D.C., March 9, 1893"; "Brigadier General Frank Wheaton, Commander, Department of Texas, to Adjutant General's Office, Washington, D.C., March 24, 1893"; "Brigadier General Frank Wheaton, Commander, Department of Texas, to Adjutant General's Office, Washington, D.C., April 15, 1893"; "Brigadier General Frank Wheaton, Commander, Department of Texas, to Adjutant General's Office, Washington, D.C., April 21, 1893," Letters Sent by Headquarters, Department of Texas, Roll 10, vol. 31; "Bandits Captured," *Daily Herald* (Brownsville), March 7, 1893, 1; "Catrino Garza's Private Secretary Arrested by Sheriff Shely," *Daily Herald* (Brownsville), March 10, 1893, 3; "Rounding Them Up," *Daily Herald* (Brownsville), March 20, 1893, 3; Swanson, *Seminole, Lipan, Cherokee, Creek, Indian Scouts Enlistment Records, Fort Clark*, 26.

8. "Lieutenant Colonel James P. Martin, Assistant Adjutant General (AAG), Department of Texas, to Commander, Fort McIntosh, April 15, 1893"; "Lieutenant Colonel James P. Martin, Assistant Adjutant General (AAG), Department of Texas, to Commander, Fort McIntosh, April 24, 1893"; "Brigadier General Frank Wheaton, Commander, Department of Texas,

to Adjutant General's Office, Washington, D.C., June 15 and 21, 1893," Letters Sent by Headquarters, Department of Texas, Roll 10, vol. 31; Post Returns, Fort Ringgold, Texas, April–June 1893; Post Returns, Fort McIntosh, Texas, April–June 1893; Regimental Returns, Third Cavalry, April–June 1893; Regimental Returns, Twenty-Third Infantry, April–May 1893.

9. National Archives and Records Administration, Records of the United States Army Adjutant General's Office, 1780–1917, Record Group 391, Records of the United States Regular Army Mobile Units, 1821–1942, Returns from Regular Army Cavalry Regiments, 1833–1916, NARA Microfilm No. 744, roll 55, Regimental Returns, Fifth Cavalry, 1886–1893, Regimental Returns, Fifth Cavalry, June–August 1893; Post Returns, Fort Ringgold, Texas, June–August 1893; Post Returns, Fort McIntosh, Texas, June–August 1893.

10. Regimental Returns, Seventh Cavalry, July 1893.

11. "Report of Brig. Gen. Wheaton, August 18, 1893," 143 (quote); "Major Arthur MacArthur, Assistant Adjutant General (AAG), Department of Texas, to Mr. W. W. Shely, Captain Joseph Shely, San Antonio, Texas, December 26, 1893," Letters Sent by Headquarters, Department of Texas, Roll 10, vol. 31.

12. "Report of the Secretary of War, November 27, 1893," House Exec. Docs., no. 1, vol. 2, pt. 2, 53rd Cong., 2nd sess., serial 3198, 7; Post Returns, Fort Ringgold, Texas, June 1893; Regimental Returns, Third Cavalry, December 1892–July 1893; Regimental Returns, Seventh Cavalry, December 1892–July 1893; Regimental Returns, Eighteenth Infantry, December 1892–July 1893; Regimental Returns, Twenty-Third Infantry, December 1892–July 1893; "Body Recovered," *Daily Herald* (Brownsville), June 28, 1893, 3.

13. Regimental Returns, Third Cavalry, June 1893; Post Returns, Fort Ringgold, Texas, June 1893, December 1893 (quote); "Señor Cayetano Romero, Mexican Legation of Mexico, Washington, D.C., to Mr. Gresham [Secretary of State Walter Q. Gresham] April 28, 1893"; "Señor Cayetano Romero, Mexican Legation of Mexico, Washington, D.C., to Mr. Gresham, June 9, 1893"; "Brigadier General Frank Wheaton, Commander, Department of Texas, to Adjutant General's Office, Washington,

D.C., July 8, 1893," US Department of State, *Papers Relating to the Foreign Relations of the United States . . . 1893*, 448–49, 453–55.

14. "Report of the Secretary of War, November 27, 1893," 4–5 (first quote); "Report of Brig. Gen. Wheaton, August 18, 1893, 143–44 (second quote).

15. For details on the names and legal results of the revolutionists' arrests and trials, see the Appendix: "List of *Insurrectos*, 1890–1893." "Alejandro Gonzales Arrested and Bailed," *Daily Herald* (Brownsville), May 22, 1893, 1; "Gonzales Heavily Fined," *Daily Herald* (Brownsville), May 27, 1893, 2; "Alejandro Gonzales," *Galveston Daily News*, May 17, 1893, 3; "Three Garzaites," *Fort Worth Daily Gazette*, December 20, 1892, 1; "Going to Prison," *Daily Herald* (Brownsville), February 2, 1893, 2; Valentine J. Belfiglio, "Antonio Mateo Bruni (1856–1931)," in Tyler et al., eds., *The New Handbook of Texas*, 1:784.

16. James Davenport Whelpley, "End of Border Outlawry," *Harper's Weekly*, June 27, 1896, 636 (quote), at https://babel.hathitrust.org/cgi/pt?id=mdp.39015023106241&view=1up&seq=623&skin=2021; Daniel S. Margolies, *Spaces of Law in American Foreign Relations: Extradition and Extraterritoriality in the Borderlands and Beyond, 1877–1898* (Athens: University of Georgia Press, 2011), 309–310; Claudia Hazlewood, "James Harvey McLeary (1845–1914)," in Tyler et al., eds., *The New Handbook of Texas*, 4:428.

17. "Message to the Senate and House of Representatives, December 6, 1897"; "Señor Cayetano Romero, Mexican Legation of Mexico, Washington, D.C., to Mr. Gresham, Department of State, Washington, D.C., September 28, 1897"; "John Sherman to Señor Cayetano Romero, Mexican Legation of Mexico, Washington, D.C., November 13, 1897"; "Señor Cayetano Romero, Mexican Legation of Mexico, Washington, D.C., to Mr. Sherman, Department of State, Washington, D.C., November 15, 1897," US Department of State, *Papers Relating to the Foreign Relations of the United States, with the Annual Message of the President, Transmitted to Congress December 6, 1897* (Washington, DC: Government Printing Office, 1898), xv, 405, 406 (first and second quote), 407–16.

18. "A Big Capture," *Daily Herald* (Brownsville), January 23, 1893, 3; "Another Capture," *Daily Herald* (Brownsville), January 27, 1893, 3; "Benavides Christening Certificate in Evidence," *Daily Herald* (Brownsville),

March 13, 1893, 1; "The Case of Francisco Benavides," *Daily Herald* (Brownsville), March 15, 1893, 1; "General Benavides Will Be Tried in Starr County before Being Extradited," *Daily Herald* (Brownsville), March 30, 1893, 1; "Campaign of the Border," *Daily Express* (San Antonio), May 21, 1893, 9; "Battle of San Ygnacio," *Daily Express* (San Antonio), February 12, 1893, 6; "Witness for the Defense," *Daily Express* (San Antonio), February 21, 1893, 8; "Won't Deliver Benavides," *Daily Express* (San Antonio), June 7, 1893, 1; "Testimony of a Soldier," *Daily Express* (San Antonio), February 15, 1893, 6; "Skirmish at San Ygnacio," *Daily Express* (San Antonio), February 16, 1893, 8.

19. "Message of the President, December 9, 1891," *Papers Relating to the Foreign Relations of the United States, with the Annual Message of the President, Transmitted to Congress, December 9, 1891* (Washington, DC: Government Printing Office, 1892), vi–vii; Adjutant General's Office, *Official Army Register for 1911*, 15, 165; "Cuban Revolutionist," *Daily Herald* (Brownsville), March 9, 1893, 1; "Border Troubles," *Daily Herald* (Brownsville), May 18, 1893, 1; Smith, *The Old Army in the Big Bend of Texas, 1911–1921: The Last Cavalry Frontier*, 35–36, 53, 82. For excellent treatments of the Philippine Insurrection, see Brian McAllister Linn, *The Philippine War, 1899–1902* (Lawrence: University Press of Kansas, 2000), and John M. Gates, *Schoolbooks and Krags: The United States Army in the Philippines, 1889–1902* (Westport, CT: Greenwood Press, 1973).

20. Militia Bureau, War Department, *Report on Mobilization of the Organized Militia and National Guard of the United States, 1916* (Washington, DC: Government Printing Office, 1916), 156; Charles H. Harris III and Louis R. Sadler, *The Great Call Up: The Guard, the Border, and the Mexican Revolution* (Norman: University of Oklahoma Press, 2015), 82, 118, 166, 176, 251, 268–99.

Notes to the Appendix

1. Aieto, Raiel. "Many Pleas of Guilty," *Daily Express* (San Antonio), May 4, 1893, 5.
2. Ajala, Monsicio. "In Federal Court," *Daily Express* (San Antonio), November 14, 1893, 8.

3. Alvido, Natiridad. "Garza Revolutionist," *Galveston Daily News*, May 17, 1892, 7.
4. Ansaleo, Motello. "Many Pleas of Guilty," *Daily Express* (San Antonio), May 4, 1893, 5.
5. Arambula, Andres. "Brigadier General Frank Wheaton, Commander, Department of Texas, to Adjutant General's Office, Washington, D.C., March 24, 1893," National Archives and Records Administration (NARA), Records of the United States Army Adjutant General's Office, 1780–1917, Record Group 393, Records of US Army Continental Commands, 1821–1920, NARA Microfilm No. M1114, Letters Sent by Headquarters, Department of Texas, 1870–1894 and 1897–1898, Roll 10, vol. 31, January–December 1893; "Many Pleas of Guilty," *Daily Express* (San Antonio), May 4, 1893, 5.
6. Arsola, Mateo. "Captain Henry Jackson, Seventh Cavalry, letter, April 12, 1893," Lewis, *A Guide to the Microfilm Edition of the Garza Revolution*, 21, at https://media2.proquest.com/documents/103936.pdf.
7. Barrera, Juan. "In Federal Court," *Daily Express* (San Antonio), November 14, 1893, 8.
8. Bazan, Victoriano. "Munoz Convicted," *Daily Express* (San Antonio), May 26, 1892, 6.
9. Belmontez, Feleciano. "In Federal Court," *Daily Express* (San Antonio), November 14, 1893, 8.
10. Benavides, Cayetano. "Many Pleas of Guilty," *Daily Express* (San Antonio), May 4, 1893, 5.
11. Benavides, Cresencio. "Captain John G. Bourke, Troop C, Third Cavalry, letter, April 3, 1892," Lewis, *A Guide to the Microfilm Edition of the Garza Revolution*, 11.
12. Benavides, Esperidion. "Many Pleas of Guilty," *Daily Express* (San Antonio), May 4, 1893, 5.
13. Benavides, Estevan. "More Garza News," *Daily Herald* (Brownsville), February 8, 1893, 3; "Many Pleas of Guilty," *Daily Express* (San Antonio), May 4, 1893, 5.
14. Benavides, Francisco. "Report of Brig. Gen. Wheaton, August 18, 1893," 143, in "Report of the Secretary of War, November 27, 1893," House Exec. Docs., no. 1, pt. 2, vol. 2, 53rd Cong., 2nd sess., serial 3198; "Brigadier

General Frank Wheaton, Commander, Department of Texas, to Adjutant General's Office, Washington, D.C., January 25, 1893," Letters Sent by Headquarters, Department of Texas, Roll 10, Vol. 31; "Another Capture," *Daily Herald* (Brownsville), January 27, 1893, 3; "Benavides Christening Certificate in Evidence," *Daily Herald* (Brownsville), March 13, 1893, 1; "The Case of Francisco Benavides," *Daily Herald* (Brownsville), March 15, 1893, 1; "General Benavides Will Be Tried in Starr County before Being Extradited," *Daily Herald* (Brownsville), March 30, 1893, 1; "Campaign of the Border," *Daily Express* (San Antonio), May 21, 1893, 9; "Battle of San Ygnacio," *Daily Express* (San Antonio), February 12, 1893, 6; "Witness for the Defense," *Daily Express* (San Antonio), February 21, 1893, 8; "Won't Deliver Benavides," *Daily Express* (San Antonio), June 7, 1893, 1; James Davenport Whelpley, "End of Border Outlawry," *Harper's Weekly*, June 27, 1896, 636, at https://babel.hathitrust.org/cgi/pt?id=mdp.39015023106241&view=1up&seq=623&skin=2021; Margolies, *Spaces of Law in American Foreign Relations*, 309–10.

15. Benavides, José María. "Lieutenant Colonel James P. Martin, Assistant Adjutant General (AAG), Department of Texas, to Lieutenant Stephen O'Conner, Camp at San Ygnacio, Texas, June 26, 1893," Letters Sent by Headquarters, Department of Texas, Roll 10, Vol. 31.

16. Bermadez, Leander. "In Federal Court," *Daily Express* (San Antonio), November 14, 1893, 8.

17. Brecina, Jesus. "Many Pleas of Guilty," *Daily Express* (San Antonio), May 4, 1893, 5.

18. Briseno, Josne. "Thirty-Two Prisoners Brought in from the Border," *Daily Herald* (Brownsville), May 4, 1893, 1.

19. Bruni, Antonio Mateo. Young, *Catarino Garza's Revolution on the Texas-Mexico Border*, 157, 169, 230; Valentine J. Belfiglio, "Antonio Mateo Bruni (1856–1931)," In Tyler et al., eds., *The New Handbook of Texas*, 1.784; "Revolutionists Arraigned." *Daily Express* (San Antonio), May 17, 1892, 6; "Munoz Convicted," *Daily Express* (San Antonio), May 26, 1892, 6.

20. Cadena, Apelinio "Pablo." "Lieutenant Herbert J. Slocum, Seventh Cavalry, telegram, February 8, 1893," Lewis, *A Guide to the Microfilm Edition of the Garza Revolution*, 19; "More Garza News," *Daily Herald* (Brownsville), February 8, 1893, 3.

21. Cadena, Refugio. "Revolutionists Captured," *Daily Herald* (Brownsville), February 21, 1893, 1.
22. Cadena, Santos. "Lieutenant Herbert J. Slocum, Seventh Cavalry, telegram, February 8, 1893," Lewis, *A Guide to the Microfilm Edition of the Garza Revolution*, 19; "More Garza News," *Daily Herald* (Brownsville), February 8, 1893, 3; "Thirty-Two Prisoners Brought in from the Border," *Daily Herald* (Brownsville), May 4, 1893, 1; "Many Pleas of Guilty," *Daily Express* (San Antonio), May 4, 1893, 5.
23. Cadlor, Guadalupe C. "Report of Brigadier General Stanley, September 12, 1890," in "Report of the Secretary of War, 1890," House Exec. Docs., no. 1, vol. 2, pt. 2, 51st Cong., 2nd sess., serial 2831, 184–185; "General Sandoval Acquitted," *Galveston Daily News*, December 23, 1890, 1.
24. Cantu, Lucio. "Six of the Border Outlaws Captured by Sheriff Shely," *Daily Herald* (Brownsville), March 23, 1893, 1; "The Revolution Over," *The Galveston Daily News*, March 13, 1893, 1; "Many Pleas of Guilty," *Daily Express* (San Antonio), May 4, 1893, 5.
25. Cantu, Victor. "Thirty-two Prisoners Brought in from the Border," *Daily Herald* (Brownsville), May 4, 1893, 1.
26. Castillo, Molena. "In Federal Court," *Daily Express* (San Antonio), November 14, 1893, 8.
27. Cavazos, Bartolo. "Many Pleas of Guilty," *Daily Express* (San Antonio), May 4, 1893, 5.
28. Chacon, Jesus. "Many Pleas of Guilty," *Daily Express* (San Antonio), May 4, 1893, 5.
29. Cuellar, Tomás. "Brigadier General Frank Wheaton, Commander, Department of Texas, to Adjutant General's Office, Washington, D.C., March 9, 1893," Letters Sent by Headquarters, Department of Texas, Roll 10, Vol. 31; "Captain George K. Hunter, Troop K, Third Cavalry, telegram, March 8, 1893," Lewis, *A Guide to the Microfilm Edition of the Garza Revolution*, 20; "Campaign of the Border," *Daily Express* (San Antonio), May 21, 1893, 9; "The Revolution Over," *Galveston Daily News*, March 13, 1893, 1.
30. Duque, Juan. "Bandits Captured," *Daily Herald* (Brownsville), March 7, 1893, 1; James Davenport Whelpley, "End of Border Outlawry," *Harper's*

Weekly, June 27, 1896, 636, at https://babel.hathitrust.org/cgi/pt?id=mdp.39015023106241&view=1up&seq=623&skin=2021.

31. Echevarria, Cecilio. "Report of Brig. Gen. Wheaton, August 18, 1893," 140–45; "Brigadier General Frank Wheaton, Commander, Department of Texas, to Adjutant General's Office, Washington, D.C., January 25, 1893," Letters Sent by Headquarters, Department of Texas, Roll 10, Vol. 31; "Trial of Revolutionist," *Daily Herald* (Brownsville), January 26, 1893, 3; "Echevarria Case," *Daily Herald* (Brownsville), March 28, 1893, 2.

32. Elizando, Cayetano Garza. "Lieutenant Colonel James P. Martin, Assistant Adjutant General (AAG), Department of Texas, to Captain William B. Wheeler, 18th Infantry, Fort Ringgold, Texas, December 7, 1892," Letters Sent by Headquarters, Department of Texas, Roll 10, Vol. 30; Young, *Catarino Garza's Revolution on the Texas-Mexico Border*, 218. "Three Garzaites," *Fort Worth Daily Gazette*, December 20, 1892, 1; "Given the Full Penalty," *Daily Express* (San Antonio), December 20, 1892, 3; "Going to Prison," *Daily Herald* (Brownsville), February 2, 1893, 2.

33. Flores, Entiquio. "Munoz Convicted," *Daily Express* (San Antonio), May 26, 1892, 6.

34. Flores, Galvino. "The Temples of Law," *San Antonio Express News*, December 19, 1890, 6; "The Day in Courts," *San Antonio Express News*, December 20, 1890, 3; "Jury Still Out," *San Antonio Express News*, December 22, 1890, 3; "The Mills of Justice," *San Antonio Express News*, December 23, 1890, 3.

35. Flores, Jesus. "Major Alexander S. B. Keyes, Third Cavalry, telegram, April 17, 1893," Lewis, *A Guide to the Microfilm Edition of the Garza Revolution*, 21; "Thirty-Two Prisoners Brought in from the Border," *Daily Herald* (Brownsville), May 4, 1893, 1; "Many Pleas of Guilty," *Daily Express* (San Antonio), May 4, 1893, 5.

36. Flores, Juan Angel. "In Federal Court," *Daily Express* (San Antonio), November 14, 1893, 8.

37. Flores, Juan Antonio. "Three Garzaites," *Fort Worth Daily Gazette*, December 20, 1892, 1; "Going to Prison," *Daily Herald* (Brownsville), February 2, 1893, 2.

38. Flores, Juan Manuel. "Munoz Convicted," *Daily Express* (San Antonio), May 26, 1892, 6.
39. Flores, Julian. "Made a Bad Break, Garza Revolutionist Try to Cross the River," *Galveston Daily News*, May 13, 1892, 1; Young, *Catarino Garza's Revolution on the Texas-Mexico Border*, 121; "The Revolution Over," *Galveston Daily News*, March 13, 1893, 1; "Garzaites Trial," *Daily Express* (San Antonio), May 20, 1892, 3.
40. Flores, Telesforo. "Captain Henry Jackson, Seventh Cavalry, letter, April 12, 1893," Lewis, *A Guide to the Microfilm Edition of the Garza Revolution*, 21; "Thirty-Two Prisoners Brought in from the Border," *Daily Herald* (Brownsville), May 4, 1893, 1; "More Men Plead Guilty," *Daily Express* (San Antonio), May 6, 1893, 6.
41. Gaitan, Anastacio. "Thirty-two Prisoners Brought in from the Border," *Daily Herald* (Brownsville), May 4, 1893, 1.
42. Galvan, Juaqnio. "Munoz Convicted," *Daily Express* (San Antonio), May 26, 1892, 6.
43. Gamez, Pablo. "Many Pleas of Guilty," *Daily Express* (San Antonio), May 4, 1893, 5. "More Men Plead Guilty," *Daily Express* (San Antonio), May 6, 1893, 6.
44. García, Amador [Amadeo]. "Report of Brigadier General Stanley, September 12, 1890," 184–85; "General Sandoval Acquitted," *Galveston Daily News*, December 23, 1890, 1; "The Temples of Law," *San Antonio Express News*, December 19, 1890, 6; "The Day in Courts," *San Antonio Express News*, December 20, 1890, 3; "Jury Still Out," *San Antonio Express News*, December 22, 1890, 3; "The Mills of Justice," *San Antonio Express News*, December 23, 1890, 3.
45. García, Amando. "Many Pleas of Guilty," *Daily Express* (San Antonio), May 4, 1893, 5; "More Men Plead Guilty," *Daily Express* (San Antonio), May 6, 1893, 6.
46. García, Antenacio. "Many Pleas of Guilty," *Daily Express* (San Antonio), May 4, 1893, 5.
47. García, Antonio. "Federal Court Cases," *Daily Express* (San Antonio), November 11, 1893, 5.
48. García, Armando. "Brigadier General Frank Wheaton, Commander, Department of Texas, to Adjutant General's Office, Washington, D.C.,

March 9, 1893," Letters Sent by Headquarters, Department of Texas, Roll 10, Vol. 31; "The Revolution Over," *Galveston Daily News*, March 13, 1893, 1.

49. García, Delfino. "Captain George F. Chase, Third Cavalry, telegram, April 27, 1893," Lewis, *A Guide to the Microfilm Edition of the Garza Revolution*, 21.
50. García, Eusebio. "Lieutenant Stephen O'Conner, Twenty-Third, telegram, August 1, 1893," Lewis, *A Guide to the Microfilm Edition of the Garza Revolution*, 23; "In the Federal Court," *Daily Express* (San Antonio), November 14, 1893, 8.
51. García, Juan. "Munoz Convicted," *Daily Express* (San Antonio), May 26, 1892, 6.
52. García, Juan M. P. "Many Pleas of Guilty," *Daily Express* (San Antonio), May 4, 1893, 5.
53. García, Julian. "Captain Henry Jackson, Seventh Cavalry, letter, April 12, 1893," Lewis, *A Guide to the Microfilm Edition of the Garza Revolution*, 21.
54. García, Julio. "Thirty-Two Prisoners Brought in from the Border," *Daily Herald* (Brownsville), May 4, 1893, 1.
55. García, Louis. "Revolutionists Captured," *Daily Herald* (Brownsville), February 21, 1893, 1.
56. García, Nesario. "Another Capture," *Daily Herald* (Brownsville), January 27, 1893, 3.
57. García, Pedro. "Brigadier General Frank Wheaton, Commander, Department of Texas, to Adjutant General's Office, Washington, D.C., April 21, 1893," Letters Sent by Headquarters, Department of Texas, Roll 10, Vol. 31; "Major Alexander S. B. Keyes, Third Cavalry, letter, April 20, 1893," Lewis, *A Guide to the Microfilm Edition of the Garza Revolution*, 21. "Thirty-Two Prisoners Brought in from the Border," *Daily Herald* (Brownsville), May 4, 1893, 1; "The Boys in Blue," *Daily Herald* (Brownsville), April 25, 1893, 2; "More Men Plead Guilty," *Daily Express* (San Antonio), May 6, 1893, 6.
58. García, Roman. "Brigadier General Frank Wheaton, Commander, Department of Texas, to Adjutant General's Office, Washington, D.C., April 15, 1893," Letters Sent by Headquarters, Department of Texas,

Roll 10, Vol. 31; "Many Pleas of Guilty," *Daily Express* (San Antonio), May 4, 1893, 5.

59. García, Rosillio. "Thirty-Two Prisoners Brought in from the Border," *Daily Herald* (Brownsville), May 4, 1893, 1; "Many Pleas of Guilty," *Daily Express* (San Antonio), May 4, 1893, 5.
60. Garza, Bernardo de la. "Garza Revolutionaries," *Daily Express* (San Antonio), May 27, 1892, 5; "Federal Court Cases," *Daily Express* (San Antonio), November 11, 1893, 5.
61. Garza, Catarino Erasmo. Young, *Catarino Garza's Revolution on the Texas-Mexico Border*; Cuthbertson, "Catarino E. Garza and the Garza War," 335–47; Cuthbertson, "Catarino Erasmo Garza (1859–1895)," 3:106–7; Thompson, *A Wild and Vivid Land*, 131-33.
62. Garza, Frank. "Captain George K. Hunter, telegram, January 19, 1892," Lewis, *A Guide to the Microfilm Edition of the Garza Revolution*, 8.
63. Garza, Luis. "Revolutionist in Court," *Daily Express* (San Antonio), May 31, 1892, 6.
64. Garza, Rafael. "Many Pleas of Guilty," *Daily Express* (San Antonio), May 4, 1893, 5.
65. Garza, Rosalio. "Another Capture," *Daily Herald* (Brownsville), January 27, 1893, 3.
66. Garza, Theodoro. "Thirty-Two Prisoners Brought in from the Border," *Daily Herald* (Brownsville), May 4, 1893, 1.
67. Garza, Ygnacio. "Garza Revolutionaries," *Daily Express* (San Antonio), May 27, 1892, 5.
68. Golindo, Juan M. "Revolutionist in Court," *Daily Express* (San Antonio), May 31, 1892, 6.
69. González, Alejandro. Young, *Catarino Garza's Revolution on the Texas-Mexico Border*, 100, 172, 179; "Garza Revolutionaries," *Daily Express* (San Antonio), May 27, 1892, 5; "Alejandro Gonzales Arrested and Bailed," *Daily Herald* (Brownsville), May 22, 1893, 1; "Gonzales Heavily Fined," *Daily Herald* (Brownsville), May 27, 1893, 2; "Alejandro Gonzales," *Galveston Daily News*, May 17, 1893, 3.
70. González, Brunio. "In Federal Court," *Daily Express* (San Antonio), November 14, 1893, 8.

71. González, Concepcíon "Chonita." Young, *Catarino Garza's Revolution on the Texas-Mexico Border*, 54, 268–71.
72. González, Francis. "Revolutionists Arraigned." *Daily Express* (San Antonio), May 17, 1892, 6.
73. González, Francisco. "Many Pleas of Guilty," *Daily Express* (San Antonio), May 4, 1893, 5.
74. González, Manuel. "Many Pleas of Guilty," *Daily Express* (San Antonio), May 4, 1893, 5.
75. González, Pedro Peña. "Revolutionist in Court," *Daily Express* (San Antonio), May 31, 1892, 6.
76. González, Prudencio. "Report of Brig. Gen. Wheaton, August 18, 1893," 143; "Brigadier General Frank Wheaton, Commander, Department of Texas, to Adjutant General's Office, Washington, D.C., January 25, 1893," Letters Sent by Headquarters, Department of Texas, Roll 10, Vol. 31; "Talk with Captain Shely," *Daily Herald* (Brownsville), February 1, 1893, 1; "Prudencio Gonzales Trial," *Daily Herald* (Brownsville), April 25, 1893, 3; "Many Pleas of Guilty," *Daily Express* (San Antonio), May 4, 1893, 5; "Campaign of the Border," *Daily Express* (San Antonio), May 21, 1893, 9.
77. González, Vicente M. "The Temples of Law," *San Antonio Express News*, December 19, 1890, 6; "The Day in Courts," *San Antonio Express News*, December 20, 1890, 3; "Jury Still Out," *San Antonio Express News*, December 22, 1890, 3; "The Mills of Justice," *San Antonio Express News*, December 23, 1890, 3.
78. Guebarra, Gregorio. "Brigadier General Frank Wheaton, Commander, Department of Texas, to Adjutant General's Office, Washington, D.C., February 24, 1893," Letters Sent by Headquarters, Department of Texas, Roll 10, Vol. 31; "The Revolution Over," *Galveston Daily News*, March 13, 1893, 1; "Many Pleas of Guilty," *Daily Express* (San Antonio), May 4, 1893, 5.
79. Guerra, Antonio. "Many Pleas of Guilty," *Daily Express* (San Antonio), May 4, 1893, 5; "In the Federal Court," *Daily Express* (San Antonio), November 14, 1893, 8.
80. Guerra, Jesus. Whelpley, "End of Border Outlawry," 636, at https://babel.hathitrust.org/cgi/pt?id=mdp.39015023106241&view=1up&seq=623&skin

=2021; "Señor Cayetano Romero, Mexican Legation of Mexico, Washington, D.C., to Mr. Gresham, Department of State, Washington, D.C., September 28, 1897"; "John Sherman to Señor Cayetano Romero, Mexican Legation of Mexico, Washington, D.C., November 13, 1897"; "Señor Cayetano Romero, Mexican Legation of Mexico, Washington, D.C., to Mr. Sherman, Department of State, Washington, D.C., November 15, 1897," US Department of State, *Papers Relating to the Foreign Relations of the United States, with the Annual Message of the President, Transmitted to Congress December 6, 1897* (Washington, DC: Government Printing Office, 1898), xv, 405, 406 (first and second quote), 407–16.

81. Guerra, Juan. "Captain William B. Wheeler, Eighteenth Infantry, telegram, March 13, 1893," Lewis, *A Guide to the Microfilm Edition of the Garza Revolution*, 20; "Thirty-Two Prisoners Brought in from the Border," *Daily Herald* (Brownsville), May 4, 1893, 1.

82. Guerra, Juan. "Brigadier General Frank Wheaton, Commander, Department of Texas, to Adjutant General's Office, Washington, D.C., March 14, 1893," Letters Sent by Headquarters, Department of Texas, Roll 10, Vol. 31.

83. Guerra, Melcher. "Report of Brigadier General Stanley, September 12, 1890," 184–85; "General Sandoval Acquitted," *Galveston Daily News*, December 23, 1890, 1; "The Temples of Law," *San Antonio Express News*, December 19, 1890, 6; "The Day in Courts," *San Antonio Express News*, December 20, 1890, 3; "Jury Still Out," *San Antonio Express News*, December 22, 1890, 3; "The Mills of Justice," *San Antonio Express News*, December 23, 1890, 3.

84. Gutiérrez, Amador. "The Temples of Law," *San Antonio Express News*, December 19, 1890, 6; "The Day in Courts," *San Antonio Express News*, December 20, 1890, 3; "Jury Still Out," *San Antonio Express News*, December 22, 1890, 3; "The Mills of Justice," *San Antonio Express News*, December 23, 1890, 3.

85. Gutiérrez, Clemente. "Brigadier General Frank Wheaton, Commander, Department of Texas, to Adjutant General's Office, Washington, D.C., February 24, 1893," Letters Sent by Headquarters, Department of Texas, Roll 10, Vol. 31; "Campaign of the Border," *Daily Express* (San Antonio), May 21, 1893, 9; "The Revolution Over," *Galveston Daily News*, March 13,

1893, 1; "Many Pleas of Guilty," *Daily Express* (San Antonio), May 4, 1893, 5; "More Men Plead Guilty," *Daily Express* (San Antonio), May 6, 1893, 6.

86. Gutiérrez, Epifano. "In Federal Court," *Daily Express* (San Antonio), November 14, 1893, 8.
87. Gutiérrez, Labrado. "In Federal Court," *Daily Express* (San Antonio), November 14, 1893, 8.
88. Gutiérrez, Liberado. "Six of the Border Outlaws Captured by Sheriff Shely," *Daily Herald* (Brownsville), March 23, 1893, 1; "The Revolution Over," *Galveston Daily News*, March 13, 1893, 1; "Many Pleas of Guilty," *Daily Express* (San Antonio), May 4, 1893, 5.
89. Gutiérrez, Liberdad. "Brigadier General Frank Wheaton, Commander, Department of Texas, to Adjutant General's Office, Washington, D.C., February 24, 1893," Letters Sent by Headquarters, Department of Texas, Roll 10, Vol. 31.
90. Gutiérrez, Porfirio. "Brigadier General Frank Wheaton, Commander, Department of Texas, to Adjutant General's Office, Washington, D.C., March 9, 1893," Letters Sent by Headquarters, Department of Texas, Roll 10, Vol. 31.
91. Gutiérrez (Gutierras), Procopio. "Captain George K. Hunter, Troop K, Third Cavalry, telegram, March 8, 1893," Lewis, *A Guide to the Microfilm Edition of the Garza Revolution*, 20; "Campaign of the Border," *Daily Express* (San Antonio), May 21, 1893, 9; "The Revolution Over," *Galveston Daily News*, March 13, 1893, 1.
92. Hernandez, Dario. "Captain Oscar Elting, telegram, February 13, 1893," Lewis, *A Guide to the Microfilm Edition of the Garza Revolution*, 19.
93. Hernandez, David. "Border Disturbers Captured," *Daily Herald* (Brownsville), February 20, 1893, 1.
94. Hernandez, Nicholas. "Federal Court Notes," *Daily Herald* (Brownsville), June 17, 1893, 3.
95. Leal, Geraldo. "Lieutenant Stephen O'Conner, Twenty-Third, telegram, February 15, 1893," Lewis, *A Guide to the Microfilm Edition of the Garza Revolution*, 19; "Border Disturbers Captured," *Daily Herald* (Brownsville), February 20, 1893, 1.

96. Lemon. Serstones. "Major Alexander S. B. Keyes, Third Cavalry, letter, August 2, 1893," Lewis, *A Guide to the Microfilm Edition of the Garza Revolution*, 23.
97. Longorio, Pablo. "Captain John G. Bourke, Troop C, Third Cavalry, letter, April 3, 1892," Lewis, *A Guide to the Microfilm Edition of the Garza Revolution*, 11; Young, *Catarino Garza's Revolution on the Texas-Mexico Border*, 180–82; "Battle of San Ygnacio," *Daily Express* (San Antonio), February 12, 1893, 6.
98. Longorio, Sixto. "Brigadier General David S. Stanley, Commander, Department of Texas, to Major General Schofield, Washington, D.C., January 1, 1892, and January 9, 1892"; "Lieutenant Colonel James P. Martin, Assistant Adjutant General (AAG), Department of Texas, to Capt. Geo. K. Hunter, 3rd Cavalry, Camp at Los Angeles, Encinal Co. Texas, February 14, 1893," Letters Sent by Headquarters, Department of Texas, Roll 10, Vol. 30 and Vol. 31; Young, *Catarino Garza's Revolution on the Texas-Mexico Border*, 171; "Revolutionists Arraigned." *Daily Express* (San Antonio), May 17, 1892, 6.
99. López, Abelarjo. "The Temples of Law," *San Antonio Express News*, December 19, 1890, 6; "The Day in Courts," *San Antonio Express News*, December 20, 1890, 3; "Jury Still Out," *San Antonio Express News*, December 22, 1890, 3; "The Mills of Justice," *San Antonio Express News*, December 23, 1890, 3.
100. López, Amostacio. "Six of the Border Outlaws Captured by Sheriff Shely," *Daily Herald* (Brownsville), March 23, 1893, 1.
101. López, Hymio. "Munoz Convicted," *Daily Express* (San Antonio), May 26, 1892, 6.
102. López, Leonidas. "Garzaites Trial," *Daily Express* (San Antonio), May 20, 1892, 3; "Munoz Convicted," *Daily Express* (San Antonio), May 26, 1892, 6.
103. López, Manuel. "Many Pleas of Guilty," *Daily Express* (San Antonio), May 4, 1893, 5.
104. López, Teodoro G. "More Men Plead Guilty," *Daily Express* (San Antonio), May 6, 1893, 6.
105. López, Victoriano. "Major Lewis T. Morris, letter, January 28, 1892," Lewis, *A Guide to the Microfilm Edition of the Garza Revolution*, 8; "The

Garza Cases," *Galveston Daily News*, May 27, 1892, 3; "Garza Revolutionaries," *Daily Express* (San Antonio), May 27, 1892, 5.

106. Magro, Abeham [Abram]. "Thirty-Two Prisoners Brought in from the Border," *Daily Herald* (Brownsville), May 4, 1893, 1; "More Men Plead Guilty," *Daily Express* (San Antonio), May 6, 1893, 6.

107. Maldonado, Juan. "Brigadier General Frank Wheaton, Commander, Department of Texas, to Adjutant General's Office, Washington, D.C., March 14, 1893," Letters Sent by Headquarters, Department of Texas, Roll 10, Vol. 31; "Captain William B. Wheeler, Eighteenth Infantry, telegram, March 13, 1893," Lewis, *A Guide to the Microfilm Edition of the Garza Revolution*, 20; "Thirty-Two Prisoners Brought in from the Border," *Daily Herald* (Brownsville), May 4, 1893, 1.

108. Margo, Estavano. "Bandits Captured," *Daily Herald* (Brownsville), March 7, 1893, 1.

109. Martínez, Ensebio. "Revolutionist Arrested," *Daily Herald* (Brownsville), June 8, 1893, 3.

110. Martínez, Eusabio M., alias Mangus de Aqua. "Report of Brig. Gen. Wheaton, August 18, 1893," 143; "Brigadier General Frank Wheaton, Commander, Department of Texas, to Adjutant General's Office, Washington, D.C., February 24, 1893," Letters Sent by Headquarters, Department of Texas, Roll 10, Vol. 31.

111. Martínez, Felipe. "Alejandro Gonzales," *Galveston Daily News*, May 17, 1893, 3.

112. Martínez, Mateo. "The Garza Cases," *Galveston Daily News*, May 27, 1892, 3; "Garza Revolutionaries," *Daily Express* (San Antonio), May 27, 1892, 5.

113. Martínez, Maximo. "Report of Brig. Gen. Wheaton, August 18, 1893," 143; "Brigadier General Frank Wheaton, Commander, Department of Texas, to Adjutant General's Office, Washington, D.C., March 24, 1893"; "Brigadier General Frank Wheaton, Commander, Department of Texas, to Adjutant General's Office, Washington, D.C., December 17, 1892," Letters Sent by Headquarters, Department of Texas, Roll 10, Vol. 30 and Vol. 31; Young, *Catarino Garza's Revolution on the Texas-Mexico Border*, 179; "Maximo Martinez," *Daily Herald* (Brownsville), June 6, 1893, 1; "Maximo Martinez Sentenced," *Daily Express* (San Antonio), June 2, 1893, 6.

114. Martivero, Evaristo. "Brigadier General Frank Wheaton, Commander, Department of Texas, to Adjutant General's Office, Washington, D.C., March 24, 1893," Letters Sent by Headquarters, Department of Texas, Roll 10, Vol. 31.
115. Mendoza, Anastacio. "Many Pleas of Guilty," *Daily Express* (San Antonio), May 4, 1893, 5.
116. Mendoza, Francisco L. "Garza Revolutionaries," *Daily Express* (San Antonio), May 27, 1892, 5.
117. Mendoza, Pedro. "Many Pleas of Guilty," *Daily Express* (San Antonio), May 4, 1893, 5.
118. Molina, Jacabo. "Revolutionists Arraigned," *Daily Express* (San Antonio), May 17, 1892, 6; "Munoz Convicted," *Daily Express* (San Antonio), May 26, 1892, 6.
119. Mongao, Innocencio. "In Federal Court," *Daily Express* (San Antonio), November 14, 1893, 8.
120. Montevino, Avisto. "Many Pleas of Guilty," *Daily Express* (San Antonio), May 4, 1893, 5.
121. Morales, Felipe. "Six of the Border Outlaws Captured by Sheriff Shely," *Daily Herald* (Brownsville), March 23, 1893, 1.
122. Morales, José María. "Brigadier General Frank Wheaton, Commander, Department of Texas, to Adjutant General's Office, Washington, D.C., February 24, 1893," Letters Sent by Headquarters, Department of Texas, Roll 10, Vol. 31; Young, *Catarino Garza's Revolution on the Texas-Mexico Border*, 31; "The Revolution Over," *Galveston Daily News*, March 13, 1893, 1; "Many Pleas of Guilty," *Daily Express* (San Antonio), May 4, 1893, 5; "More Men Plead Guilty," *Daily Express* (San Antonio), May 6, 1893, 6.
123. Moreno, Severino. "More Garza News," *Daily Herald* (Brownsville), February 8, 1893, 3; "Thirty-Two Prisoners Brought in from the Border," *Daily Herald* (Brownsville), May 4, 1893, 1.
124. Moya, Electorio. "Federal Court Notes," *Daily Herald* (Brownsville), June 19, 1893, 3.
125. Moya, Teodoro. "Federal Court Notes," *Daily Herald* (Brownsville), June 19, 1893, 3.
126. Muñoz, Pablo. "Brigadier General David S. Stanley, Commander, Department of Texas, to Major General Schofield, Washington, D.C.,

January 3, 1892," Letters Sent by Headquarters, Department of Texas, Roll 10, Vol. 30; "Trying a Garzaite," *Galveston Daily News*, May 20, 1892, 4; "Trial of Garza's Lieutenant," *Galveston Daily News*, May 25, 1892, 4; "The First in Sixty Years," *Galveston Daily News*, May 26, 1892, 3; "The Garza Cases," *Galveston Daily News*, May 27, 1892, 3; "Pablo Munoz Sentenced," *Galveston Daily News*, May 28, 1892, 5; "Revolutionists Arraigned," *Daily Express* (San Antonio), May 17, 1892, 6; "Garzaites Trial," *Daily Express* (San Antonio), May 20, 1892, 3; "Trial of Munoz," *Daily Express* (San Antonio), May 21, 1892, 6; "Munoz Convicted," *Daily Express* (San Antonio), May 26, 1892, 6; "From the Border," *Daily Express* (San Antonio), May 28, 1892, 6.

127. Natividad, Alvado. "Revolutionists Arraigned," *Daily Express* (San Antonio), May 17, 1892, 6.
128. Nieto, Rafael. "The Revolution Over," *Galveston Daily News*, March 13, 1893, 1; "More Men Plead Guilty," *Daily Express* (San Antonio), May 6, 1893, 6.
129. Ortiz, Espiridion. "Six of the Border Outlaws Captured by Sheriff Shely," *Daily Herald* (Brownsville), March 23, 1893, 1; "More Men Plead Guilty," *Daily Express* (San Antonio), May 6, 1893, 6.
130. Palacio, Porician. Lewis, *A Guide to the Microfilm Edition of the Garza Revolution*, 9; "Found at Last," *Fort Worth Daily Gazette*, December 25, 1892, 2; "Escaped from the Bandits," *Daily Herald* (Brownsville), January 16, 1893, 2.
131. Palacios, Antonio. "Captain Henry Jackson, Seventh Cavalry, letter, March 3, 1893," Lewis, *A Guide to the Microfilm Edition of the Garza Revolution*, 20.
132. Palacios, Florencio. "Garza Man Surrenders," *Daily Herald* (Brownsville), June 8, 1893, 3; "Federal Court Cases," *Daily Express* (San Antonio), November 11, 1893, 5.
133. Paz, Ramón. "Lieutenant Colonel James P. Martin, Assistant Adjutant General (AAG), Department of Texas, to Judge T. S. Maxey, Austin, Texas, March 5, 1893," Letters Sent by Headquarters, Department of Texas, Roll 10, Vol. 31; "Judge T. S. Maxey, letter, February 27, 1893," Lewis, *A Guide to the Microfilm Edition of the Garza Revolution*, 20.

134. Peña, Juan. "Revolutionist in Court," *Daily Express* (San Antonio), May 31, 1892, 6.
135. Peña, Navato. "Federal Court Notes," *Daily Herald* (Brownsville), June 15, 1893, 3; "More Garzaites," *Daily Express* (San Antonio), June 12, 1893, 8.
136. Peña, Zeon. "Garzaites Trial," *Daily Express* (San Antonio), May 20, 1892, 3.
137. Pérez, Juan García. "Revolutionist in Court," *Daily Express* (San Antonio), May 31, 1892, 6.
138. Pérez, Monico, alias Alezando Perez. "The Garza Cases," *Galveston Daily News*, May 27, 1892, 3.
139. Pisusias, Rafael. "In Federal Court," *Daily Express* (San Antonio), November 14, 1893, 8.
140. Poletio, Florentino. "Brigadier General David S. Stanley, Commander, Department of Texas, to Major General Schofield, Washington, D.C., February 2, 1892," Letters Sent by Headquarters, Department of Texas, Roll 10, Vol. 30.
141. Ponze, Aurelio. "Thirty-Two Prisoners Brought in from the Border," *Daily Herald* (Brownsville), May 4, 1893, 1.
142. Quellar, Fortunatio. "Major Lewis T. Morris, letter, January 28, 1892," Lewis, *A Guide to the Microfilm Edition of the Garza Revolution*, 8.
143. Ramírez, Ensenio. "Ensenio Ramirez," *Daily Herald* (Brownsville), June 17, 1893, 3.
144. Ramírez, Eusabio. "In Federal Court," *Daily Express* (San Antonio), November 14, 1893, 8.
145. Ramírez, Francisco. "The Garza Cases," *Galveston Daily News*, May 27, 1892, 3; "Witness for the Defense," *Daily Express* (San Antonio), February 21, 1893, 8; "Garza Revolutionaries," *Daily Express* (San Antonio), May 27, 1892, 5.
146. Ramírez, Jesus. "Another Capture," *Daily Herald* (Brownsville), January 27, 1893, 3; "Campaign of the Border," *Daily Express* (San Antonio), May 21, 1893, 9.
147. Ramírez, Rafael. "Brigadier General Frank Wheaton, Commander, Department of Texas, to Adjutant General's Office, Washington, D.C., March 9, 1893," Letters Sent by Headquarters, Department of Texas,

Roll 10, Vol. 31; "Major Alexander S. B. Keyes, Third Cavalry, telegram, March 9, 1893," Lewis, *A Guide to the Microfilm Edition of the Garza Revolution,* 20; "Catarino Garza's Private Secretary Arrested by Sheriff Shely," *Daily Herald* (Brownsville), March 10, 1893, 3; "Campaign of the Border," *Daily Express* (San Antonio), May 21, 1893, 9; "Battle of San Ygnacio," *Daily Express* (San Antonio), February 12, 1893, 6; "Testimony of a Soldier," *Daily Express* (San Antonio), February 15, 1893, 6; "Skirmish at San Ygnacio," *Daily Express* (San Antonio), February 16, 1893, 8.

148. Ramírez, Secandio (Secundino). "Brigadier General Frank Wheaton, Commander, Department of Texas, to Adjutant General's Office, Washington, D.C., March 14, 1893," Letters Sent by Headquarters, Department of Texas, Roll 10, Vol. 31; "Captain William B. Wheeler, Eighteenth Infantry, telegram, March 13, 1893," Lewis, *A Guide to the Microfilm Edition of the Garza Revolution,* 20; "Thirty-Two Prisoners Brought in from the Border," *Daily Herald* (Brownsville), May 4, 1893, 1.

149. Ramírez, Ygnacio. "Garzaites Trial," *Daily Express* (San Antonio), May 20, 1892, 3; "Garza Revolutionaries," *Daily Express* (San Antonio), May 27, 1892, 5.

150. Ramón, Severiano M. "Another Capture," *Daily Herald* (Brownsville), February 6, 1893, 2.

151. Rangel, Jesus. "Revolutionists Arraigned," *Daily Express* (San Antonio), May 17, 1892, 6; "Munoz Convicted," *Daily Express* (San Antonio), May 26, 1892, 6.

152. Regilado, Juan Sanches. "Thirty-Two Prisoners Brought in from the Border," *Daily Herald* (Brownsville), May 4, 1893, 1.

153. Rendon, Benito. "Garzaites Trial," *Daily Express* (San Antonio), May 20, 1892, 3; "Munoz Convicted," *Daily Express* (San Antonio), May 26, 1892, 6.

154. Reyna, Francisco. "Revolutionist in Court," *Daily Express* (San Antonio), May 31, 1892, 6.

155. Rios, Macario. "The Garza Cases," *Galveston Daily News,* May 27, 1892, 3; "Garza Revolutionaries," *Daily Express* (San Antonio), May 27, 1892, 5.

156. Rodriguez, Guillermo. "Federal Court Notes," *Daily Herald* (Brownsville), June 19, 1893, 3.

157. Rodriguez, Mieigio. "In Federal Court," *Daily Express* (San Antonio), November 14, 1893, 8.

158. Rodriguez, Moreliano (Molentino). "Garza Revolutionist," *Galveston Daily News*, May 17, 1892, 7; "Revolutionists Arraigned," *Daily Express* (San Antonio), May 17, 1892, 6.
159. Rodriguez, Narciso. "Thirty-Two Prisoners Brought in from the Border," *Daily Herald* (Brownsville), May 4, 1893, 1.
160. Rodriguez, Victor. "Lieutenant Colonel James P. Martin, Assistant Adjutant General (AAG), Department of Texas, to Commanding Officers, Fort Brown, Fort McIntosh, Fort Ringgold, Camp at Eagle Pass, Texas, December 20, 1891, telegram," Letters Sent by Headquarters, Department of Texas, Roll 9, Vol. 29.
161. Roman, Eustoigio. "Revolutionists Arraigned," *Daily Express* (San Antonio), May 17, 1892, 6.
162. Rosa, Santos. "Another Capture," *Daily Herald* (Brownsville), January 27, 1893, 3; "Thirty-Two Prisoners Brought in from the Border," *Daily Herald* (Brownsville), May 4, 1893, 1; "Many Pleas of Guilty," *Daily Express* (San Antonio), May 4, 1893, 5.
163. Ruiz, Inez. Whelpley, "End of Border Outlawry," 636, at https://babel.hathitrust.org/cgi/pt?id=mdp.39015023106241&view=1up&seq=623&skin=2021.
164. Sais, Cesario. "The Garza Cases," *Galveston Daily News*, May 27, 1892, 3.
165. Sais, Geraldo. "Maximo Martinez Sentenced," *Daily Express* (San Antonio), June 2, 1893, 6.
166. Saiz, Severiano. "Another Capture," *Daily Herald* (Brownsville), January 27, 1893, 3; "Thirty-Two Prisoners Brought in from the Border," *Daily Herald* (Brownsville), May 4, 1893, 1; "Many Pleas of Guilty," *Daily Express* (San Antonio), May 4, 1893, 5; "Revolutionists Arraigned," *Daily Express* (San Antonio), May 17, 1892, 6.
167. Salazar, Devincio. "Six of the Border Outlaws Captured by Sheriff Shely," *Daily Herald* (Brownsville), March 23, 1893, 1.
168. Salazar, Dioneus (Deonecio, Dionitio). "Brigadier General Frank Wheaton, Commander, Department of Texas, to Adjutant General's Office, Washington, D.C., February 24, 1893," Letters Sent by Headquarters, Department of Texas, Roll 10, Vol. 31; "The Revolution Over," *Galveston Daily News*, March 13, 1893, 1; "More Men Plead Guilty," *Daily Express* (San Antonio), May 6, 1893, 6.

169. Salinas, Cecillio. "Three Garzaites," *Fort Worth Daily Gazette*, December 20, 1892, 1; "Going to Prison," *Daily Herald* (Brownsville), February 2, 1893, 2.
170. Salinas, Felipe. "Thirty-Two Prisoners Brought in from the Border," *Daily Herald* (Brownsville), May 4, 1893, 1.
171. Salinas, Fernandez. "Brigadier General Frank Wheaton, Commander, Department of Texas, to Adjutant General's Office, Washington, D.C., March 9, 1893," Letters Sent by Headquarters, Department of Texas, Roll 10, Vol. 31; "Major Alexander S. B. Keyes, Third Cavalry, telegram, March 9, 1893," Lewis, *A Guide to the Microfilm Edition of the Garza Revolution*, 20; "Catarino Garza's Private Secretary Arrested by Sheriff Shely," *Daily Herald* (Brownsville), March 10, 1893, 3; "Thirty-Two Prisoners Brought in from the Border," *Daily Herald* (Brownsville), May 4, 1893, 1; "Many Pleas of Guilty," *Daily Express* (San Antonio), May 4, 1893, 5.
172. Salinas, Luis. "Thirty-Two Prisoners Brought in from the Border," *Daily Herald* (Brownsville), May 4, 1893, 1.
173. Salinas, Maximo. "Munoz Convicted," *Daily Express* (San Antonio), May 26, 1892, 6.
174. Sánchez, Aciano. "Brigadier General Frank Wheaton, Commander, Department of Texas, to Adjutant General's Office, Washington, D.C., August 5, 1893," Letters Sent by Headquarters, Department of Texas, Roll 10, Vol. 31.
175. Sánchez, Astano. "In Federal Court," *Daily Express* (San Antonio), November 14, 1893, 8.
176. Sánchez, Juan. "More Men Plead Guilty," *Daily Express* (San Antonio), May 6, 1893, 6.
177. Sánchez, Luis. "Revolutionist in Court," *Daily Express* (San Antonio), May 31, 1892, 6.
178. Sandoval, Francisco Ruíz. "Report of Brigadier General Stanley, September 12, 1890," 184–85; Young, *Catarino Garza's Revolution on the Texas-Mexico Border*, 64, 78–102, 112, 116, 195, 200; "Sandoval's Case," *Fort Worth Daily Gazette*, December 20, 1890, 2; "Sandoval's Case," *Fort Worth Daily Gazette*, December 22, 1890, 2; "The Trial of Mexican Revolutionist," *Galveston Daily News*, June 27, 1890, 2; "General Sandoval Acquitted," *Galveston Daily News*, December 23, 1890, 1.

179. Sandoval, Jesus "Chico." "Brigadier General Frank Wheaton, Commander, Department of Texas, to Adjutant General's Office, Washington, D.C., March 14, 1893," Letters Sent by Headquarters, Department of Texas, Roll 10, Vol. 31; "Captain William B. Wheeler, Eighteenth Infantry, telegram, March 13, 1893," Lewis, *A Guide to the Microfilm Edition of the Garza Revolution*, 20.

180. Sandoval, Marco. "Federal Court Notes," *Daily Herald* (Brownsville), June 15, 1893, 3; "More Garzaites," *Daily Express* (San Antonio), June 12, 1893, 8.

181. Sandoval, Procopio. "Brigadier General Frank Wheaton, Commander, Department of Texas, to Adjutant General's Office, Washington, D.C., March 14, 1893," Letters Sent by Headquarters, Department of Texas, Roll 10, Vol. 31; "Thirty-Two Prisoners Brought in from the Border," *Daily Herald* (Brownsville), May 4, 1893, 1; "More Men Plead Guilty," *Daily Express* (San Antonio), May 6, 1893, 6.

182. Sandrez, Abren C. "Many Pleas of Guilty," *Daily Express* (San Antonio), May 4, 1893, 5.

183. Santos, Feverion de los. "Lieutenant John T. Knight, Troop I, Third Cavalry, letter, February 18, 1892," Lewis, *A Guide to the Microfilm Edition of the Garza Revolution*, 8.

184. Sarate, Juan Manuel. "Thirty-two Prisoners Brought in from the Border," *Daily Herald* (Brownsville), May 4, 1893, 1.

185. Sias, Americano. "Many Pleas of Guilty," *Daily Express* (San Antonio), May 4, 1893, 5.

186. Soto, José María. "Many Pleas of Guilty," *Daily Express* (San Antonio), May 4, 1893, 5.

187. Soto, Juan Manuel. "Thirty-Two Prisoners Brought in from the Border," *Daily Herald* (Brownsville), May 4, 1893, 1.

188. Stringer, Abalado. "Made a Bad Break, Garza Revolutionist Try to Cross the River," *Galveston Daily News*, May 13, 1892, 1.

189. Trapito, Tebucio. "In Federal Court," *Daily Express* (San Antonio), November 14, 1893, 8.

190. Treviño, Amelito. "The Revolution Over," *Galveston Daily News*, March 13, 1893, 1.

191. Treviño, Anaclito. "Brigadier General Frank Wheaton, Commander, Department of Texas, to Adjutant General's Office, Washington, D.C., February 24, 1893," Letters Sent by Headquarters, Department of Texas, Roll 10, Vol. 31; Many Pleas of Guilty," *Daily Express* (San Antonio), May 4, 1893, 5; "More Men Plead Guilty," *Daily Express* (San Antonio), May 6, 1893, 6.
192. Treviño, Donaciano. "More Men Plead Guilty," *Daily Express* (San Antonio), May 6, 1893, 6.
193. Treviño, Felipe. "Brigadier General Frank Wheaton, Commander, Department of Texas, to Adjutant General's Office, Washington, D.C., August 5, 1893," Letters Sent by Headquarters, Department of Texas, Roll 10, Vol. 31.
194. Treviño, Juan. "Lieutenant Thomas M. Corcoran, Seventh Cavalry, telegram, June 23, 1893," Lewis, *A Guide to the Microfilm Edition of the Garza Revolution*, 22.
195. Treviño, Victoriano. "Captain Henry Jackson, Seventh Cavalry, letter, April 12, 1893," Lewis, *A Guide to the Microfilm Edition of the Garza Revolution*, 21; "Thirty-two Prisoners Brought in from the Border," *Daily Herald* (Brownsville), May 4, 1893, 1.
196. Uribe, Santiago. "Captain Henry Jackson, Seventh Cavalry, letter, April 12, 1893," Lewis, *A Guide to the Microfilm Edition of the Garza Revolution*, 21.
197. Usilio, Santiago. "Many Pleas of Guilty," *Daily Express* (San Antonio), May 4, 1893, 5.
198. Valdez, Rafael. "Bandits Captured," *Daily Herald* (Brownsville), March 7, 1893, 1; "Revolutionists Arraigned," *Daily Express* (San Antonio), May 17, 1893, 6.
199. Varrera, Seario. "Thirty-Two Prisoners Brought in from the Border," *Daily Herald* (Brownsville), May 4, 1893, 1.
200. Vasquez, Feliciano. "Federal Court Notes," *Daily Herald* (Brownsville), June 19, 1893, 3.
201. Vela, Anicelo. "Lieutenant Stephen O'Conner, Twenty-Third, telegram, August 1, 1893," Lewis, *A Guide to the Microfilm Edition of the Garza Revolution*, 23.

202. Vela, Justo. "Brigadier General Frank Wheaton, Commander, Department of Texas, to Adjutant General's Office, Washington, D.C., August 5, 1893," Letters Sent by Headquarters, Department of Texas, Roll 10, Vol. 31.
203. Venavidce, Espiridion. "Thirty-Two Prisoners Brought in from the Border," *Daily Herald* (Brownsville), May 4, 1893, 1.
204. Vidrue, Juan Garza. "Garzaites Trial," *Daily Express* (San Antonio), May 20, 1892, 3.
205. Ybanez, Carmen. "Three Garzaites," *Fort Worth Daily Gazette*, December 20, 1892, 1; "Given the Full Penalty," *Daily Express* (San Antonio), December 20, 1892, 3; "Going to Prison," *Daily Herald* (Brownsville), February 2, 1893, 2.
206. Ybanes, Blas. "Brigadier General Frank Wheaton, Commander, Department of Texas, to Adjutant General's Office, Washington, D.C., March 14, 1893," Letters Sent by Headquarters, Department of Texas, Roll 10, Vol. 31; "Thirty-Two Prisoners Brought in from the Border," *Daily Herald* (Brownsville), May 4, 1893, 1; "Many Pleas of Guilty," *Daily Express* (San Antonio), May 4, 1893, 5.
207. Zapata, Alberto. "In Federal Court," *Daily Express* (San Antonio), November 14, 1893, 8.
208. Zapata, Juan Garza. "Munoz Convicted," *Daily Express* (San Antonio), May 26, 1892, 6.
209. Zarmosa, Porfirio. "Garza Revolutionaries," *Daily Express* (San Antonio), May 27, 1892, 5.
210. Zarrate, Juan Manuel. "Brigadier General Frank Wheaton, Commander, Department of Texas, to Adjutant General's Office, Washington, D.C., March 24, 1893," Letters Sent by Headquarters, Department of Texas, Roll 10, Vol. 31.

▼ ▼ ▼

BIBLIOGRAPHY

US Government Archives and Documents

National Archives and Records Administration (NARA), Washington, DC

Records of US Army Continental Commands, 1821–1920, Record Group 393, Part 1

"Blueprint Maps of Rio Grande Frontier, Department of Texas," RG393-I, E, 15W2, Map Case 91A, Drawer 4, "Map of the Rio Grande Frontier, Texas, East of Fort McIntosh and South of the Mex. National R.R. Prepared in the Engineer Office, Department of Texas, San Antonio, Texas, December 17, 1892. Official: H. L. Ripley 1st Lieut. 3rd Cavalry, Acting Engineer Officer."

"Letters and Reports Relating to the Garza Revolution, Entry 4877, Box 2 1893."

"Map of the Rio Grande Frontier, Texas, East of Fort McIntosh and South of the Mex. National R.R. Prepared in the Engineer Office, Department of Texas, San Antonio, Texas, February 17, 1893. Official: H. L. Ripley 1st Lieut. 3rd Cavalry, Acting Engineer Officer."

"Map showing the present location of United States and Mexican troops along the lower Rio Grande Frontier, with all available means of communication by rail, water, stage, telegraph (Military and Commercial), and telephone, between all important points. Drawn by 1' Lt. T. W. Griffith, 18' U.S. Inf. under the direction of Col. Anson Mills, 3' U.S. Cavalry. March 8, 1893."

National Archives Records Administration (NARA) Microfilm Series

Records of the US Army Adjutant General's Office, 1780–1917, Record Group 94
    Returns from US Military Posts, 1800–1916, Microfilm No. M617
        Post Returns, Fort Brown, Texas, January 1887–December 1902, roll 153.
        Post Returns, Fort Clark, Texas, January 1882–December 1892, roll 215.
        Post Returns, Fort McIntosh, Texas, January 1881–December 1891, roll 683.
        Post Returns, Fort McIntosh, Texas, January 1892–December 1902, roll 684.
        Post Returns, Fort Ringgold, Texas, January 1885–December 1894, roll 1022.
        Post Returns, Fort Sam Houston, Texas, September 1890–December 1900, roll 1079.
        Post Returns, San Antonio, Texas, January 1883–August 1890, roll 1085.

    Returns from Regular Army Infantry Regiments, June 1821–December 1916, Microfilm No. M665
        Regimental Returns, Eighteenth Infantry Regiment, January 1890–December 1897, roll 196.
        Regimental Returns, Twenty-Third Infantry Regiment, January 1891–December 1897, roll 239.

Records of the US Regular Army Mobile Units, 1821–1942, Record Group 391
    Returns from Regular Army Cavalry Regiments, 1833–1916, Microfilm No. 744.
        Regimental Returns, Third Cavalry, 1885–1893, roll 32.
        Regimental Returns, Fifth Cavalry, 1886–1893, roll 55.
        Regimental Returns, Seventh Cavalry, 1889–1896, roll 74.

Records of the US Army Adjutant General's Office, 1780–1917, Record Group 94
    NARA Microfilm No. M233 "Register of Enlistments, 1798–1914"
        Vol. 1885–1890, A–K, roll 44.
        Vol. 1891–1892, A–Z, roll 46.

Records of the US Army Adjutant General's Office, 1780–1917, Record Group 393. Records of US Army Continental Commands, 1821–1920, NARA Microfilm No. M1114.

Letters Sent by Headquarters, Department of Texas, 1870–1894 and 1897–1898. (Letters and telegrams arranged by date.)

Vol. 27, January 2, 1888–December 31, 1888, roll 9

"Lieutenant O. M. Smith, Assistant Adjutant General (AAG), Department of Texas, to Commanding Officer Fort Ringgold, September 25, 1888, telegram."

"Brigadier David S. Stanley to Adjutant General's Office, Division of the Missouri, September 27, 1888, telegram."

Vol. 29, January 2, 1890–December 31, 1891, roll 9

"Lieutenant David J. Rumbough, aide-de-camp, Commanding General, Department of Texas, to Commanding Officer, Fort McIntosh, Telegram, 10:20 pm, June 24, 1890."

"Brigadier General David S. Stanley, Commander, Department of Texas, to Dr. P. Ornelas, Consul of Republic of Mexico, San Antonio, Tex., June 25, 1890."

"Brigadier General David S. Stanley, Commander, Department of Texas, to Adjutant General's Office, Washington, D.C., telegram, January 27, 1891."

"Second Lieutenant Daniel B. Devore, aide-de-camp, Commanding General, Department of Texas, to Captain Henry W. Wessells Jr., Fort Sam Houston, Texas, September 9, 1891."

"Lieutenant Colonel James P. Martin, Assistant Adjutant General (AAG), Department of Texas, to Commanding Officer, Fort Ringgold, Tex., September 16, 1891, telegram."

"Lieutenant Colonel James P. Martin, Assistant Adjutant General (AAG), Department of Texas, to Commanding Officer, Fort Brown, Tex., September 17, 1891, telegram."

"Lieutenant Colonel James P. Martin, Assistant Adjutant General (AAG), Department of Texas, to Commanding Officer, Fort McIntosh, Tex., September 17, 1891, telegram,"

"Lieutenant Colonel James P. Martin, Assistant Adjutant General (AAG), Department of Texas, to Commanding Officer, Fort Ringgold, Tex., September 17, 1891, telegram."

"Brigadier General David S. Stanley, Commander, Department of Texas, to Adjutant General's Office, Washington, D.C., September 18, 1891."

"Brigadier General David S. Stanley, Commander, Department of Texas, to Dr. Plutarco Ornelas, Mexican Consul, San Antonio, Tex., September 18, 1891."

"Lieutenant Colonel James P. Martin, Assistant Adjutant General (AAG), Department of Texas, to Commanding Officer, Fort Bliss, Tex., September 21, 1891."

"Lieutenant Colonel James P. Martin, Assistant Adjutant General (AAG), Department of Texas, to Capt. Johnson, 3rd Cav. in field near Santa Maria, September 23, 1891."

"Lieutenant Colonel James P. Martin, Assistant Adjutant General (AAG), Department of Texas, to Lt. S. A. Dyer, U.S. Army at Corpus Christi, Texas, September 26, 1891."

"Lieutenant Colonel James P. Martin, Assistant Adjutant General (AAG), Department of Texas, to Commanding Officer Fort McIntosh, October 2, 1891."

"Lieutenant Colonel James P. Martin, Assistant Adjutant General (AAG), Department of Texas, to Lt. S. A. Dyer, U.S. Army at San Diego, Texas, October 20, 1891."

"Lieutenant Colonel James P. Martin, Assistant Adjutant General (AAG), Department of Texas, to Commanding Officer, Fort Ringgold, Tex., November 2, 1891."

"Lieutenant Colonel James P. Martin, Assistant Adjutant General (AAG), Department of Texas, to Post Commanders, November 10, 1891."

"Brigadier General David S. Stanley, Commander, Department of Texas, to Adjutant General's Office, Washington, D.C., December 23, 1891."

"Brigadier General David S. Stanley, Commander, Department of Texas, to Commanding Officer, Fort Ringgold, Tex., December 23, 1891, telegram."

"Lieutenant Colonel James P. Martin, Assistant Adjutant General (AAG), Department of Texas, to Colonel Morrow, Fort McIntosh, Tex., December 23, 1891."

"Brigadier General Frank Wheaton, Commander, Department of Texas, to Dr. Plutarco Ornelas, Mexican Consul, San Antonio, Tex., December 24, 1891."

"Lieutenant Colonel James P. Martin, Assistant Adjutant General (AAG), Department of Texas, to Commanding Officer, Fort Ringgold, Tex., December 24, 1891, telegram."

"Brigadier General David S. Stanley, Commander, Department of Texas, to Commanding Officer, Fort Ringgold, Tex., December 26, 1891, telegram."

Vol. 30, January 1892–December 1892, roll 10

"Brigadier General David S. Stanley, Commander, Department of Texas, to Major General Schofield, Washington, D.C., January 1, 1892."

"Brigadier General David S. Stanley, Commander, Department of Texas, to Major General Schofield, Washington, D.C., January 3, 1892."

"Brigadier General David S. Stanley, Commander, Department of Texas, to Major General Schofield, Washington, D.C., January 5, 1892."

"Brigadier General David S. Stanley, Commander, Department of Texas, to Major General Schofield, Washington, D.C., January 9, 1892."

"Brigadier General David S. Stanley, Commander, Department of Texas, to Adjutant General's Office, Washington, D.C., January 21, 1892."

"Brigadier General David S. Stanley, Commander, Department of Texas, to Major General Schofield, Washington, D.C., February 2, 1892."

"Brigadier General David S. Stanley, Commander, Department of Texas, to His Excellency Governor J. S. Hogg, Austin, Texas, February 25, 1892."

"Lieutenant Colonel James P. Martin, Assistant Adjutant General (AAG), Department of Texas, to Chief Quartermaster, Department of Texas, February 26, 1892."

"Brigadier General David S. Stanley, Commander, Department of Texas, to His Excellency Governor J. S. Hogg, Austin, Texas, March 1, 1892."

"Lieutenant Colonel James P. Martin, Assistant Adjutant General (AAG), Department of Texas, to Commanding Officer, Fort Clark, Tex., May 3, 1892."

"Lieutenant Colonel James P. Martin, Assistant Adjutant General (AAG), Department of Texas, to Commanding Officer, Fort Ringgold, July 20, 1892."

"Lieutenant Colonel James P. Martin, Assistant Adjutant General (AAG), Department of Texas, to Lieut. P. G. Lowe, 18th Infantry, Commander, Seminole-Negro Indian Scouts, Camp at Polvo, Tex., July 20, 1892."

"Lieutenant Colonel James P. Martin, Assistant Adjutant General (AAG), Department of Texas, to Captain William B. Wheeler, 18th Infantry, Fort Ringgold, Tex., September 22, 1892."

"Lieutenant Colonel James P. Martin, Assistant Adjutant General (AAG), Department of Texas, to Captain William B. Wheeler, 18th Infantry, Fort Ringgold, Tex., November 10, 1892."

"Brigadier General Frank Wheaton, Commander, Department of Texas, to Adjutant General's Office, Washington, D.C., December 5, 1892."

"Lieutenant Colonel James P. Martin, Assistant Adjutant General (AAG), Department of Texas, to Captain William B. Wheeler, 18th Infantry, Fort Ringgold, Tex., December 7, 1892."

"Brigadier General Frank Wheaton, Commander, Department of Texas, to Adjutant General's Office, Washington, D.C., December 17, 1892."

"Assistant Adjutant General (AAG), Department of Texas, to Captain George F. Chase, Third Cavalry, Fort Sam Houston, Tex., December 17, 1892."

"Assistant Adjutant General (AAG), Department of Texas, to Commanding Officer, Fort McIntosh, Tex., December 19, 1892."

"Brigadier General Frank Wheaton, Commander, Department of Texas, to Major General Schofield, Washington, D.C., December 23, 1892."

"Lieutenant Colonel James P. Martin, Assistant Adjutant General (AAG), Department of Texas, to Commanding Officer, Fort McIntosh, Tex., December 23, 1892."

"Assistant Adjutant General (AAG), Department of Texas, to Commanding Officer, Fort McIntosh, Tex., December 27, 1892."

"Assistant Adjutant General (AAG), Department of Texas, to Captain Henry Jackson, Seventh Cavalry, December 28, 1892."

"Lieutenant Colonel James P. Martin, Assistant Adjutant General (AAG), Department of Texas, to Captain Oscar Elting, Troop E, Third Cavalry, San Ignacio, Tex., December 28, 1892."

"Brigadier General Frank Wheaton, Commander, Department of Texas, to Adjutant General's Office, Washington, D.C., December 30, 1892."

"Lieutenant Colonel James P. Martin, Assistant Adjutant General (AAG), Department of Texas, to Captain Oscar Elting, Troop E, Third Cavalry, San Ignacio, Tex., December 30, 1892."

"Brigadier General Frank Wheaton, Commander, Department of Texas, to Chief Signal Officer, Washington, D.C., December 31, 1892."

Vol. 31, January 1893–December 1893, roll 10

"Brigadier General Frank Wheaton, Commander, Department of Texas, to Adjutant General's Office, Washington, D.C., January 23, 1893."

"Brigadier General Frank Wheaton, Commander, Department of Texas, to Adjutant General's Office, Washington, D.C., January 25, 1893."

"Lieutenant Colonel James P. Martin, Assistant Adjutant General (AAG), Department of Texas, to Commanding Officer, Fort McIntosh, Fort Ringgold, Camps at Carrizo, San Ygnacio, February 2, 1893."

"Lieutenant Colonel James P. Martin, Assistant Adjutant General (AAG), Department of Texas, to Capt. Geo. K. Hunter, 3rd Cavalry, Camp at Los Angeles, Encinal Co., Texas, February 14, 1893."

"Lieutenant Colonel James P. Martin, Assistant Adjutant General (AAG), Department of Texas, to Major Alexander S. B. Keyes, Third Cavalry, Fort Ringgold, Tex., February 20, 1893."

"Brigadier General Frank Wheaton, Commander, to Adjutant General's Office, Washington, D.C., February 24, 1893."

"Brigadier General Frank Wheaton, Commander, Department of Texas, to Adjutant General's Office, Washington, D.C., March 9, 1893."

"Brigadier General Frank Wheaton, Commander, Department of Texas, to Adjutant General's Office, Washington, D.C., March 24, 1893."

"Brigadier General Frank Wheaton, Commander, Department of Texas, to Adjutant General's Office, Washington, D.C., April 15, 1893."

"Lieutenant Colonel James P. Martin, Assistant Adjutant General (AAG), Department of Texas, to Commander, Fort McIntosh, April 15, 1893."

"Brigadier General Frank Wheaton, Commander, Department of Texas, to Adjutant General's Office, Washington, D.C., April 21, 1893."

"Lieutenant Colonel James P. Martin, Assistant Adjutant General (AAG), Department of Texas, to Commander, Fort McIntosh, April 24, 1893."

"Lieutenant Colonel James P. Martin, Assistant Adjutant General (AAG), Department of Texas, to Commanding Officer, Fort Ringgold, Tex., May 6, 1893."

"Brigadier General Frank Wheaton, Commander, Department of Texas, to Adjutant General's Office, Washington, D.C., June 15, 1893."

"Brigadier General Frank Wheaton, Commander, Department of Texas, to Adjutant General's Office, Washington, D.C., June 21, 1893."

"Department of Texas Circular, August 5, 1893."

"Lieutenant Colonel James P. Martin, Assistant Adjutant General (AAG), Department of Texas, to Adjutant General, Washington, D.C., August 22, 1893."

"Major Arthur MacArthur, Assistant Adjutant General (AAG), to Mr. W. W. Shely, Captain Joseph Shely, San Antonio, Tex., December 26, 1893."

US Army

Adjutant General's Office. *General Court-Martial Orders, Adjutant General's Office, 1883*. Washington, DC: Government Printing Office, 1884.

Adjutant General's Office. *General Court-Martial Orders, Adjutant General's Office, 1885*. Washington, DC: Government Printing Office, 1886.

Adjutant General's Office. *Official Army Register for 1911*. Washington, DC: War Department Document No. 383, Adjutant General's Office, December 1, 1910.

Heitman, Francis B. *Historical Register and Dictionary of the United States Army*. 2 vols. Washington, DC: Government Printing Office, 1903.

Militia Bureau, War Department. *Report on Mobilization of the Organized Militia and National Guard of the United States, 1916.* Washington, DC: Government Printing Office, 1916.

Secretary of the Interior

Secretary of the Interior. *Official Register of the United States, Containing a List of Officers and Employés in the Civil, Military, and Naval Service on the First of July, 1891.* 2 vols. Washington, DC: Government Printing Office, 1892.

US Bureau of the Census

Ninth Census of the United States, 1870, NARA Microfilm Publication M593, roll 1609, Wilson County, Texas, Precinct 4.

Tenth Census of the United States, 1880, NARA Microfilm Publication T9, roll 1332, Webb County, Texas, Precinct 3, Enumeration District 145.

Twelfth Census of the United States, 1900, NARA Microfilm Publication T623, Starr County, Texas, Justice Precinct 01, Enumeration District 074.

US Department of State

US Department of State. *Papers Relating to the Foreign Relations of the United States, with the Annual Message of the President, Transmitted to Congress December 9, 1891.* Washington, DC: Government Printing Office, 1892.
"Message of the President, December 9, 1891."

US Department of State. *Papers Relating to the Foreign Relations of the United States, with the Annual Message of the President, Transmitted to Congress December 5, 1892.* Washington, DC: Government Printing Office, 1893.
"Message to the Senate and House of Representatives, December 6, 1892."

US Department of State. *Papers Relating to the Foreign Relations of the United States, with the Annual Message of the President, Transmitted to Congress December 3, 1893.* Washington, DC: Government Printing Office, 1894. (Letters listed by date.)

"Señor Cayetano Romero, Mexican Legation of Mexico, Washington, D.C., to Mr. Foster, Department of State, Washington, D.C., December 13, 1892."

"Señor Cayetano Romero, Mexican Legation of Mexico, Washington, D.C., to Mr. Foster, Department of State, Washington, D.C., December 14, 1892."

"Señor Alberto Leal, Consulate of Mexico, Rio Grande City, Tex. to Señor Mariscal, December 16, 1892."

"John W. Foster, Headquarters, Department of State, Washington, D.C., to Señor Cayetano Romero, Mexican Legation of Mexico, Washington, D.C., December 27, 1892."

"Señor Cayetano Romero, Mexican Legation of Mexico, Washington, D.C., to Mr. Foster, Department of State, Washington, D.C., January 1, 1893."

"John W. Foster, Headquarters, Department of State, Washington, D.C., to Señor Cayetano Romero, Mexican Legation of Mexico, Washington, D.C., January 4, 1893."

"General Schofield to Secretary of War S. B. Elkins, January 17, 1893."

"John W. Foster, Headquarters, Department of State, Washington, D.C., to Señor Cayetano Romero, Mexican Legation of Mexico, Washington, D.C., January 19, 1893."

"Secretary of War S. B. Elkins to Secretary of State John W. Foster, January 19, 1893."

"General Schofield to Mr. Lamont, February 20, 1893."

"Señor Cayetano Romero, Mexican Legation of Mexico, Washington, D.C., to Mr. Gresham, April 28, 1893."

"Señor Cayetano Romero, Mexican Legation of Mexico, Washington, D.C., to Mr. Gresham, June 9, 1893."

"Brigadier General Frank Wheaton, Commander, Department of Texas, to Adjutant General's Office, Washington, D.C., July 8, 1893."

US Department of State. *Papers Relating to the Foreign Relations of the United States, with the Annual Message of the President, Transmitted to Congress December 6, 1897.* Washington, DC: Government Printing Office, 1898. (Letters arranged by date.)

"Message to the Senate and House of Representatives, December 6, 1897."

"Señor Cayetano Romero, Mexican Legation of Mexico, Washington, D.C., to Mr. Gresham, Department of State, Washington, D.C., September 28, 1897."

"John Sherman to Señor Cayetano Romero, Mexican Legation of Mexico, Washington, D.C., November 13, 1897."

"Señor Cayetano Romero, Mexican Legation of Mexico, Washington, D.C., to Mr. Sherman, Department of State, Washington, D.C., November 15, 1897."

House and Senate Executive Documents

51st Congress, 2nd Session

"Report of Brigadier General Stanley, September 12, 1890," in "Report of the Secretary of War, 1890," House Exec. Docs., no. 1, vol. 2, pt. 2, serial 2831.

"Report of the Major-General Commanding the Army, October 23, 1890," in "Report of the Secretary of War, 1890," House Exec. Docs., no. 1, vol. 2, pt. 2, serial 2831.

"Report of the Quartermaster-General, October 9, 1890," in "Report of the Secretary of War, 1890," House Exec. Docs., no. 1, vol. 2, pt. 2, serial 2831.

"Report of the Secretary of War, November 15, 1890," House Exec. Docs., no. 1, vol. 2, pt. 2, serial 2831.

52nd Congress, 1st Session

"Report of Major-General Commanding the Army, September 24, 1891," in "Report of the Secretary of War, 1891," House Exec. Docs., no. 1, vol. 1, serial 2921.

"Report of Brig. Gen. Stanley, September 9, 1891," in "Report of the Secretary of War, 1891," House Exec. Docs., no. 1, vol. 1, serial 2921.

52nd Congress, 2nd Session

"Report of Brig. Gen. Wheaton, September 13, 1892," in "Report of the Secretary of War, 1892," House Exec. Docs., no. 1, vol. 1, pt. 2, serial 3077.

"Report of the Chief Signal Officer, October 10, 1892," in "Report of the Secretary of War, 1892." House Exec. Docs., no. 1, vol. 1, pt. 2, serial 3077.

"Report of Major-General Commanding the Army, September 30, 1892," in "Report of the Secretary of War, 1892," House Exec. Docs., no. 1, vol. 1, pt. 2, serial 3077.

53rd Congress, 2nd Session
"Report of Brig. Gen. Wheaton, August 18, 1893," in "Report of the Secretary of War, November 27, 1893," House Exec. Docs., no. 1, vol. 2, pt.2, serial 3198.
"Report of the Chief Signal Officer, October 9, 1893," in "Report of the Secretary of War, November 27, 1893," House Exec. Docs., no. 1, vol. 2, pt. 2, vol. 2, serial 3198.
"Report of the Secretary of War, November 27, 1893." House Exec. Docs., no. 1, vol. 2, pt. 2, serial 3198.

53rd Congress, 3rd Session
"Report of the Chief Signal Officer, October 1, 1894," in "Report of the Secretary of War, November 26, 1894," House Exec. Docs., no. 1, vol. 4, pt. 2, serial 3295.

54th Congress, 1st Session
"Report of the Chief Signal Officer, October 1, 1895," in "Report of the Secretary of War, November 26, 1895," House Exec. Docs., vol. 3, no. 2, serial 3370.

54th Congress, 2nd Session
"Report of the Chief Signal Officer, 30 Sept. 1896," in "Report of the Secretary of War, November 24, 1896," House Exec. Docs., no. 2, vol. 2, serial 3478.

56th Congress, 2nd Session
"Report of the Chief Signal Officer, October 5, 1900," in "Report of the Secretary of War, November 30, 1900," House Exec. Docs., no. 2, vol. 2, serial 4071.

Archives

Center of Southwest Studies, Fort Lewis College, Durango, Colorado. Microfilm Collection 1, entry 032
"John Gregory Bourke Diary"

Vol. 102, March 7, 1891–May 16, 1891, roll 8.
Vol. 103, May 16, 1891–July 2, 1891, roll 8.
Vol. 104, July 2, 1891–September 12, 1891, roll 8.
Vol. 105, September 12, 1891–September 19, 1891, roll 8.
Vol. 106, September 19, 1891–November 14, 1891, roll 8.
Vol. 107, November 14, 1891–January 25, 1892, roll 8.
Vol. 108, January 25, 1892–June 24, 1892, roll 8.
Vol. 109, June 24, 1892–December 23, 1892, roll 8.
Vol. 110, December 23, 1892–February 8, 1893, roll 9.
Vol. 111, February 8, 1893–May 13, 1893, roll 9.

Books

Anders, Evan. "Manuel Guerra (1856–1915)." In *The New Handbook of Texas*, ed. Ron Tyler, Douglas E. Barnett, Roy R. Barkley, Penelope C. Anderson, and Mark F. Odintz, 3:369. Austin: Texas State Historical Association, 1996.

Baulch, Joe R. "Garza War." In *The New Handbook of Texas*, ed. Ron Tyler, Douglas E. Barnett, Roy R. Barkley, Penelope C. Anderson, and Mark F. Odintz, 3:13. Austin: Texas State Historical Association, 1996.

Belfiglio, Valentine J. "Antonio Mateo Bruni (1856–1931)." In *The New Handbook of Texas*, ed. Ron Tyler, Douglas E. Barnett, Roy R. Barkley, Penelope C. Anderson, and Mark F. Odintz, 1:784. Austin: Texas State Historical Association, 1996.

Bourke, John G. *Our Neutrality Laws*. Fort Ethan Allen, VT: private printing, 1895.

Carlson, Paul H. *"Pecos Bill": A Military Biography of William R. Shafter*. College Station: Texas A&M University Press, 1989.

Cuthbertson, Gilbert M. "Catarino Erasmo Garza (1859–1895)." In *The New Handbook of Texas*, ed. Ron Tyler, Douglas E. Barnett, Roy R. Barkley, Penelope C. Anderson, and Mark F. Odintz, 3:106–7. Austin: Texas State Historical Association, 1996.

Cutrer, Thomas W. "David Sloan Stanley." In *The New Handbook of Texas*, ed. Ron Tyler, Douglas E. Barnett, Roy R. Barkley, Penelope C. Anderson, and Mark F. Odintz, 4:57–58. Austin: Texas State Historical Association, 1996.

De León, Arnoldo. *They Called Them Greasers: Anglo Attitudes toward Mexicans in Texas, 1821–1900*. Austin: University of Texas Press, 1983.

Essen, Emmett M. *Shavetails and Bell Sharps: The History of the U.S. Army Mule*. Lincoln: University of Nebraska Press, 1997.

Fordyce, Samuel W., IV, ed. *An American General: The Memoirs of David Sloan Stanley*. Santa Barbara, CA: Narrative Press, 2003.

Garza, Alicia A. "Rio Grande City Riot of 1888." In *The New Handbook of Texas*, ed. Ron Tyler, Douglas E. Barnett, Roy R. Barkley, Penelope C. Anderson, and Mark F. Odintz, 5:585. Austin: Texas State Historical Association, 1996.

Gates, John M. *Schoolbooks and Krags: The United States Army in the Philippines, 1889–1902*. Westport, CT: Greenwood Press, 1973.

Haragan, Donald R. "Weather Modification." In *The New Handbook of Texas*, ed. Ron Tyler, Douglas E. Barnett, Roy R. Barkley, Penelope C. Anderson, and Mark F. Odintz, 6:859–60. Austin: Texas State Historical Association, 1996.

Harris, Charles H., III, and Louis R. Sadler. *The Great Call-Up: The Guard, the Border, and the Mexican Revolution*. Norman: University of Oklahoma Press, 2015.

Hazlewood, Claudia. "James Harvey McLeary (1845–1914)." In *The New Handbook of Texas*, ed. Ron Tyler, Douglas E. Barnett, Roy R. Barkley, Penelope C. Anderson, and Mark F. Odintz, 4:428. Austin: Texas State Historical Association, 1996.

Hughes, James B., Jr. *Mexican Military Arms: The Cartridge Period, 1866–1967*. Houston: Deep River Armory, 1968.

Krieger, Margery H. "Bethel Coopwood (1827–1907)." In *The New Handbook of Texas*, ed. Ron Tyler, Douglas E. Barnett, Roy R. Barkley, Penelope C. Anderson, and Mark F. Odintz, 2:316. Austin: Texas State Historical Association, 1996.

Kwakwa, Edward K. *The International Law of Armed Conflict: Personal and Material Fields of Application*. Boston: Kluwer Academic, 1992.

Leiker, James N. *Racial Borders: Black Soldiers along the Rio Grande*. College Station: Texas A&M University Press, 2002.

Linn, Brian McAllister. *The Philippine War, 1899–1902*. Lawrence: University Press of Kansas, 2000.

Margolies, Daniel S. *Spaces of Law in American Foreign Relations: Extradition and Extraterritoriality in the Borderlands and Beyond, 1877–1898*. Athens: University of Georgia Press, 2011.

May, Robert E. *Manifest Destiny's Underworld: Filibustering in Antebellum America.* Chapel Hill: University of North Carolina Press, 2002.

Neal, Charles M., Jr. *Valor across the Lone Star: The Congressional Medal of Honor in Frontier Texas.* Foreword by Jerry Thompson. Austin: Texas State Historical Association, 2002.

Parsons, Chuck. *Texas Ranger Lee Hall: From the Red River to the Rio Grande.* Denton: University of North Texas Press, 2020.

Petrie, John N. *American Neutrality in the 20th Century: The Impossible Dream.* McNair Paper 33 (Washington, DC: National Defense University, Institute for Strategic Studies, January 1953).

Porter, Joseph C. "John G. Bourke." In Paul Andrew Hutton, *Soldiers West: Biographies from the Military Frontier*, 137–57. Lincoln: University of Nebraska Press, 1989.

Porter, Joseph C. "John Gregory Bourke (1846–1896)." In *The New Handbook of Texas*, ed. Ron Tyler, Douglas E. Barnett, Roy R. Barkley, Penelope C. Anderson, and Mark F. Odintz, 1:662. Austin: Texas State Historical Association, 1996.

Porter, Joseph C. *Paper Medicine Man: John Gregory Bourke and His American West.* Norman: University of Oklahoma Press, 1986.

Samuels, Peggy, and Harold Samuels. *Frederic Remington: A Biography.* Garden City, NY: Doubleday and Company, 1982.

Smith, Thomas T. *The Old Army in Texas: A Research Guide to the U.S. Army in Nineteenth-Century Texas.* 2nd ed. Austin: Texas State Historical Association, 2020.

Smith, Thomas T. *The Old Army in the Big Bend of Texas, 1911–1921: The Last Cavalry Frontier.* Austin: Texas State Historical Association, 2018.

Smith, Thomas T. *The U.S. Army and the Texas Frontier Economy, 1845–1900.* College Station: Texas A&M University Press, 1999.

Smith, Thomas T., Jerry D. Thompson, Robert Wooster, and Ben E. Pingenot, eds. *The Reminiscences of Major General Zenas R. Bliss, 1854–1876.* Austin: Texas State Historical Association, 2007.

Spellman, Paul N. *Captain J. A. Brooks, Texas Ranger.* Denton: University of North Texas Press, 2007.

Stanley, D. S. *Personal Memoirs of Major General D. S. Stanley, U.S.A.* Cambridge, MA: Harvard University Press, 1917.

Swanson, Don A. *Seminole, Lipan, Cherokee, Creek, Indian Scouts Enlistment Records, Fort Clark.* Bronte, TX: Ames-American Printing Co., n.d.

Thompson, Jerry. *A Wild and Vivid Land: An Illustrated History of the South Texas Border.* Austin: Texas State Historical Association, 1997.

Thompson, Jerry, ed. *Fifty Miles and a Fight: Major Peter Heintzelman's Journal of Texas and the Cortina War.* Austin: Texas State Historical Association, 1998.

Tise, Sammy. *Texas County Sheriffs.* Hallettsville, TX: Tise Genealogical Research, 1989.

Tyler, Ron, Douglas E. Barnett, Roy R. Barkley, Penelope C. Anderson, and Mark F. Odintz, eds. *The New Handbook of Texas.* 6 vols. Austin: Texas State Historical Association, 1996.

Uglow, Loyd. *A Military History of Texas.* Denton: University of North Texas Press, 2022.

Wallace, Ernest. *Ranald S. Mackenzie on the Texas Frontier.* Foreword by David J. Murrah. College Station: Texas A&M University Press, 1993.

Warner, Ezra J. *Generals in Blue: The Lives of the Union Commanders.* Baton Rouge: Louisiana State University Press, 1964.

Webb, Walter Prescott. "Thomas Sheldon Maxey (1846–1921)." In *The New Handbook of Texas*, ed. Ron Tyler, Douglas E. Barnett, Roy R. Barkley, Penelope C. Anderson, and Mark F. Odintz, 4:581. Austin: Texas State Historical Association, 1996.

West Point Alumni Foundation. *The Register of Graduates and Former Cadets of the United States Military Academy 1802–1970, Cullum Memorial Edition.* West Point, NY: West Point Alumni Foundation, 1970.

Wooster, Robert. *The American Military Frontiers: The United States Army in the West, 1783–1900.* Albuquerque: University of New Mexico Press, 2009.

Young, Elliott. *Catarino Garza's Revolution on the Texas-Mexico Border.* Durham, NC: Duke University Press, 2004.

Newspapers

Newspapers were generally accessed through the Portal to Texas History, University of North Texas Libraries' Digital Projects Unit, at http://texashistory

.unt.edu/search. The San Antonio *Express* was researched through the microfilm copies at San Antonio Public Library, Central Library, Texana Collections. Articles are arranged by newspaper and date.

The Daily Herald (Brownsville, TX)
"The Military Telegraph Line." January 16, 1893, 3.
"Escaped from the Bandits." January 16, 1893, 2.
"A Big Capture." January 23, 1893, 3.
"Commenced Construction." January 24, 1893, 3.
"Another Capture." January 27, 1893, 3.
"Mexico." January 30, 1893, 2.
"Going to Prison." February 2, 1893, 2.
"Another Capture." February 6, 1893, 2.
"More Garza News." February 8, 1893, 3.
"A Suggestion by Major Morris." February 9, 1893, 2.
"The Dead Bandit." February 25, 1893, 3.
"Capt. Bourke Accused of Working the Third Degree." March 3, 1893, 1.
"Rio Grande City Notes." March 6, 1893, 3.
"Bandits Captured." March 7, 1893, 1.
"Cuban Revolutionist." March 9, 1893, 1;
"Capt. Bourke Arrives." March 9, 1893, 1;
"Starr County Attorney Protests to the Governor." March 10, 1893, 2.
"Catrino Garza's Private Secretary Arrested by Sheriff Shely." March 10, 1893, 3.
"Rounding Them Up." March 20, 1893, 3.
"No Successor Appointed." March 31, 1893, 3.
"News by Wire." April 16, 1893, 2.
"Military Items." May 8, 1893, 3.
"The Right Man in the Right Place." May 17, 1893, 3.
"Border Troubles." May 18, 1893, 1.
"Alejandro Gonzales Arrested and Bailed." May 22, 1893, 1.
"Gonzales Heavily Fined." May 27, 1893, 2.
"Body Recovered." June 28, 1893, 3.
"Material for Construction." August 16, 1893, 3.

El Paso International Daily Times
"The Rain Maker's Record." September 16, 1891, 4.

The Galveston Daily News
"Revolution in Mexico." June 24, 1890, 6.
"The Trial of Mexican Revolutionist." June 27, 1890, 2.
"General Sandoval Acquitted." December 23, 1890, 1.
"Invading Mexico." September 17, 1891, 1.
"A Skirmish with Garza." December 23, 1891, 1.
"Corporal Edstrom's Funeral." January 2, 1892, 2.
"Fight with Garza's Men." January 2, 1891,
"Made a Bad Break, Garza Revolutionist Try to Cross the River." May 13, 1892, 1.
"Garza Revolutionist." May 17, 1892, 7.
"Trying a Garzaite." May 20, 1892, 4.
"Trial of Garza's Lieutenant." May 25, 1892, 4.
"The First in Sixty Years." May 26, 1892, 3.
"The Garza Cases." May 27, 1892, 3.
"Pablo Munoz Sentenced." May 28, 1892, 5.
"The Revolution Over." March 13, 1893, 1.
"Alejandro Gonzales." May 17, 1893, 3.

Fort Worth Daily Gazette
"Arrest Expected for Violation of the United States Neutrality Law." June 25, 1890, 2.
"Nipped in the Bud." June 26, 1890, 2.
"Sandoval's Case." December 20, 1890, 2.
"Sandoval's Case." December 22, 1890, 1.
"Rain Makers." September 19, 1891, 1.
"Dangerous." September 17, 1891, 7.
"Another Account." September 17, 1891, 7.
"Only a Namesake." September 18, 1891, 1.
"A Plan of Revolution." September 18, 1891, 1.
"The Garza Affair." September 19, 1891, 1.
"No Revolution." September 23, 1891, 1.

"Suspicious Mexican." November 15, 1891, 8.
"Held as Suspects." November 16, 1891, 7.
"Worse, More of It." March 3, 1892, 3.
"Talk It Over." March 1, 1892, 8.
"Rain Experiments." March 3, 1892, 3.
"The Fricke Case." March 4, 1892, 4.
"Freebooters." December 13, 1892, 1.
"Bandits Battle." December 14, 1892, 1.
"He Was a Traitor." December 15, 1892, 1.
"The Men Roasters." December 17, 1892, 1.
"Lonely Woman." December 16, 1892, 1.
"The Cause of the Trouble." December 16, 1892, 1.
"Three Garzaites." December 20, 1892, 1.
"No Truth in It." December 21, 1892, 1.
"Where Are They?" December 24, 1892, 1.
"A Soldier Died." December 24, 1892, 1.
"Found at Last." December 25, 1892, 2.
"The Border War." December 27, 1892, 1.
"Capt. J. G. Bourke." December 29, 1892, 1.

The New York Times
"Garza's Men Growing Bolder; They Shot and Killed a Scout from Ambush." February 3, 1892, 1.

New York Tribune
"The News This Morning." July 18, 1900, 8.

San Antonio Express News
"The Temples of Law." December 19, 1890, 6.
"The Day in Courts." December 20, 1890, 3.
"Jury Still Out." December 22, 1890, 3.
"The Mills of Justice." December 23, 1890, 3.

The Daily Express (San Antonio)
"Corporal Edstrom's Funeral." January 1, 1892, 2.

"Revolutionists Arraigned." May 17, 1892, 6.
"Garza at Key West." May 18, 1892, 5.
"Garzaites Trial." May 20, 1892, 3.
"Trial of Munoz." May 21, 1892, 6.
"Rest Their Case." May 24, 1892, 6.
"Ended the Trial." May 25, 1892, 6.
"Munoz Convicted." May 26, 1892, 6.
"Garza Revolutionaries." May 27, 1892, 5.
"From the Border." May 28, 1892, 6.
"Revolutionist in Court." May 31, 1892, 6.
"Given the Full Penalty." December 20, 1892, 3.
"The Chase for Garza." January 1, 1893, 1.
"Story of Two Captives." February 11, 1893, 3.
"Battle of San Ygnacio." February 12, 1893, 6.
"Story of the Fight." February 14, 1893, 6.
"Testimony of a Soldier." February 15, 1893, 6.
"Skirmish at San Ygnacio." February 16, 1893, 8.
"Witness for the Defense." February 21, 1893, 8.
"Many Pleas of Guilty." May 4, 1893, 5.
"More Men Plead Guilty." May 6, 1893, 6.
"Campaign of the Border." May 21, 1893, 9.
"Maximo Martinez Sentenced." June 2, 1893, 6.
"Won't Deliver Benavides." June 7, 1893, 1.
"More Garzaites." June 12, 1893, 8.
"Federal Court Cases." November 11, 1893, 5.
"In the Federal Court." November 14, 1893, 8.
"Garza Is in Luck." December 17, 1893, 6.

Magazines and Periodicals

Cuthbertson, Gilbert M. "Catarino E. Garza and the Garza War." *Texana* 12 (1974): 335–47.

Davis, Richard Harding. "West from a Car Window: Part I, From San Antonio to Corpus Christi." *Harper's Weekly*, March 5, 1892, 220–22.

Davis, Richard Harding. "West from a Car Window: Part II, Our Troops on the Border." *Harper's Weekly*, March 26, 1892, 294.

Gwynne, S. C. "Rain of Error." *Texas Monthly*, August 2003, 39–46.

Hodge, F. W. "John Gregory Bourke." *American Anthropologist* 9 (July 1896): 245–48.

Hunter, J. M., ed. "The Garza Revolution in 1890." *Frontier Times* 19 (January 1942): 135–36.

Lobel, Jules. "The Rise and Decline of the Neutrality Act: Sovereignty and Congressional War Powers in United States Foreign Policy." *Harvard International Law Journal* 24 (Summer 1983): 1–71.

Speed, Jno. Gilmer. "The Hunt for Garza." *Harper's Weekly*, January 30, 1892, 103, 113.

Whelpley, James Davenport. "End of Border Outlawry." *Harper's Weekly*, June 27, 1896, 636.

Internet Sources

"Bexar County, Texas Probate Records, 1837–1913." "Texas, U.S. Wills and Probate Records, 1833–1974." Ancestry.com.

Eckel, Jennifer. "Andrew Jackson Evans (1832–1897)." In *The New Handbook of Texas*, ed. Ron Tyler, Douglas E. Barnett, Roy R. Barkley, Penelope C. Anderson, and Mark F. Odintz. Austin: Texas State Historical Association, 1996. https://www.tshaonline.org/handbook/entries/evans-andrew-jackson.

"Find a Grave." Ancestry.com.

Lewis, Daniel. *A Guide to the Microfilm Edition of the Garza Revolution, 1891–1893: Records of the U.S. Army Continental Commands, Department of Texas*. Bethesda, MD: UPA Collection, LexisNexis, Reed Elsevier 2009. https://media2.proquest.com/documents/103936.pdf.

Office of the Quartermaster General. "U.S. National Cemetery Interment Control Forms" and "U.S. Military Burial Registers, 1768–1921, Record Book of Interments in the Post Cemetery, Fort McIntosh, Texas." Ancestry.com.

Office of the Quartermaster General. 1774–1985, National Archives Record Group 92, "U.S. Burial Registers, Military Posts and National Cemeteries,

1862–1960," "Record Book of Fort Ringgold, Tex. Cemetery," and "Record Book of National Cemetery at Alexandria, Louisiana," 118. Ancestry.com.

Olson, Theodore B. "Overview of the Neutrality Act: Memorandum of Opinion for the Attorney General, September 24, 1984," 209–18. https://www.justice.gov/file/23671.

Stopka, Christina, comp. "Partial List of Texas Ranger Company and Unit Commanders." Texas Ranger Research Center. https://www.texasranger.org/wp-content/uploads/2019/10/HISTORY_RangerCommanders2019.pdf.

U.S. Marshals Service. "Deputy U.S. Marshal Rufus B. Glover." https://www.odmp.org/officer/19659-deputy-us-marshal-rufus-b-glover.

"Warren Washington 'Wash' Shely." Ancestry.com. https://www.ancestry.com/mediaui/tree/40645530/person/28070962537/media/.

INDEX

References to illustrations appear in italic type.

Adair, Samuel E., 62
Agualeguas, Mexico, 22–23
Aieto, Raiel, 69
Ajala, Monsicio, 69
Alamo Heights, San Antonio, Tex., 15
Alexandria National Cemetery, Pineville, La., 25
Alvido, Natiridad, 69
Anamosa, Iowa, 82
Andrus, Edwin P., 62
Ansaleo, Motello, 69
Aqua Nueva, Tex., 77
Arambula, Andres, 69
Arctic, 53
Argyle Hotel, San Antonio, Tex., 15
Arlington National Cemetery, 32
Arnold, James, 70, 83
Arsola, Mateo, 69
Arthur, Chester A., 29
Avis, Edward S., 51

Bañados, Manuel, 24
Banda, Honsel A., 59–60
Barnhill, Pink, 60, 75–76, 85, 87
Barrera, Juan, 69
Battle of Franklin, 8
Battle of Stone's River, 15
Battle of Wounded Knee, 13, 25, 49

Bazan, Victoriano, 69
Beach, William D., 26
Belmontez, Feleciano, 69
Benavides, Cayetano, 70
Benavides, Cresencio, 70
Benavides, Esperidion, 70
Benavides, Estevan, 70
Benavides, Francisco (*El Tuerto*), 5, 46–47, 58, 66–67, 70–71, 77, 85
Benavides, Grecencio, 32
Benavides, José María, 71
Benavides, Marcial, 56, 84
Bermadez, Leander, 71
Bessie (steamship), 54
Bexar County jail, 65, 69, 74–77, 82, 85, 87–88, 91
Big Bend of Texas, 36, 49
Bliss, Zenas R., 36
Boarman, Alexander, 69, 71, 73–77, 80–88, 90–91
Bocos del Toro, Colombia, 33, 76
Boer War, 30
Bourke, John Gregory, 1, 10, 15–16, 18, 20–25, 27, 29–30, 32–34, 36–37, *43*, 50–51, 58–60, 114n5
Brackett, Albert G., 9
Brecina, Jesus, 71
Brewster County, Tex., 23

Briseno, Josne, 71
Broeter, I. H., 34
Brooks, James A., 25–26, 58
Brownsville, Tex., 10, 16–17, 30, 54, 80, 83, 86, 90
Bruni, Antonio Mateo, 65, 71
Bruni Ranch, Tex., 30, 56
Buchel County, Tex., 23
Bullis, John L., 36

Cadena, Apelinio "Pablo," 71
Cadena, Refugio, 71
Cadena, Santos, 71
Cadlor, Guadalupe C., 71
Caldwell, Frank M., 61
California, 31
Callahan Expedition, 6
Callahan, James H., 6
Camargo, Mexico, 6, 18–19, 53, 58
Camp at Eagle Pass, Tex., 9–10, 23, 29–30
Camp Del Rio, Tex., 14
Camp Peña Colorado, Tex., 23, 49
Camp Rice, Tex., 15
Cantu, Lucio, 72
Cantu, Victor, 72
"Captain Francis H. Hardie, G Troop Third United States Cavalry" (Remington), *41*
Carbajal, José María, 6
Carranza, Venustiano, 68
Carrizo (Zapata), Tex., 14, 19–23, 26, 30, 33, 46, 49, 51–52, 60, 62–63, 69, 73–75, 77–79, 82–84, 87, 89–90
Carter, Jesse McI., 19, 30, 51
Casa Blanca, Tex., 22
Casas Blancas, Tex., 66–67, 70–71
Castiglione, Kathline "Kat," 2
Castillo, Molena, 72
Cavazos, Bartolo, 72
Center of Southwest Studies, Fort Lewis College, Durango, Colo., 2
Cerón, Luis, 11

Cerralvo, Mexico, 22
Chacon, Jesus, 72
Charco Redondo, Tex., 27
Chase, George F., 26, 29, 32–33, 49, 51, 55, 57, 61, 72, 74, 79–80, 83, 87, 88
Chicago, Ill., 60, 63
Chihuahuan Desert, Mexico, 28
Chilean Civil War, 67
Civil War, U. S., 5–6, 15, 35
Clark, David L., 2
Clayton, Powell, Jr., 62
Clendenin, David R., 17
Cleveland, Grover, 35, 70, 82
Cleveland, Ohio, 25
Cloud, Benjamin G., 63
Colombia, 13, 67
Colombian Revolution, 13, 33, 67, 76
Colorado Ranch, Tex., 27, 29
Columbus, N.Mex., 68
Congressional Medal of Honor, 8, 15, 36, 49
Conner, Carolina, 16
Conrad, Julius T., 57, 61
Constitutional Army, 5, 28, 37, 75
Constitution of the United States, 8
Cooper, Samuel, 35
Coopwood, Bethel, 12–13
Corbarruvias, Manuel, 46
Corcoran, Thomas M., 51, 62, 90
Corpus Christi, Tex., 15–16, 30, 67
Cortina, Juan Nepomuceno, 6
Cortina War, 6
Cory, John E., 64
Costa Rica, 33
Cox, W. E., 66, 70
Crews, Andrew D., 2
Crook, George, 1, 15, 34
Cuban Revolution, 66–67, 78
Cuellar, J. C. "Lino," 32
Cuellar, Lena, 81
Cuellar, Tomás, 72
Cuero, Tex., 33
Cusack, Joseph E., 62

Daily Herald, Brownsville, Tex., 58–60
Daly, Henry W., 32
Davis, Jacqueline B., 2
Davis, Richard Harding, 30–31
Delores, Mexico, 18
Del Rio, Tex., 1
Detroit, Mich., 73, 83, 86, 88, 91
De Waelsche, Matt, 2
Díaz, Porfirio, 5, 7, 10–12, 20, 68
Dickman, Joseph T., 57–58, 61, 67, 70, 72, 77
Diez y Seis de Septiembre, 18
Downs, Walter, 58, 60, 70, 72, 75–76, 85, 87
Drew, George A., 36
Duque, Juan, 65, 72
Durango, Colo., 2
Duval County, Tex., 70
Dyer, Shubiel A., 15
Dyrenforth, Robert St. George, 14–15, 97n2

Eagle Nest Crossing, Tex., 36
Eagle Pass, Tex., 9, 14, 16
Echavarria, Cecilio, 58, 72
Edgerly, Winfield S., 49, 51
Edinburg, Tex., 9, 14
Edstrom, Charles H., 24–25, 34, 75
Edwards, James H., 60
Eighth Cavalry, 28, 67
Eighteenth Infantry, 8, 21, 24, 29, 51–52, 63
El Alazán, Tex., 50
El Chinaco (newspaper), 13
El Clovis Ranch, Tex., 70
Elizando, Cayetano Garza, 73
Elkins, Stephen B., 46, 50
El Paso, Tex., 15, 23, 62
Elting, Oscar, 49, 51–52, 61
Evans, Andrew J. "Jack", 33, 36–37, 107n33

Fandango Creek, 27
Fenton, Charles W., 51
Ferguson, Henry T., 29

Fifth Cavalry, 8, 62, 63
Fifth Infantry, 8–10, 14, 21, 30
First Cavalry, 30, 35
Flores, Entiquio, 73
Flores, Galvino, 73
Flores, Jesus, 73
Flores, Juan Angel, 73
Flores, Juan Antonio, 73
Flores, Juan Manuel, 73
Flores, Julian, 35, 73, 85, 89
Flores, Telesforo, 73–74
Florida, 36
Foley County, Tex., 23
Forbush, William C., 62
Fort Bliss, Tex., 15, 23, 53
Fort Brown, Tex., 10, 14, 19, 20–21, 23, 26, 51, 54
Fort Chadbourne, Tex., 8
Fort Clark, Tex., 6–7, 9–10, 23, 35–36, 53–54
Fort D. A. Russell, Wyo., 52
Fort Davis, Tex., 14
Fort Duncan, Tex., 6, 9, 36
Fort Elliott, Tex., 14
Fort Hancock, Tex., 23, 53, 62
Fort Leavenworth, Kans., 21
Fort McIntosh, Tex., 9–12, 14–15, 19–20, 23, 26, 29, 32, 48–55, 61, 63
Fort Reno, Oklahoma Territory, 62
Fort Riley, Kans., 49, 54, 62, 64
Fort Ringgold, Tex., 1, 9–10, 14–25, 32, 36, 48, 50–54, 59, 61–63, 70, 75, 80, 83, 86, 88–90
Fort Sam Houston, Tex., 9, 26, 28, 49, 61
Fort Sam Houston National Cemetery, 50
Fort Worth Daily Gazette, 20
Foster, John W., 48–49, 52–53
Foster, S. T., 85
Fricke, Paul, 34–35
Fourth Cavalry, 6

Gaitan, Anastacio, 74
Galvan, Juaqnio, 74

Galveston Daily News, 20
Gamez, Pablo, 74
García, Amador [Amadeo], 74
García, Amando, 74
García, Antenacio, 74
García, Antonio, 74
García, Armando, 74
García, Delfino, 74
García, Eusebio, 74
García, Juan, 74–75
García, Juan M. P., 75
García, Julian, 75
García, Julio, 75
García, Lorenzo, 22
García, Louis, 75
García, Nesario, 75
García, Pedro, 75
García. Roman, 75
García, Rosillio, 75
Garza, Bernardo de la, 75
Garza, Catarino Erasmo, 5, 11, 16–20, 22, 27–28, 33, 37, *38*, 65, 75–77, 83, 88
Garza, Encarnación, 33
Garza, Frank, 76
Garza, Luis, 76
Garza, Rafael, 76
Garza, Rosalio, 76
Garza, Theodoro, 76
Garza, Tomás, 24
Garza, Ygnacio, 76
Garza Raid, 18–19
"Garza Revolutionists in the Texas Chaparral" (Remington), *39*
Georgia, 36
Geronimo Campaign, 32
Glenn Springs, Tex., 28
Gloria, Mexico, 53
Glover, Rufus B., 32, 46, 61, 81, 85
Golindo, Juan M., 76
Gonzáles, Alejandro, 17–18, 29–30, 34, 65, 76–77
González, Brunio, 77
González, Concepcíon "Chonita," 17, 77

González, Francis, 77
González, Francisco, 77
González, Jose F., 22
González, Manuel, 77
González, Pedro Peña, 77
González, Prudencio, 58, 77
González, Vicente M., 77
Gordon, Sam, 64
Granjenato Ranch, Tex., 29
Greely, Adolphus W., 53–54
Gresham, Walter Q., 63, 66, 70, 77–78, 82
Griffith, Thomas W., 51
Guebarra, Gregorio, 78
Guerra, Antonio, 78
Guerra, Jesus, 65–66, 78
Guerra, Juan, 79
Guerra, Melcher, 79
Guerra, Rosendo, 56, 84
Guerrero, Julian, 58
Guerrero, Mexico, 11, 22, 46, 53, 79–80
Gulf of Mexico, 23
Gutiérrez, Amador, 79
Gutiérrez, Clemente, 79
Gutiérrez, Epifano, 79
Gutiérrez, Labrado, 79
Gutiérrez, Liberado, 79
Gutiérrez, Liberdad, 79
Gutiérrez, Porofiio, 79
Gutiérrez, [Gutierras], Procopio, 79

Hall, Edward F., 55–56, 72, 74, 76, 78, 81–82, 84–85, 89
Hall, William P., 62
Hardie, Francis H., 12, 19, 21, 23–24, 26–27, 30–32, *41*, 48, 51, 53, 61, 80
Hardie, James A., 31
Harper's Weekly, 30–31, *39–41*
Hatch, Everard E., 51
Havana, Cuba, 33
Havana, Tex., 29, 62
Haynes, Robert A., 26
Hays, Charles E., 24, 29, 51
Heard, John W., 29, 61

Hebbronville, Tex., 29
Hedekin, Charles A., 12, 48, 51, 56, 61, 84
Hernandez, Dario, 80
Hernandez, David, 80
Hernandez, Nicholas, 80
Hernández, Nieves, 22
Hidalgo, Father Miguel, 18
Hidalgo, Tex., 62
Hidalgo County, Tex., 23
Hogg, James S., 34, 60
Houston, Tex., 33
Howard, Brian P., 2
Huerta, Victoriano, 68
Hughes, John R., 16
Hunter, George K., 26, 30, 49, 51, 61, 76

Idaho, 25
Iglesias, Eugene, 11–12, 71, 73–74, 77, 79, 80, 84, 88
Indian tribes. *See* Native American tribes
Indiana, 27
Indio, Tex., 30
Ireland, 6
Irish Fenian Brotherhood, 5

Jackson, Henry, 49–52, 60–62, 69, 72–75, 78–79, 82–84, 87, 89–90
Jeff Davis County, Tex., 23
Jim Hogg County, Tex., 29
Jodon, Florent B., 37
Jodon, John, 22, 35
Johnson, John B., 19, 30, 51
Jones, Frank, 84, 88
July, John, 61, 91

Kansas, 61–62
Kendziorski, Nik, 2
Key West, Fla., 33, 67
Keyes, Alexander S. B., 48, 63, 73, 80
Kibbetts, Bobby, 36
Kibbetts, John, 36
King Ranch, Tex., 15
Kinney County, Tex., 23

Knight, John T., 26, 30, 33, 89
Kraup, Frederick P., 58

La Grulla, Tex., 18, 21, 24, 59–60, 73
La Mecca, Mexico, 35, 73, 89
Lamont, Daniel S., 63–64
Langhorne, George Tayloe, 10, 18–19, 22, 27–29, 37, *44*, 51, 67, 83, 103n19
Langtry, Tex., 14
Laredo, Tex., 9, 11, 12, 18, 48–49, 52, 56, 63, 65, 71, 80–81, 84–85
La Retama, Tex., 61
Las Comitas, Tex., 51
Las Cuevitas Ranch, Tex., 28, 83
Las Guerras, Mexico, 53
Las Islas, Tex., 12, 71, 74, 77, 79, 88
Las Mujeres Ranch, Tex., 86
Leal, Geraldo, 80
Lemon, Serstones, 80
Libres Fronterizos Regiment, 35, 73, 85
Longorio, Pablo, 32, 80
Longorio, Sixto, 26–27, 80
Lopeño, Tex., 51, 56
López, Abelarjo, 80
López, Amostacio, 80
López, Hymio, 80
López, Leonidas, 81
López, Manuel, 81
López, Teodoro G., 81
López, Victoriano, 81
Los Angeles, Tex., 23, 26–27, 30, 50–51, 61
Los Fieles Zaragozans Regiment, 37
Lowe, Percival G., 5–6, 81
Loyd, David, 24
Lynch, Patrick, 50, 63

Mabry, Woodford H., 25, 34
MacArthur, Arthur, *44*
Mackay, James O., 51, 61
Mackenzie, Ranald S., 6–7
Madden, John F., 30
Magro, Abeham [Abram], 81
Maine, 5

Maldonado, Juan, 81
Margo, Estavano, 81
martial law. *See* US Army
Martínez, Basillio, 47
Martínez, Ensebio, 81
Martínez, Eusabio M. (*Mangus de Aqua*), 46–47, 60–61, 81
Martínez, Felipe, 81
Martínez, Mateo, 82
Martínez, Maximo, 46, 61, 82
Martínez, Paulino, 13
Martínez, Refugio, 47
Martínez, Tomás, 47
Martivero, Evaristo, 82
Matamoros, Mexico, 16, 34, 53
Maverick County, Tex., 16, 23
Maxey, Thomas S., 33, 37, 65, 70–84, 86–91, 107n33
McCleary, James Harvey, 65
McKinley, William, 66, 78
Mckrone, Patrick, 30–31, *41*
McNeel, James S., 25, 33
Mendoza, Anastacio, 82
Mendoza, Francisco L., 82
Mendoza, Pedro, 82
Meno, Gonzalo. *See* Sandoval, Marco
Mexican-American War, 10
Mexican Army, 7, 13, 16, 24, 72; strength on the border, 52–53; tactics, 59; weapons, 46–47
Mexican Army, cavalry, Third Squadron, Sixth Cavalry Regiment, 46; Fourth Cavalry Regiment, 53; Sixth Cavalry Regiment, 46
Mexican Army, infantry, Third Auxiliaries, 53; Fourth Auxiliaries, 53; Fifth Auxiliary Battalion, 53; Fifth Infantry Squadron, 52; Sixth Infantry Battalion, 53; Thirteenth Regiment, 52; Tamaulipas Auxiliary, 53
Mexican Constitution of 1857, 20
"Mexican Guide" (Remington), *40*
Mexican Independence 1821, 18

Mexican Legation, Washington, DC, 48–49, 52, 63, 66, 78
Mexican National Guard, 16
Mexican National Railroad, 29–30, 50
Mexican Revolution of 1910, 1, 67
Mexico, 66
Mexico City, 7
Midland, Tex., 15
Mier, Mexico, 22, 35, 53, 70, 73, 85
Miller, William H. H., 35–36
Molina, Jacabo, 82
Mongao, Innocencio, 82
Monterrey, Mexico, 22
Montevino, Avisto, 82
Morales, Felipe, 83
Morales, Francisco, 47
Morales, José María, 83
Moreno, Juan, 32
Moreno, Severino, 83
Morris, Louis T., 58–59, 81
Morrow, Albert P., 19, 29
Morton, Charles, 9–10
Moya, Electorio, 83
Moya, Teodoro, 83
Mulas Ranch, Tex., 75–76, 85, 87
Muñoz, Pablo, 28, 37, 67, 83

Nassau, Bahamas, 33
National Guard, 67
Native Americans, 6, 13
Native American tribes, Apache, 15; Cheyenne, 15; Kickapoo, 6; Lipan Apache, 6, 50; Nez Percé, 15; Sioux, 13, 15, 25, 49
Natividad, Alvado, 83
Neff, Albert, 63
neutrality laws, United States, 5, 7–8, 12–13, 37, 55, 64–67, 69–91; Neutrality Act of 1794, 8; Neutrality Act of 1817, 8
New Orleans, La., 33
New Rochelle, N.Y., 31
New York, 5, 32
New York Tribune, 13

Nieto, Rafael, 83
Nueces County, Tex., 19, 34
Nuevo Laredo, Mexico, 52
Nuevo León, Mexico, 11, 16, 22, 52

O'Conner, Stephen, 29, 49, 51, 61, 71, 74, 90
Oklahoma, 25
Oklahoma Territory, 61–62
Olney, Richard, 66, 78
Omaha, Nebr., 15
Ornelas, Dr. Plutarco, 11, 19, 48, 72–73, 77
Ortiz, Espiridion, 83

Palacio, Porician, 55–56, 84
Palacios, Antonio, 84
Palacios, Florencio, 84
Palito Blanco Ranch, Tex., 17–19, 29, 32–34, 65, 76, 80
Parras, Mexico, 22–23
Paul, Charles R., 51
Paz, Ramón, 84
Pecos County, Tex., 23, 84, 88
Pecos River, 36
Peña, Juan, 84
Peña, Navato, 84
Peña Ranch, Tex., 71
Peña Station, Tex., 29–30
Peña, Zeon, 84
Pérez, Juan García, 84
Pérez, Monico, alias Alezando Perez, 84
Pershing Expedition of 1916, 68
Pershing, John J., 68
Philadelphia, Pa., 15
Philippine Insurrection, 67
Philippines, 67
Piedras Negras, Mexico, 6
Pineville, La., 25
Pisusias, Rafael, 84
Pittsburg, Pa., 25
Plan Revolucionario, 20
Poletio, Florentino, 85
Pollard, William, 63

Polvo, Tex., 23
Ponze, Aurelio, 85
Posse Comitatus Act of 1878, 7, 59
Post at San Antonio, Tex., 8–9
Potrancias Ranch, Tex., 51
Presidio County, Tex., 23
Presidio del Norte, Tex., 23
Price, Larkin F., 34, 66, 74, 77–78, 82
Prieto Ranch, Tex., 28
Proctor, Redfield, 13
Puerto Limón, Costa Rica, 33
Purington, George A., 29

Quellar, Fortunatio, 85

Ramírez, Ensenio, 85
Ramírez, Eusabio, 85
Ramírez, Francisco (Insurrecto), 85
Ramírez, Francisco (Mexican calvary trooper), 47
Ramírez, Jesus, 85
Ramírez, Rafael, 47, 84
Ramírez, Secandio [Secundino], 85
Ramírez, Ygnacio, 85
Ramón, Severiano M., 86
Randall, Edward L., 18–19
Rangel, Jesus, 86
Realitos, Tex., 33, 51, 61
Recéndez, Abraham, 16
Reconstruction, 59
Regilado, Juan Sanches, 86
Remington, Frederic S., 31, *39–41*
Remolina, Mexico, 6–7
Rendado, Tex., 26–27, 29, 51, 61
Rendon, Benito, 86
Retamal Springs, Tex., 24–27, 34, 75, 88
Reyes, Bernardo, 11–12, 16–17, 52
Reyna, Francisco, 86
Reynosa, Mexico, 53
Rhode Island, 35
Richardson, E. B., 34
Ringgold Barracks. *See* Fort Ringgold, Tex.

Rio Grande, 9–10, 22–23, 30, 52, 59, 62, 66–67, 70–71
Rio Grande City, Tex., 9, 16, 22, 25, 37, 48, 58, 72, 75–76, 85, 87, 90
Rio Grande City Riot of 1888, 16–17
Rio Grande Valley, 10–12, 50
Rios, Macario, 86
Rivers, Tyree R., 49, 51, 80
Roberts, Benjamin F., 64
Rodriguez, Guillermo, 86
Rodriguez, Mieigio, 86
Rodriguez, Moreliano [Molentino], 86
Rodriguez, Narciso, 86
Rodriguez, Victor, 86
Roma, Tex., 21, 50, 52, 75
Roman, Eustoigio, 86
Romero, Cayetano, 48–49, 52–53, 63, 66, 78
Rosa, Santos, 97
Ruiz, Inez, 65, 87

Sais, Cesario, 87
Sais, Geraldo, 87
Saiz, Severiano, 87
Salazar, Devincio, 87
Salazar, Dioneus (*also* Deonecio, Dionitio), 87
Salinas, Cecillio, 88
Salinas, Felipe, 88
Salinas, Fernandez, 61, 88
Salinas, Luis, 88
Salinas, Maximo, 88
Salinas, Pablo, 47
Salineño, Tex., 30, 51, 62
Sample, George W., 63
San Antonio, Tex., 9–11, 15, 17, 37, 48–50, 53, 65–67, 69, 71–85, 88–91
San Antonio Viejo, Tex., 29
San Bartola Ranch, Tex., 80
San Diego, Calif., 67
San Diego, Tex., 15, 17, 29, 32, 76
San Francisco Creek, 23
San Ignacio, Mexico, 46, 52, 55, 66

San Ignacio Raid, 5, 46–49, 52, 55, 58, 61, 64–66, 70, 72, 77–80, 82–85, 87–90
San Juan College, Matamoros, Mexico, 16
San Juan River, 18
San Miguel, Mexico, 19, 53
San Pedro, Tex., 62
San Ygnacio, Tex., 5, 29, 46–49, 51–52, 56, 61–62, 64, 71, 85–86, 88
Sánchez, Aciano, 88
Sánchez, Astano, 88
Sánchez, Juan, 88
Sánchez, Luis, 88
Sandoval, Francisco Ruíz, 5, 11–13, 18, 20, 71, 74, 79, 88
Sandoval, Jesus "Chico," 88
Sandoval, Marco, alias Gonzalo Meno, 88
Sandoval, Procopio, 89
Sandoval Raid, 5, 11–12, 71, 73–74, 77, 79, 80, 88
Sandrez, Abren C., 89
Santa Maria, Tex., 10, 14, 21, 30, 50–51
Santos, Feverion de los, 33, 89
Santos, Jose María, 32
Sarate, Juan Manuel, 89
Schofield, John M., 13, 23, 36, 46, 49–50, 52–53, 59, 63
Sebree, Victor, 16–17
Second Dragoons, 8
Segura, Rutillio, 46–47
Seminole-Negro Indian Scouts. *See* US Army, units
Seventh Cavalry, 29, 49, 51, 62–63
Second Infantry, 35
Seminole-Negro Indian Scouts, detachment of, 36, 50–51, 59–61, 63–64, 81, 91
Shafter, William R., 7
Shely, Josephus "Joe," 13, *42*, 55, 57, 62, 69, 74–75, 77–79, 81–82, 84, 88, 90, 112n13
Shely, Warren Washington "Wash", 17, 28, 37, *42*, 55, 57–58, 60–62, 66, 72–73, 75–76, 79–81, 83, 85, 87–90, 112n13

Sherman, John, 66, 78
Short, Walter C., 29
Sias, Americano, 89
Singer Sewing Machine Company, 16
Siteetastonachy (Snake Warrior). See Kibbitts, John
Slocum, Herbert J., 49, 51, 62, 71
Soledad Ranch, Tex., 32, 61
Soto, José María, 89
Soto, Juan Manuel, 89
Spain, 66–67, 78
Spanish-American War, 30
Stanley, David Sloan, 8, 11, 13–14, 17, 19–20, 23, 25–29, 33–35, 44
Starr County, Tex., 17, 23, 28, 36, 55, 57–58, 60, 62, 66, 70, 72–73, 75, 79, 81, 83, 85, 88–90
Starr County jail, 76–77
Steever, Edgar Z., 9, 12–13, 71, 73–74, 77, 79–80, 88
St. Louis, Mo., 16
Stringer, Abalado "Mogro," 35, 89
Summerlin, Robert L., 34, 83
Sutton, Warner P., 22
Swain, Hugh, 19, 51, 61

Tamaulipas, Mexico, 11
Tejada, Lerdo de, 5
Telegraph. See US Army, military telegraph
Texas Rangers, 6
Third Artillery, 9
Third Cavalry, 8–10, 15, 18–19, 21, 24, 26, 29, 31, 51, 61, 63, 64, 67
"Third Cavalry Troopers Searching a Suspected Revolutionist" (Remington), *40*
Thirteenth Infantry, 8
Thomas, Early D., 62
Tisdale, Shelby, 21
Toy, Frederick E., 49
Trapito, Tebucio, alias Tebucio González, 89

Treaty of Guadalupe Hidalgo, 66–67, 71
Treviño, Amelito, 89
Treviño, Anaclito, 89
Treviño, Donaciano, 89
Treviño, Felipe, 89
Treviño, Juan, 90
Treviño, Victoriano, 90
"Trumpeter Tyler, Third Cavalry" (Remington), *41*
Twenty-third Infantry, 8–9, 15, 18–19, 21, 28, 49, 51, 63
Tyler, Trumpeter. See Mckrone, Patrick

Uña de Gato Ranch, Tex., 21
"United States Cavalry Hunting for Garza on the Rio Grande" (Remington), *39*
United States Military Academy, West Point, N.Y., 1, 8, 15, 31
Upham, John J., 10
Uribe, Santiago, 90
US Army: cost of, 67; courts-martial, 29, 64; deaths of soldiers, 24, 50, 63; desertion of soldiers, 62–63; disease within, 63; drunkenness of, 29; equipment of, 31; mapping, 23; martial law, 58–59, military telegraph, 51, 53–54; pack mules, 32–33, 52; rations, 31; scouts, guides, and spies, 32, 50, 54–55, 57, 62; strength, 8–9; strength in Texas, 8, 9, 14, 20, 53; strength in South Texas, 9, 20, 26, 52, 53, 63; suicides within, 63; tactics of, 30, 50–52, 59, 64; weapons of, 27, 35–36
US Army, headquarters, Department of the East, 14; Department of the Missouri, 14; Department of Texas, 8, 11, 14, 21, 28, 35, 48, 54, 64
US Bureau of Ethnology, 16
US Congress, 8
US Department of Agriculture, 15
US Department of Justice, 55
US Department of State, 48, 55, 59, 60, 65

US Federal Court, Western District of Texas, 2, 64–65, 69–90
US Supreme Court, 65–66, 72, 78, 87
Usilio, Santiago, 90

Valdez, Rafael, 90
Val Verde County, Tex., 23
Van Riper, William, 26
Varrera, Seario, 90
Vasquez, Feliciano, 90
Vela, Anicelo, 90
Vela, Justo, 90
Venavidce, Espiridion, 90
Veracruz, Mexico, 68
Vestal, Solomon P., 62
Victorio, Chihenne Apache, 7
Vidrue, Juan Garza, 90
Villa, Francisco "Pancho", 68
volunteer regiments, Fifteenth Pennsylvania Cavalry, 15; Second Rhode Island Infantry, 35; Sixth Pennsylvania Cavalry, 29; Twenty-sixth US Volunteer Infantry, 67; Thirty-ninth US Volunteer Infantry, 67

Wade, James F., 62
Walker, Kirby, 57, 61
Walker, Samuel Allen, 27–28, 103n19
Ward, Private John (Warrior), 36
War Department, 14, 17, 25, 36, 48, 49–50, 53, 55, 59
Washington, DC, 16, 50
Webb County, Tex., 23, 30, 65, 71, 80, 84
Wessells, Henry W. Jr., 28–30
West, Parker W., 10, 48, 50–51, 70, 75, 79, 81, 83, 85–86, 88–90
West Point. *See* United States Military Academy
Wheaton, Frank, 35–36, *44*, *45*, 46, 48–55, 57, 60–61, 63–64
Wheeler, William B., 21–22, 29, 36–37, 51, 79
Williams, Robert C., 30
Wilson County, Tex., 55
Woodruff, Edward C., 9–10
Wooster, Robert, 2
World's Columbian Exposition, 60
Wreford, Sam P., 54
Wyoming, 25

Ybanes, Blas, 90
Ybanez, Carmen, 91

Zapata, Alberto, 91
Zapata County, Tex., 23, 26, 48–49, 57
Zapata, Juan Garza, 91
Zapata, Tex. *See* Carrizo, Tex.
Zarmosa, Porfirio, 91
Zarrate, Juan Manuel, 61, 91

www.ingramcontent.com/pod-product-compliance
Lightning Source LLC
Chambersburg PA
CBHW020932180426
43192CB00036B/893